D0338126

The
Eliminationists

The
Eliminationists

How Hate Talk Radicalized
the American Right

David Neiwert

 PoliPointPress

The Eliminationists: How Hate Talk Radicalized the American Right
Copyright © 2009 by David Neiwert

All rights reserved, including the right to reproduction in whole, in part, or in any form.

14 13 12 11 10 09   1 2 3 4 5

Production management: BookMatters
Book design: BookMatters
Cover design: Naylor Design, Inc.

LIBRARY OF CONGRESS CATALOGING-IN-PUBLICATION DATA
Neiwert, David A., 1956–
   The eliminationists : how hate talk radicalized the American right /
   David Neiwert.
      p.   cm.
   Includes bibliographical references and index.
   ISBN 978-0-9815769-8-5
   1. Right-wing extremists—United States.   2. Radicalism—
   United States.   I. Title.
HN90.R3N43   2009
320.520973—dc22   2009004889

Published by:
PoliPointPress, LLC
P.O. Box 3008
Sausalito, CA 94966-3008
(415) 339-4100
www.p3books.com

Distributed by Ingram Publisher Services

Printed in the United States of America

Contents

Introduction
Unleashing the Demonic

LIBERAL HUNTING PERMIT

No Bag Limit—Tagging Not Required. May be used while under the influence of Alcohol. May be used to Hunt Liberals at Gay Pride Parades, Democrat Conventions, Union Rallys, Handgun Control Meetings, News media Association, Lesbian Luncheons and Hollywood Functions. MAY HUNT DAY OR NIGHT WITH OR WITHOUT DOGS.

> *A bumper sticker available at some conservative Web sites,*
> *spotted near a gay-pride parade in San Francisco.*[1]

In July of 2008, a graying, mustachioed man from the Knoxville suburb of Powell, Tennessee, sat down and wrote out by hand a four-page manifesto describing his hatred of all things liberal and his belief that "all liberals should be killed."

When he was done, Jim David Adkisson drove his little Ford Escape to the parking lot of the Tennessee Valley Unitarian Universalist Church in Knoxville. A few days before, the church had attracted media attention for its efforts to open a local coffee shop for gays and lesbians. Leaving the manifesto on the seat of the car, he walked inside the church carrying a guitar case stuffed with a shotgun and 76 rounds of ammunition.

The congregants were enjoying the opening scene from the

church's production of the musical *Annie Jr.* when Adkisson, in a hallway outside the sanctuary, abruptly opened the guitar case, pulled out the shotgun, fired off a harmless round that startled everyone, then walked into the sanctuary and began firing indiscriminately. Witnesses report he was saying "hateful things." An unsuspecting 61-year-old grandmother and retired schoolteacher named Linda Kraeger was hit in the face with a shotgun blast. A 60-year-old foster father named Greg McKendry got up to shield others from the attack and was hit in the chest.

When Adkisson stopped to reload, a group of men, who had already begun closing around him, tackled him and wrested away his gun. Adkisson complained that the men were hurting him. "The only thing he said was he was asking us to get off of him, that he wasn't doing anything," said Jamie Parkey, one of the men who tackled him. "We just looked at each other incredulously, like 'How dare you?' "[2]

Greg McKendry was dead at the scene. Linda Kraeger died the next day. Seven other congregants were wounded.

A detective who interviewed Adkisson and examined his four-page manifesto reported to his superiors that Adkisson targeted the church "because of its liberal teachings and his belief that all liberals should be killed because they were ruining the country, and that he felt that the Democrats had tied his country's hands in the war on terror and they had ruined every institution in America with the aid of media outlets."

When the detective interviewed Adkisson, he said he'd decided that since "he could not get to the leaders of the liberal movement that he would then target those that had voted them in to office."[3]

Knoxville's police chief told reporters the next day that Adkisson was motivated by his "hatred of the liberal movement" and "liberals in general, as well as gays." He was also frustrated by his inability to get a job, a problem he also blamed on liberals. His neighbors in Powell described Adkisson as "a Confederate" and a "believer in the Old South."[4]

When detectives went to Adkisson's home in Powell, they found—scattered among the ammunition, guns, and brass knuckles—books written by leading conservative pundits: *Liberalism Is a Mental Disorder* by Michael Savage, *Let Freedom Ring* by Sean Hannity, and *The O'Reilly Factor* by Bill O'Reilly, among others. Adkisson's manifesto, released some months later to the public, was largely a distillation of these works, ranting about how "Liberals have attack'd every major institution that made America great.... Liberals are evil, they embrace the tenets of Karl Marx, they're Marxist, socialist, communists."

And then he went the next step, in the logic of anger:

> This was a symbolic killing. Who I wanted to kill was every Democrat in the Senate & House, the 100 people in Bernard Goldberg's book. I'd like to kill everyone in the mainstream media. But I know those people were inaccessible to me. I couldn't get to the generals & high ranking officers of the Marxist movement so I went after the foot soldiers, the chickenshit liberals that vote in these traitorous people [*sic*]. Someone had to get the ball rolling. I volunteered. I hope others do the same. It's the only way we can rid America of this cancerous pestilence....
>
> If decent patriotic Americans could vote three times in every election we couldn't stem this tide of liberalism that's destroying America. Liberals are a pest like termites. Millions of them. Each little bite contributes to the downfall of this great Nation. The only way we can rid ourselves of this evil is Kill them in the streets. Kill them where they gather.
>
> I'd like to encourage other like minded people to do what I've done. If life aint worth living anymore don't just Kill yourself, do something for your country before you go. Go Kill Liberals. [5]

The events that sunny Sunday left the church's pastor, Rev. Chris Buice, with a shattered congregation. "People were killed in the sanctuary of my church, which should be the holy place, the safe place. People were injured," he told PBS's Rick Karr a couple of weeks later. "A man came in here, totally dehumanized us—members of our church were not human to him. Where did he get that? Where did he get that sense that we were not human?"[6]

Shortly after John McCain's second debate appearance with Barack Obama on October 7, 2008—a debate most observers thought Obama won handily—Republican officials from his campaign told reporters they intended to mount a more aggressive series of attacks against the Democratic front-runner, who was widening his lead in the polls. According to the *Washington Post*, they believed that "to win in November they must shift the conversation back to questions about the Democrat's judgment, honesty and personal associations."[7]

Within days, McCain and his running mate, Alaska Governor Sarah Palin, began aggressively attacking Obama for his past associations with radical leftist William Ayers and his supposed lack of trustworthiness. Palin accused Obama of "palling around with terrorists," while McCain told a crowd, "We've all heard what he's said. But it's less clear what he's done, or what he will do."

The anger stirred up at these rallies became palpable in concrete ways. At one Palin rally, the governor was blaming the media for a series of disastrous television network interviews she had recently given. At one point, supporters began turning on members of the press crew in attendance, even haranguing a camera crew covering the event. One Palin backer turned viciously on a black member of the TV crew and told him, "Sit down, boy!" Attendees at McCain rallies began shouting out "Terrorist!" when Obama's name was mentioned, and one attendee reportedly shouted out "Kill him!" when Palin was describing Ayers's ties to Obama (though the Secret Service later insisted the report was unfounded).[8] A camera crew at a Palin rally in Ohio interviewed some of the people attending and came away with a series of chilling remarks:[9]

> I'm afraid if he wins, the blacks will take over. He's not a Christian! This is a Christian nation! What is our country gonna end up like?

> He's related to a known terrorist, for one.

> He must support terrorists! You know, uh, if it walks like a duck and quacks like a duck, it must be a duck. And that to me is Obama.

> Obama and his wife, I'm concerned that they could be anti-white. That he might hide that.

> I don't like the fact that he thinks us white people are trash . . . because we're not!

When Obama confronted McCain about this kind of rhetoric at their third and final debate on October 15, McCain demurred that he consistently decried this kind of talk from his campaign, and he defended his supporters "categorically" as "the most dedicated, patriotic men and women that are in this nation." Then he went on not only to dredge up the William Ayers association again but also to accuse Obama of aiding and abetting a community-activist group, ACORN—which had been recently in the news over irregularities involving its voter-registration efforts. He said ACORN was "maybe perpetrating one of the greatest frauds in voter history in this country, maybe destroying the fabric of democracy."

Almost overnight, ACORN offices at various locales around the country were vandalized. A community activist in Cleveland received an email warning that she was "going to have her life ended," and an ACORN staffer in Rhode Island got a phoned-in death threat complete with racial epithets. Voice mails came pouring in, too:

> Hi, I was just calling to let you all know that Barack Obama needs to get hung. He's a fucking nigger, and he's a piece of shit. You guys are fraudulent, and you need to go to hell. All the niggers on oak trees. They're gonna get all hung, honeys, they're gonna get assassinated, they're gonna get killed.
>
> You liberal idiots. Dumb shits. Welfare bums. You guys just fucking come to our country, consume every natural resource there is, and make a lot of babies. That's all you guys do. And then suck up the welfare and expect everyone else to pay for your hospital bills for your kids. I just say let your kids die. That's the best move. Just let your children die. Forget about paying for hospital bills for them. I'm not gonna do it. You guys are lowlifes. And I hope you all die.

Then there were the emails like this one:

> You blue gums are not going to steal the election.
>
> All of you porch monkeys need to go back to Africa.[10]

McCain and Palin shortly began ratcheting back their rhetoric, especially after polls showed that such tactics were losing rather than gaining votes. But the fuse had been lit: threats and intimidating behavior continued to be reported around the country. In Ohio, a barn covered with pro-Obama signs was vandalized twice, the first time with racial epithets.[11] In Sacramento, vandals scrawled "White Power," "KKK" and "Nigger" over the front of a large homemade Obama display. In Idaho Falls, a large Obama sign had a Nazi swastika painted on it.[12] In Tennessee, two neo-Nazi "skinheads" were arrested for plotting to assassinate Obama; according to federal agents, they planned to kill 102 black people in a murderous spree that would culminate in a suicidal attack on Obama.[13]

As of the date of this writing, nothing indicated that the election's outcome would put this fuse out. Indeed, the Southern Poverty Law Center reported that it had recorded more than 200 hate-related incidents sparked by Obama's election in the weeks immediately following.[14]

These seemingly disparate incidents—the shooting in Kentucky and the increase of hateful speech in the campaign—received prominent coverage in the national news, but few noted the deep and significant connection between them. After all, what does yet another random "lone wolf" shooting spree in a public venue have to do with election-year rhetoric on the presidential campaign trail?

What connects them is that they are both manifestations of one of the most troubling aspects of modern American politics: the impulse to demonize our political adversaries, and the consequences of that demonization on our discourse and our body politic. This impulse has coursed through American politics since its beginnings, and it certainly exists on all sides of the nation's political aisles today.

But more particularly, both episodes reflect a trend that has manifested itself with increasing intensity in the past decade: the positing of elimination as the solution to political disagreement. Rather than engaging in a dialogue over political and cultural issues, one side simply dehumanizes its opponents and suggests, and at times demands, their excision. This tendency is almost singularly peculiar to the American Right. It manifests itself in many venues: on radio talk shows and in political speeches, in bestselling books and babbling blogs. Most of all, we can feel it on the ground:

in our everyday lives, in our encounters, big and small, with each other.

The little Tualatin pancake house was an Oregon woman's favorite breakfast spot because the owner, who often doubled as waitress, had always been friendly to her family, often carrying her youngest son about and serving them with a ready smile. But one morning in 2004, she went there alone for a cup of coffee and a side order of bacon, and wound up fleeing in fear.

An older couple in one of the booths next to hers was playing a card game; they told the waitress they were playing "Al Gore Gin," which they explained meant you could make up the rules as you went along and "anything goes." When the waitress came to the woman's table to fill her cup with an amused look on her face, the woman remarked that it sounded more like a "Bush game" to her. Overhearing this, the card-playing couple started talking loudly about the virtues of President Bush.

Soon the occupants of another booth—three men, one middle-aged and two in their twenties—began chiming in loudly. In the process of declaiming the virtues of the president, the older man turned to the woman and remarked, "I hate all you fucking Democrats. You fucking deserve to die. Hopefully, we can kill the fucking bunch of you soon."

The woman quickly got up, paid for her meal, and left, shaking and shaken. As she did so, she noticed that no one said anything to the man, who had turned to the others and carried on with his tirade.[15]

Timothy Burke, a history professor at Swarthmore College near Philadelphia, probably felt perfectly comfortable driving around campus with a John Kerry sticker affixed to his bumper. But he wasn't prepared for what could happen on the drive home.

Burke lives only about a five-minute drive from campus along a narrow and winding road. He was heading home for lunch one day when he suddenly found he was being aggressively tailgated by a man in a pickup truck, which pulled up to within inches of his rear bumper and stayed there at 45 miles per hour. Burke slowed gradually as he approached the turnoff to his residential street. The pickup stayed right behind him, following him as he made his turn.

Driving slowly through the neighborhood, Burke was further surprised when the truck suddenly passed him on the left at high speed. Burke turned into his driveway as the pickup came to a screeching halt at the stop sign some 75 feet down the street. Burke got out of his car and stared with amazement at the man, who suddenly shifted the truck back into reverse toward Burke's home while simultaneously shouting incoherently out his window at Burke. Burke yelled at him, "Why were you tailgating me like that? I was already going well over the speed limit!"

"Because you're a fucking faggot, fucker! You fuck! I should have fucking hit you! I should hit you now!" The man, a fiftyish fellow with a walrus mustache, continued on in this vein, until Burke yelled back, "What is your FUCKING problem? What did I do to you?"

The man pointed to his car and the Kerry-Edwards sticker. "You faggot, you voted for that war criminal! I'm going to beat the shit out of you." Burke noticed the man turning a shade of purple and realized he wasn't just putting on a show. He pulled out his cell phone to call the police just as the man screeched away, still yelling, his tires smoking. Burke spent about ten minutes "kind of trembling as the adrenaline drain[ed] away."[16]

Another college professor, Tony Van Der Meer, teaches African studies at the University of Massachusetts in Boston. He had a similar up-close encounter with someone who thought he ought to be shot, though in this case, the aggressor was an on-campus National Guard recruiter. And in the ensuing melee, Van Der Meer was the one tackled by three police officers and arrested.

For Van Der Meer, it all began with a typical cross-campus stroll on his way to lunch in early April 2003. As he entered the lobby of the school's McCormick Building, he saw one of his students, a senior named Tony Naro, in an angry exchange with a Guard recruiter (who was never identified). Naro, who was handing out leaflets commemorating Martin Luther King Jr.'s assassination, later said the recruiter started the conflict by heckling him. "He called me a [expletive] communist," said Naro.

Someone called the campus police because, according to the police report, someone else was "blocking the guardsmen from handing out informational pamphlets."

Naro spotted Van Der Meer and called him over for help; the professor suggested he move elsewhere, away from the recruiters, to avoid trouble. At this point, one of the recruiters, who had been reading one of Naro's fliers, turned to the young man and told him he ought to be "shot in the head like King." Van Der Meer upbraided the recruiter for talking that way to a student. The recruiter replied that Van Der Meer "should be shot, too." A shouting match erupted. One report said that Van Der Meer responded, "No. You should be shot in the head."

At this point the police intervened, and Van Der Meer took the brunt of it. He was pushed to the ground by the campus officer, tackled by three cops, and handcuffed. The police claimed in their report that Van Der Meer had initiated the contact with the officer by pushing him in the chest, but this was not corroborated by a single witness. Some 12 witnesses later attested that Van Der Meer had not touched anyone until the first officer pushed him down.

Deanna Brunetti, who was selling class rings in the lobby, told authorities that she heard the guardsman say to Van Der Meer, "You should be shot in the head, you and all you peacemaker people." She added, "I saw the cop grab the black man by the lapel and push him to the ground. He almost pushed the black man into my table. I didn't see the black man raise a finger to the officer. Not once."

Eventually, Suffolk County prosecutors dropped the charges against Van Der Meer.[17]

Such incidents—the nasty personal encounters, the ugliness at campaign rallies, the violent acts of "lone wolf" gunmen—are anything but rare. If you're a liberal in America—or for that matter, anyone who happens to have run afoul of the conservative movement and its followers—you probably have similar tales to tell about unexpected and brutal viciousness from otherwise ordinary, everyday people, nearly all of them political conservatives, nearly all directed at their various enemies: liberals, Latinos, Muslims, and just about anyone who disagrees with them.

What motivates this kind of talk and behavior is called *eliminationism*: a politics and a culture that shuns dialogue and the democratic exchange of ideas in favor of the pursuit of outright elimination of the opposing side, either through suppression, exile, and ejection, or extermination.

Rhetorically, eliminationism takes on certain distinctive shapes. It always depicts its opposition as beyond the pale, the embodiment of evil itself, unfit for participation in their vision of society, and thus worthy of elimination. It often further depicts its designated Enemy as vermin (especially rats and cockroaches) or diseases, and disease-like cancers on the body politic. A close corollary—but not as nakedly eliminationist—is the claim that opponents are traitors or criminals and that they pose a threat to our national security.

Eliminationism is often voiced as crude "jokes," a sense of humor inevitably predicated on venomous hatred. And such rhetoric—we know as surely as we know that night follows day—eventually begets action, with inevitably tragic results.

Two key factors distinguish eliminationist rhetoric from other political hyperbole:

1. It is *focused on an enemy within*, people who constitute entire blocs of the citizen populace.
2. It advocates the excision and extermination of those entire blocs by violent or civil means.

Eliminationism—including the rhetoric that precedes it and fuels it—expresses a kind of self-hatred. In an American culture that advertises itself as predicated on equal opportunity, eliminationism runs precisely counter to those ideals. Eliminationists, at heart, hate the very idea of an inclusive America.

The origins of such hatred, like slavery and war, are man's most ancient and savage impulses: the desire to dominate others, through violence if necessary. The expressions of such hatred go largely unnoticed and unexamined, perhaps because they expose a side of human nature so ugly we prefer not to even recognize its existence. Only recently have we even coined a term like eliminationism with which to frame it.

The term was first used meaningfully by historian Daniel Jonah Goldhagen in his controversial text *Hitler's Willing Executioners: Ordinary Germans and the Holocaust*. According to Goldhagen, "eliminationist antisemitism" had a unique life in German culture and eventually was the driving force behind the Holocaust.[18] Goldhagen never provides a concise definition of the word, but rather offers a massively detailed description of the eliminationist world view:

The eliminationist mind-set that characterized virtually all who spoke out on the "Jewish Problem" from the end of the eighteenth century onward was another constant in Germans' thinking about Jews. For Germany to be properly ordered, regulated, and, for many, safeguarded, Jewishness had to be eliminated from German society. What "elimination"—in the sense of successfully ridding Germany of Jewishness—meant, and the manner in which this was to be done, was unclear and hazy to many, and found no consensus during the period of modern German antisemitism. But the necessity of the elimination of Jewishness was clear to all. It followed from the conception of the Jews as alien invaders of the German body social. If two people are conceived of as binary opposites, with the qualities of goodness inhering in one people, and those of evil in the other, then the exorcism of that evil from the shared social and temporal space, by whatever means, would be urgent, an imperative. "The German Volk," asserted one antisemite before the midpoint of the century, "needs only to topple the Jew" in order to become "united and free."[19]

Hitler's Willing Executioners is an important and impressive piece of scholarship, particularly in the extent to which it catalogues the willing participation of the "ordinary" citizenry in so many murderous acts, as well the hatemongering that precipitated those acts. His identification of "eliminationism" as a central impulse of the Nazi project was not only heavily borne out by the evidence but was an important insight into the underlying psychology of fascism.

The eliminationist project is in many ways the signature of fascism, partly because it proceeds naturally from fascism's embrace of what Oxford Brookes scholar Roger Griffin calls *palingenesis*, or a Phoenix-like national rebirth, as its core myth.[20] The Nazi example clearly demonstrates how eliminationist rhetoric has consistently preceded, and heralded, the eventual assumption of the eliminationist project; indeed, such rhetoric has played a critical role in giving *permission* for it to proceed, by creating the cultural and psychological conditions that enable the subsequent violence.

Goldhagen focuses almost solely on the Holocaust and the virulently anti-Semitic form of eliminationism that took root in Europe prior to World War II. However, we can see eliminationism playing a role in human history throughout the ages— including its special role in American history and the shaping of American culture, right up to the present.

At the time I read Goldhagen's text, I was engaged in a historical research project about the internment of Japanese Americans during World War II.[21] I was struck by the similarity between Goldhagen's description of the buildup to Nazi power and the rhetoric and behavior of Americans for the 40 and more years preceding the internment toward Asians generally and the Japanese specifically.

A peek into the darker corners of American history tells us that this phenomenon has not been restricted to Asians. Eliminationist rhetoric, followed and accompanied by an actual campaign of often violent eliminationism, has infused the most shameful episodes of our history as a nation: the destruction of the Native American peoples; the subjugation of African Americans from slavery to Jim Crow—the lynching era and "sundown towns"; and the nativist anti-immigrant campaigns of various eras that targeted ethnic minorities—from the Irish to the Germans to the Italians and the Asians, and today, the Latinos. It lives today in the form of hate crimes and hateful rhetoric directed against gays and lesbians, Muslims, and various other minorities.

More recently, eliminationism has been directed not only at these minorities but also at the "liberals" who are perceived as their enablers: antiwar activists, environmentalists, guardians of civil rights. Indications are that the hateful rhetoric and its poisonous consequences are starting to spread.

I began observing this phenomenon back in 2003 at my blog *Orcinus,* almost as an offhand observation. I asked readers to chip in and tell me their own experiences and to link me to others' stories of the same kind. It was like tapping into a high-voltage power line. Comments poured in to my blog, accompanied by as many if not more emails.

Such incidents are difficult to catalog or quantify. Only on occasion (as in the Van Der Meer case) do matters ever get reported in the press; indeed, it's rare that police are even called or involved. But judging from the outpouring at *Orcinus* and elsewhere, eliminationist rhetoric, as far as many progressives are concerned, has so deeply infected the popular discourse that it is indeed poisoning how we treat each other in our daily lives.

Incidents like those described above—a representative sampling of more than a hundred stories I've collected—are not occurring in a vacuum. People are acting out in an eliminationist manner because they have been inundated with, and have naturally internalized, a broad range of eliminationist ideas and talking points. Such speech is being bandied about in every cultural bandwidth— from talk radio, to the local press and in letters to the editor, to blogs and national mainstream media. And while my readers helped me catalog ugly incidents, they also helped me compile examples of eliminationist rhetoric, and this list is perhaps even more impressive.

Herewith, a sampling:

> If I had one dirty bomb I could eliminate all the liberals in Fresno at once.
>
> *Fresno City Council member Jerry Duncan,*
> *in an email to his colleagues.*

If I were given a choice of pressing one of two buttons—one to do away with terrorism or another to do away with those Democrats up in Washington—I wouldn't even have to think about it. I would do away with the Democrats, and do this country a favor.

> *William G. Koehlke, Letter to the editor, published in* the Athens Banner-Herald *on Saturday, March 15, 2003.*

I am a United States sailor. I have chosen to defend my country and the freedom some take for granted. I love my country, my family, my freedom. Only by the blood which was shed by the service members before me did we receive this freedom.

There are some, though, who do not appreciate this freedom. I call these people traitors; they call themselves protesters. They are nothing more than an infectious disease that infests the minds and hearts of the Americans we are defending. It consumes the honor and courage within its host until it kills the very patriotism that made this country.

No cure exists for this disease. Never will everyone be satisfied. But let it be known what this guardian of America's freedom thinks of these protesters: Traitors should be hanged. I hold our enemies in higher standing. At least they are willing to fight for their beliefs and the country they love.

> *Derik L. Jobe, Sonar Technician, U.S. Navy, Letter to the editor,* Amarillo Globe News, *Amarillo, Texas, December 3, 2003.*[22]

I don't really consider the Democrat party a party of the people anymore, nor do I consider the socialist Democrats (they are not "liberal," that's just a euphemism for socialist anymore) "nice people who are misguided." I consider them to be pure, raw evil, who want to destroy everything rational or beautiful in sight: success, prosperity, even the very security of the country.

> *Conservative blogger Amber Pawlik, June 2004.*[23]

WASHINGTON—January 6, 2004. A paramilitary organization calling itself the Christian Liberation Front changed the balance of power in Washington by a pair of brutal attacks this afternoon. A force estimated at about 200 CLF commandos stormed the Supreme Court building, killing 35 people, including five Supreme Court Justices. At the same time, a contingent of 1,000 CLF paramilitaries attacked the Hart Senate Office Building, where a Senate Democratic Caucus meeting was being held. Approximately 50 people were killed in the attack. Once the commandos had seized the building, they systematically killed Democratic senators from states with Republican governors.

> Conservative blogger Mark Byron, "The Usefulness of
> Civil Disobedience," an essay describing a "fantasy
> episode" that "has a following in the darker parts
> of my mind," November 13, 2003.[24]

For many decades, conservative citizens and like-minded political leaders (starting with President Calvin Coolidge) have been denigrated by the vilest of lies and characterizations from hordes of liberals who now won't even admit that they are liberals—because the word connotes such moral stink and political silliness. As a class, liberals no longer are merely the vigorous opponents of the Right; they are spiteful enemies of civilization's core decency and traditions. . . .

That is why the unthinkable must become thinkable. If the so-called "Red States" (those that voted for George W. Bush) cannot be respected or at least tolerated by the "Blue States" (those that voted for Al Gore and John Kerry), then the most disparate of them must live apart—not by secession of the former (a majority), but by expulsion of the latter.

> Mike Thompson, Human Events, November 3, 2004,
> in a "satire" titled "Declaration of Expulsion:
> A Modest Proposal."[25]

Instead of sitting around, incessantly sniping at President Bush and the U.S. Military, sipping "liberal coward broth," hating America and Conservatives, the wacko liberal poison Left-Wing Nuts— and the rest of The Enemy Within™—should be rounded-up and put into "re-education camps" and forced to watch 24 hour, nonstop TV news footage of 9/11, Sodomy Insane's rape/torture/murder rooms, and the unearthing of Iraqi mass graves. Those hard-core Lefty wacko filth who can't be converted, should be summarily tried and locked away for life; no chance of parole. They're a waste of oxygen and a "clear and present danger" to America, as is the murderous, degenerate cult of Islam. Free and unfettered speech is guaranteed under the First Amendment, but actively working and trying to destroy this Nation, in a time of war, when our very lives are in peril, is a treasonous and seditious offense, and should be treated as such, and punished by death. The much-maligned Patriot Act provides for that very situation, and should be implemented post haste. All verminous, hate-America, liberal-socialist-commie filth should be contained and selectively eliminated.

John Shelley, "Liberal Broth," an essay at his personal Web site, July 30, 2004.[26]

Eliminationism has become an endemic feature of modern movement conservatism (which, as we will see shortly, is something wholly distinct from traditional conservatism). It shows itself as an unwillingness to argue the facts or merits of issues and to demand outright the suppression or violent oppression (and ultimately the purgation) of elements deemed harmful to American society.

This kind of rhetoric is, in effect, the death of discourse itself. Instead of offering an opposing idea, it simply shuts down intellectual exchange and replaces it with the brute intention to silence and eliminate.

As we've seen from the preceding examples, a lot of eliminationist talk occurs on a small, personal level, often during chance encounters between strangers. This kind of rhetoric pops up not only in bizarre road-rage incidents, ugly public exchanges, disturbing letters to the editor, and vicious blog posts, but also from the very fonts of public information: the mass media. Figures such as Rush Limbaugh, Bill O'Reilly, Ann Coulter, Lou Dobbs, and Glenn Beck routinely engage in it and fuel the flames with bogus stories—nonsensical conspiracy theories and outrageously inflammatory misinformation—derived from fanatical far-right sources. The kind of incident Timothy Burke experienced is becoming commonplace because it's being openly encouraged by major figures in the conservative movement, both in the media and in officialdom.

A brief sampling:

> *Rush Limbaugh*: I tell people don't kill all the liberals. Leave enough so we can have two on every campus—living fossils— so we will never forget what these people stood for.[27]

> *Ann Coulter*: My only regret with Timothy McVeigh is he did not go to the New York Times Building.[28]

> *Bill O'Reilly*: Everybody got it? Dissent, fine; undermining, you're a traitor. Got it? So, all those clowns over at the liberal radio network, we could incarcerate them immediately. Will you have that done, please? Send over the FBI and just put them in chains, because they, you know, they're undermining everything and they don't care, couldn't care less.[29]

> *Michael Reagan*: There is a group that's sending letters to our troops in Iraq . . . claiming 9/11 was an inside job—oh, yeah, yeah—and that they should rethink why they're fighting. . . . Excuse me, folks, I'm going to say this: We ought to find the people who are doing this, take them out and shoot them. Really. Just find the people who are sending those letters to our troops to demoralize our troops and do what they are doing, you

take them out, they are traitors to our country, and shoot them. You have a problem with that, deal with it. But anyone who would do that doesn't deserve to live. You shoot them. You call them traitors—that's what they are—and you shoot them dead. I'll pay for the bullet.[30]

Michael Barone: Our covert enemies are harder to identify, for they live in large numbers within our midst. And in terms of intentions, they are not enemies in the sense that they consciously wish to destroy our society. On the contrary, they enjoy our freedoms and often call for their expansion. But they have also been working, over many years, to undermine faith in our society and confidence in its goodness. These covert enemies are those among our elites who have promoted the ideas labeled as multiculturalism, moral relativism and . . . transnationalism.[31]

Dinesh D'Souza: There is no way to restore the culture without winning the war on terror. Conversely, the only way to win the war on terror is to win the culture war. Thus we arrive at a sobering truth. In order to crush the Islamic radicals abroad, we must defeat the enemy at home.[32]

David Horowitz: Make no mistake about it, there is a war going on in this country. The aggressors in this war are Democrats, liberals and leftists who began a scorched earth campaign against President Bush before the initiation of hostilities in Iraq.[33]

Kathleen Parker: Here's a note I got recently from a friend and former Delta Force member, who has been observing American politics from the trenches: "These bastards like Clark and Kerry and that incipient ass, Dean, and Gephardt and Kucinich and that absolute mental midget Sharpton, race baiter, should all be lined up and shot." [34]

These are examples of nationally broadcast instances of the rhetoric of elimination, sometimes under the guise of "humor." Through such statements, underlying attitudes are transmitted to a wide audience and the generally passive acceptance with which they are received sends a powerful message: that such talk, and its accompanying hateful worldview, is acceptable. Likewise, silence on the part of decent mainstream conservatives sounds to the kind of people who would act on this rhetoric like tacit approval.

The threats haven't been restricted to ordinary citizens and protesters. One of the more disturbing examples of a public target of such ire involved 9/11 Commission member Jamie Gorelick. She was bombarded with death threats, including a phoned-in bomb threat at her home and hundreds of what she called "very vile" emails.[35] All this occurred after then–Attorney General John Ashcroft accused Gorelick of authoring a memo that he and other conservatives blamed for creating a bureaucratic "wall" they said caused the intelligence failures leading to 9/11 (a dubious claim at best, considering that Ashcroft had previously testified elsewhere that this "wall" had existed since the 1980s).[36] The conservative noise machine leapt into action—most notably Limbaugh. He claimed that "Gorelick really ran the place while Janet Reno was the face of the Justice Department" and that she "erected a wall and . . . the Clinton administration determined that they were gonna fight terrorism not as a war but as a legal matter."[37] Right-wing operative Dick Morris chimed in on Fox News: "Of all of the public officials in the Clinton administration, and the Bush administration, the one who is most directly responsible, in my judgment, for 9/11 happening, is Jamie Gorelick."[38]

One of the favorite tactics of those who resort to threats is the hoax-anthrax letter. The recipient gets an envelope containing white powder with a note warning that it is anthrax. This is actually a concrete form of domestic terrorism, otherwise known as "piggybacking," in which terrorists emulate the acts of other terrorists, using them as a kind of launching pad. In this case, the perpetrators were using the once-real threat of anthrax mailings—the still-unsolved post-9/11 anthrax mailings of October and November 2001, which themselves were a kind of piggyback attack, riding the immediate wave of 9/11 fearfulness. Former president Bill Clinton, MSNBC talk-show host Keith Olbermann, and a number of other liberal luminaries have been recipients of such threats.

Olbermann's attacker was eventually caught and arrested. He turned out to be a 39-year-old man named Chad Castagana, who lived with his parents in Woodland Hills, California. Before he was caught, he sent out anthrax threats to various perceived liberals in the media, including Comedy Central's Jon Stewart and CBS's David Letterman, as well as various liberal politicians, including House Democratic leader Nancy Pelosi and Sen. Charles Schumer of New York. In all, he mailed 14 letters. Castagana also had a busy online life, posting at conservative Web sites like Free Republic, where he used the handle "Marc Costanzo." His profile stated: "Ann Coulter is a Goddess and I worship Laura Ingraham and Michelle Malkin."[39]

Naturally, these right-wing luminaries can't be held legally responsible for inspiring a nutcase like Castagana—but that doesn't absolve them of all culpability for inspiring such acts by him and others. "I have no idea who this loon is. I do not condone his actions or any actions like his by anyone else," wrote Malkin at her blog in response to queries about the Castagana case. But because of the clear, commonsensical connection—that is, he heard the hatemongering and constant demonization of liberals coming from these pundits and decided to act upon it—they do carry a moral and professional culpability.

All freedoms entail responsibilities, and when you do media work in America—and especially when you have a nationally prominent platform—you have not only the freedom of the press as your ally but a responsibility to the public as your burden. And chief among those responsibilities is to not abuse your power in a way that harms your fellow citizens or inspires others to harm them. It is possible, after all, to use your megaphone to lie shamelessly. You can use it to smear the good name of public officials. You can use it to rewrite history. You can use it to intimidate the "little people" who don't possess the same kind of power. And you can use it to dehumanize others, turning them into potential targets for hatefulness and violence.

Eliminationists, as we've observed, never act in a vacuum. Someone specific almost always inspires them. When Olbermann discussed the culpability of Coulter, Malkin, and Ingraham for their roles in inspiring Castagana on his show, Malkin retorted that Olbermann was using "the most desperate rhetoric to discredit and stifle our voices." She further claimed he was trying to "slime me as some sort of domestic terrorist." In reality, he was trying to hold her accountable for the domestic terrorism that her reckless rhetoric helped set off.

Ironically, Malkin has also been a leader in the contingent of the conservative movement that insists that it is liberals, not conservatives, who have been "unhinged" in their rhetoric and driving the national discourse over a cliff. This retort is standard to any mention of the Right's proclivity for eliminationist rhetoric. Malkin, in fact, wrote an entire book to support this thesis.[40]

The increasingly nasty tone of liberal rhetoric in recent years, especially on an interpersonal level, is also important to note. Some of the examples Malkin cites are ugly, indeed, as is some of the bile directed toward George W. Bush in recent years.

However, most of the examples Malkin and her fellow conservatives point to involve anger directed at a specific person—most typically, George Bush or Dick Cheney—and often for reasons related to the loss of American and civilian lives in Iraq. Few of them are *eliminationist*—that is, most do not call for the suppression and eradication of an entire class of people. Rather, the hatred is focused on a handful of individuals.

In contrast, right-wing rhetoric has been explicitly eliminationist, calling for the infliction of harm on whole blocs of American citizens: liberals, gays and lesbians, Latinos, blacks, Jews, feminists, or whatever target group is the victim *du jour* of right-wing ire. This vile form of "anti-discourse" has been coming from the most prominent figures of movement conservatism: its most popular pundits and its leading politicians. And the sheer volume and intensity of the rhetoric dwarf whatever ugliness is coming from the liberal side of the debate.

Moreover, much of the current liberal anger and nastiness is *reactive*—a response to over a decade's worth of venomous attacks on them by conservative mouthpieces, who have often reveled in their efforts to make the word "liberal" a pejorative. It often expresses outrage over some act rather than a person, something as worthy of it as the Abu Ghraib scandal or the conduct of the war in Iraq. Such reactive hostility is particularly common among people who have found themselves under attack by the Right. If movement conservatives have been behaving like the village loon, wandering about the town square and poking people in the eye with a sharp stick, they probably shouldn't be surprised when their victims respond angrily. Their wide-eyed protestations of horror at the anger they've provoked are in some ways downright comical.

So even if we can see where this kind of rhetoric, and its result-ing dysfunctional behaviors, is coming from, the question remains: Where is it taking us?

The problem with eliminationism isn't that it is simply unpleas-ant or ugly or even uncomfortable discourse, which is what can often be said of the Left's frequently charged rhetoric. The prob-lem, as we already noted, is that it implies the death of discourse, as well as its dissolution into violence and the use of force.

And what the eliminationists call jokes aren't. The humor in their statements—whatever might be funny about them—is entirely contingent on their listeners' underlying attitude about their fellow Americans, an attitude that not only demonizes them but also reduces them to subhuman level, prime targets for violent elimination. Jokes shouldn't have a concrete real-world effect, and these do: at some point members of their audience (particularly the more hate-filled and mentally unstable types) will act on them.

This is where the specter of fascism raises its head on American soil. Eliminationism has always been a signature trait of fascism, the manifestation of its embrace of the myth of national rebirth through the fiery destruction of the existing order. As we shall see, it has a long history in America; but in the context of modern mass politics, it almost always raises the red flag of incipient fascism.

Eliminationists have always minimized, for public consump-tion, the nature of the demonic beast they unleash. The propo-nents of Indian genocide in the old West couched their violent intentions in words like "protecting civilization." The advocates of lynching and Klan terror always cloaked their vicious murderous-ness in the guise of "the defense of traditional values" and particu-larly "white maidenhood." For the Nazis, the Holocaust was osten-sibly all about the "racial health" of the body politic. The same is true of modern neo-Nazis. Recall, if you will, that William Pierce often protested that *The Turner Diaries* was a mere work of fiction; but that did not prevent either Robert Mathews (the leader of the murderous neo-Nazi gang called The Order) or Oklahoma City bomber Timothy McVeigh—both of whom were ardent fans of Pierce's work—from attempting to enact its blueprint. We should remember this when Rush Limbaugh and Ann Coulter claim that they're just "entertainers" telling "jokes," and their ever-abundant apologists parrot them.

Perhaps the most disturbing facet of this trend is precisely that mainstream conservatives—button-down types who bridle at the first hint of liberal incivility—seem to have developed an extraordinary, boiled-frog kind of tolerance for the increasing ugliness of their own movement. They can produce reams of ponderous rationalizations for behavior and speech that is simply inexcusable.

These same mainstream conservatives used to be one of the key bulwarks against any kind of fascist impulse in America. Part of our political bloodstream for over a century, such impulses could never find the political space to take root because, in large part, ordinary conservatives had little in common with them. In the span of the past decade, this has increasingly ceased to be the case.

I've observed this shift through firsthand experience. I grew up in a conservative family in a conservative state—Idaho—and have lasting familial and friendship ties to many right-leaning folks. More importantly, perhaps, I also worked as a journalist in northern Idaho at a time when white supremacists, most famously the Aryan Nations at Hayden Lake, began making it their home. These people—with their Hitler worship, their swastikas, and their hatred of Jews and blacks—were genuine fascists, and their "Patriot" associates were genuine proto-fascists; that is, they represented a seedbed for nascent fascism, with all of the necessary traits in germinative form. In the course of my work, conducting interviews and exploring these people's motives and beliefs, I got to know many of them and came to be deeply familiar with their milieu and their value systems. In the process, I was disabused of many of the stereotypes surrounding them.

Not only were they not tattooed thugs with leathers but most of them seemed like perfectly normal people who led perfectly normal lives. Most of them were not hopelessly stupid, uneducated backwoods ignoramuses; indeed, some were better educated than the rest of us, and many held thoroughly detailed and often arcane belief systems based on their own logic, perhaps misguided but rational in its own way. Most of them were former conservatives who had become increasingly radicalized, drawn into the irrational parallel universe of conspiracy theories and scapegoating.

Beginning in the mid-1990s, I began observing greater and greater similarities between mainstream conservatives and these longtime denizens of the Far Right. More and more they shared the willingness—even eagerness—to embrace verifiably false information as fact, as well as subscribe to the increasing dehumanization of those they considered their enemies. Since the events of 9/11, these similarities have intensified.

It has become increasingly easy to lose track of the differences between genuine proto-fascists and mainstream conservatives, but some important ones remain. As much as movement conservatives might threaten and bluster, they lack the visceral, paranoid anger that animates so many actual fascists. They may try to talk and walk like fascists, but underneath, they lack the street violence and thuggery, the actual eliminationist enterprise that is the true fascist's hallmark. These persistent differences are a good thing, for it means that the situation is not yet irretrievable.

So I've devised a term to describe what's taking place: *para-fascism*. Para-fascists are distinct from proto-fascists in that they lack certain traits of genuine fascists in their nascent form, yet they stand as a constant threat in that they could find the means and motives to eventually turn into the real thing—if not now, perhaps even years down the road. Fascism in its previous manifestations often took root, like all pathologies, after years of subsisting on the fringe of society. So while it would be clearly incorrect to call modern conservatives "fascists," the transformation of movement conservatism has created, in essence, the groundwork for the eventual outbreak of genuine fascism. You need look no further than the ugly eliminationism now ascendant on the Right to get a good view of this reality.

It is by small steps of incremental meanness and viciousness that we lose our humanity. We have the historical example of 20th-century fascism as a reminder. The Nazis, in the end, embodied demonic inhumanity, but they didn't get that way overnight. They did this by not simply branding their opponents as the Enemy, but by denying them their essential humanity, depicting them as worse than scum—disease-laden, world-destroying vermin, in desperate need of elimination.

Eliminationism is an acute warning sign: it has historically played the role of creating *permission* for people to act out their violent impulses against its targets. More than any other facet of para-fascism, it poses the greatest specific danger of transforming it into the real thing.

This is why eliminationist rhetoric has a special quality: the distinctive odor of burning flesh. And when it hits our nostrils, we dare not ignore the warning.

1

The Politics of the Personal

There's one thing about growing up in a place like Idaho: if you can't make friends with conservatives, you won't have many friends.

I remember them in the gun shops where I hung out with my dad. Born and raised in southern Idaho, he is still an accomplished marksman and woodsman. He also was a gunsmith in his spare time, so my afternoons after school were spent in the gun shops where he picked up spare change helping out. Mostly it was a lot of older men, and the air was often an acrid mix of tobacco smoke, gunpowder, and right-wing politics. I was exposed to the NRA worldview at an early age, not to mention the John Birch Society, which was everywhere in Idaho Falls. Certainly I had it drilled into my head to be on the lookout for commies, gun-grabbers, and other loathsome forms of humanity. Most of these, I learned, were Democrats, and so even through high school I identified with all things Republican.

Mine was a typical Idaho working-class Republican family. I remember well the Goldwater bumper sticker on the '59 Ford Fairlane, our family car in 1964. When our junior high school held a mock presidential debate in 1968, I eagerly took the Nixon side. In high school I worked on the congressional campaigns of local Republicans, and I continued doing GOP campaign work in college. I paid for my first couple of years of college by doing farm work, mostly hauling irrigation pipe, and later moved up to higher-paying road construction jobs. I knew well the value of hard work. My belief in blue-collar virtues—integrity, decency, honesty, common sense, and fair play—was embedded in me like the work lines in my hands. And until I got out of college, I really believed that conservatism best embodied those values—even if it included people whose politics reflected a deep, extremist paranoia.

The Right in Idaho, in fact, had a long history of political extremism. From the mid-1950s onward, anticommunist paranoia, embodied in the John Birch Society, was a dominant political force in southern Idaho. The first time I saw Gen. Jack D. Ripper, the cigar-chewing paranoid who blows up the world in *Dr. Strangelove,* I thought the character was modeled after our neighbor down the street, the one who had the bomb shelter. He also worked at the local nuclear engineering laboratory.

The Birch Society was everywhere at the time; I saw copies of Gary Allen's eminently digestible Bircherite opus, *None Dare Call It Conspiracy,* in the homes of my parents' friends. My grandmother dated an ardent Bircherite for many years, and I used to thumb through his conspiracist library in his farmhouse just outside Twin Falls. Southern Idaho was also heavily dominated by the Mormon Church (about two-thirds of my graduating class belonged to the Church of Jesus Christ of Latter-day Saints, or LDS), and the "Church-Birch connection" was well-known and oft-remarked. When I was in high school in the early 1970s, the local Birch unit became ardently involved in the fight over our school district's dress code; they said that allowing boys to grow their hair long was part of the communist conspiracy to feminize our men. Fortunately, the district ignored them and let us grow our hair.

The Birch Society's influence even followed me to northern Idaho, where the LDS influence was significantly smaller. When I was editor of the local paper in Sandpoint, Idaho, in the late 1970s, I remember spending one evening at the home of a local businessman. I barely knew the man and wasn't sure why he had invited me to dinner, but he had made an effort to seek me out, so I went. After the meal with his wife and children, he and I retired to his den, where he got out one of those filmstrip projectors with an accompanying phonograph and proceeded to show me a Birch Society recruitment film. Afterward, I thanked him and declined any further contact. By then, I had seen enough of the Birch Society to stay away.

One of the other things about growing up in a place like Idaho is that, yes, there are racists. Neo-Nazis. White supremacists. Conspiracy-mongering survivalists. Militiamen.

You name it, we've got 'em. Not very many of 'em, mind you. Their numbers are really quite small, but they've been coming (mostly from California and Arizona) in numbers large enough to shift the political demographics in the state. And they come because the nearly all-white cultural landscape is comfortable for them.

Whatever name you want to give them, they all fit the description of genuine American proto-fascists. Some of them—the Aryan Nations folks in particular—are quite unapologetic about their beliefs. Others, like the militiamen, are geared to make inroads into the mainstream, so they do their utmost to disguise those beliefs, though they inevitably emerge when you probe just a little bit.

Idaho's image nationally has taken a real beating as a haven for racists, and for the most part this is a gross distortion of the reality. Most Idahoans are deeply embarrassed by these people and will find nearly anything else to talk about. Most people think it's unfair to judge the rest of the state by them, and the fact is, they are only a tiny faction. However, their presence poses special challenges that can't be dealt with by running away from them.

I've had some personal experience with this dilemma. When I was the editor the *Daily Bee* in Sandpoint in the late 1970s, we were faced with the tough decision of how to handle the increasing visibility of Richard Butler's neo-Nazi Church of Jesus Christ Christian, based at the Aryan Nations compound some 30 miles down the road in Hayden Lake. After much hand-wringing, we decided it was best not to give them any coverage, since publicity was what they craved, and it would only encourage their radicalism.

What we didn't understand was that the silence was interpreted as *consent*. And so, over the next several years, the Idaho Panhandle witnessed a parade of disturbing hate crimes (enough so that Idaho became one of the first states to pass a bias-crime law), ranging from the vandalization of a Jewish-owned restaurant to the harassment of mixed-race schoolchildren. There was also a procession of extraordinarily violent incidents, including the multistate rampage of murder and robbery by the neo-Nazi sect called The Order and the pipe-bombing campaigns planned by their successors. All of these acts emanated from the Aryan Nations.

By then I had moved on to other papers, but the *Bee* changed its policies on the Aryan Nations in fairly short order, as did most other newsrooms in the area that had taken similar approaches. I certainly never forgot that mistake.

In the ensuing years, I had various occasions to deal with these extremists as a journalist, especially in the 1990s when I began writing about the "Christian Patriot" movement, better known in the media as the "militia movement." I covered the 81-day standoff of the Montana Freemen in 1996 and their subsequent trials, as well as the activities of other Northwest militiamen, notably the Washington State Militia, whose leaders and core followers were arrested by federal agents on bomb-building charges the same year. I also interviewed national militia-movement leaders, like Col. James "Bo" Gritz and John Trochmann.

During that time, I also had the chance to meet and talk with a substantial number of the far-right True Believers, who form the rank and file of these movements, and it was eye-opening. Most of what you think you know about these people isn't true. Most of them aren't angry skinheads festooned with swastika tattoos. They aren't uneducated backwoods hicks, and they don't have horns growing out of their heads. Most of them are quiet, taxpaying (begrudgingly) citizens who have barbecues with their neighbors and take part in local bake sales for the football team. It's only when you start digging a little beneath the surface that you discover that they're, well, different.

By the time their numbers started increasing, they already existed along a continuum of the political landscape in Idaho. A large portion of the Patriots I met and interviewed, interestingly, started out as members of the John Birch Society, which acted as a launching pad to radicalism for many future extremists. Perhaps the most notorious instance of this was Robert Mathews, the leader of The Order, who was radicalized as a teenage Bircher and gradually became a racist assassin, overseeing the killing of Denver radio talk-show host Alan Berg and masterminding a series of bank and armored-car robberies.

Many of the leaders in the movement had Bircher backgrounds; both Trochmann, leader of the Militia of Montana, and "Bo" Gritz began as Birchers. And you could find many ex-Birchers among rank-and-file followers. One Patriot I interviewed, a man named Calvin Greenup, who had engaged in an armed standoff with authorities in Montana's Bitterroot Valley for several weeks, said he grew up with it in his school. "That was going on in this valley when I was in school," he told me. "My sixth-grade teacher, as a matter of fact, was a John Bircher. And she's the one that started me on the path of teaching me the Bill of Rights and the Constitution. John Birchers were strong then. Underground, but strong."

The conspiracist element often commingled with deeply religious beliefs of an apocalyptic nature, that secular society was intent on destroying Christianity and people like themselves. This made for a toxic combination. Randy and Vicki Weaver, the protagonists of the notorious 1992 Ruby Ridge standoff, moved to Idaho from Iowa after being radicalized by a combination of apocalyptic fundamentalism and far-right conspiracy theories.

In general, most of these people prefer to fly under the radar and blend in. If they're not off in the woods secluding themselves from society, as the Weavers were, they have normal homes in normal neighborhoods. Many of them have difficulty maintaining friendships—in large part due to their innate paranoia and snap judgments—but they still do their best to keep up appearances and maintain a low profile.

This seeming normalcy reflects a significant component of the racist Right's general strategy since the early 1980s—namely, to cast themselves in as mainstream a light as possible for the general public. Through the 1980s and 1990s, Louisiana white supremacist David Duke attempted to portray his remade Ku Klux Klan as a suit-and-tie operation out to defend downtrodden whites. The "militia movement" of the 1990s was specifically geared toward mainstreaming some of the basic tenets of their worldview (particularly notions about a looming conspiracy by nefarious internal enemies out to destroy America), though it met with only mixed success (as did Duke). Far more successful, however, in achieving a mainstream appearance were the border-watching Minutemen of the first decade of the 21st century, who were an offshoot of the militia movement.

Probably the definitive examination of "Christian Patriots"—the term by which members of many sectors of the Far Right identify themselves—was James Aho's landmark sociological study, *The Politics of Righteousness: Idaho Christian Patriotism*, which should have permanently laid to rest many myths about such followers of "extremist" belief systems. Built on his extended interviews with several hundred people, he came away with some fascinating data:

> There is no evidence that Idaho Christian patriots have less formal education than their less radical peers. Indeed, the subjects studied here have on the average spent more years in school than their more conventional neighbors. This is not to say that they have achieved a better education or that they are more intelligent. But there is nothing to support the popularly held reverse contention that Idaho Christian patriotism can be accounted for by the lack of education of its proponents.... Apart from these differences and similarities between Identity Christians and Christian Constitutionalists, Idaho's patriots in general do not seem more socially alienated from their communities than cross-sections of Americans or Idahoans.[1]

And what are the defining characteristics of these True Believers, psychologically and politically? Aho breaks them down into three key categories. First, there's dualism, or the division of reality into a "godly" spiritual realm, in which lies the "perfect," and a corrupt material world, which is "profanity, unconsciousness, and death." Second, there's "conspiratorialism," or "the psychologizing of history and the reduction of historical events to the conscious intentions of omniscient and all-powerful Benefactors and Malefactors." This mix reduces the causes of perceived social decline into a quest for scapegoats in need of elimination. And third, there's the apocalyptic belief in the imminent end of the world as we know it.[2]

Most of these characteristics, taken by themselves, seem relatively unremarkable. But when they come together they become a pathological influence on their communities and society at large.

The solutions for society's ills nearly all these people come to adopt are uniformly *eliminationist*: keep black people out of our communities; round up homosexuals and AIDS victims and put them in concentration camps; deport all the nation's 12 million illegal aliens; get rid of all the liberals. And as Aho explains, the search for an Other to scapegoat—the "quest for whom to blame and whom to eliminate"—comes to define their very agenda.

For most of my life, even into the 1990s, it was fairly easy to distinguish eliminationists from mainstream conservatives. Conservatives were people who welcomed the advances of science and education, were generally civil in their dealings with political opponents, shunned conspiracism and outrageous paranoia, and were not constantly sounding the alarm about the impending end of civilization. Religious beliefs always played a role in traditional conservatism, but the old consensus held by both liberals and conservatives—that religious freedom meant the freedom of every citizen to choose his or her creed without coercion—still held sway, for the most part.

That began to change, though, in the mid-1990s. And by the first few years of the 21st century, the differences between the mainstream Right and its fanatical fringe became thin indeed.

The convergence began in the wake of the terrorist attacks of September 11, 2001. Most strikingly, the apocalypticism already inherent in fundamentalist beliefs came leaping to the fore. A wellspring of preachers assured their flocks that they were living in the "End Times." Some even formed alliances with Israel under the assumption that Armageddon was forthcoming in the Middle East.

The inherent dualism in these beliefs took on even sharper edges, becoming more like the "exemplary dualism" of the Christian Patriots. It also spread beyond the religious zealots. It soon became common for mainstream conservatives to do the following:

- Blame liberal decadence for the terrorist attacks (conservative pundit Dinesh D'Souza devoted an entire text to this subject, fittingly titled *The Enemy at Home*).
- Promote fears about the shifting racial admixture of the American populace. This is heard most loudly in the debate over immigration, where the arrival of Latino immigrants is often characterized as an "invasion."
- Voice an animus toward pacifism (treated in such national venues as Bill O'Reilly's Fox News program as tantamount to surrender and "hating America") and feminism (Rush Limbaugh's infamous reference to "feminazis" being only the most famous of the sneers).

Likewise, the right-wing propensity for conspiracy theories took on a life of its own and entered the mainstream after 9/11.

The immigration debate provided a convenient venue: it became possible for millions of Americans to learn from right-wing pundits, from Michelle Malkin to CNN's Lou Dobbs, about the "invasion" of America being planned by Mexican radicals under the so-called Reconquista (or reconquest) of the Southwest. This groundless conspiracy theory was first concocted in the 1990s by a white-supremacist group called American Border Patrol.

But most of the paranoia has been directed at Muslims, beginning with many right-wing Web sites—most prominently Little Green Footballs and Malkin's blog—and gradually moving into the more rarefied heights of the Beltway elite. The bloggers, Malkin especially, were prone to finding a "jihadist" conspiracy beneath every unturned rock. She reported looming "jihadi" cabals everywhere, from a memorial for the victims of one of the 9/11 hijackings, to a suicide bombing in Oklahoma, to a small clutch of Muslim clerics aboard an airline flight to Minnesota. But then we began hearing similar theories from supposedly elite right-wing thinkers, like Mark Steyn and Norman Podhoretz. Podhoretz, in his book *World War IV*, envisioned a decades-long struggle with the forces of a radical "Islamofascism," which evidently poses an existential threat surpassing that of the Soviet Union and Nazi Germany combined.

Finally, you could find the right-wing paranoid mindset turning from readily identifiable Others—like Latinos and Muslims—to their fellow American citizens, "treasonous" liberals who wanted to see America fail. Fox News' Bill O'Reilly concocted a supposed "war on Christmas" being waged against American Christians by atheists and "secular humanists." A number of religious-right figures began inveighing against a similar war against Christianity in the form of the "gay agenda." For a couple of days on his national broadcast, O'Reilly even went so far as to tout a theory about a growing cabal of pink-pistol-slinging lesbian thugs who beat up hapless men in various locales around the country. Most of all, the Enemy was increasingly identified as *liberals*. Building on years of radio-talk demonization of all things left, it became common for right-wing pundits to talk about liberals as being the "Enemy at Home," as D'Souza's book put it.

The transformation didn't happen overnight. It came in bits and pieces, small events that seemed innocuous enough at the time. Beginning in the mid-1990s, and increasingly so in the years after 9/11, figures on the mainstream Right began picking up ideas, talking points, issues, and agendas from its extremist fringes: the xenophobic, conspiracist, fanatical religious Right. These ostensibly mainstream figures would then repackage these ideas and talking points for general consumption, usually by stripping out the overt references to racism and xenophobic hatred.

These "transmitters," as sociologists call them, were often leading right-wing media luminaries, all viewed as reliable mainstream conservatives: Limbaugh, O'Reilly, Coulter, Dobbs, Malkin, Savage, and a host of imitators. Some were public officials, like Sen. Trent Lott (whose ties to the segregationist neo-Confederate movement came to public attention in 2002), Rep. Tom Tancredo, and Rep. Ron Paul (the latter a 2008 Republican presidential candidate, despite his longtime proclivity for "New World Order" conspiracy theories). Sometimes the transmissions came from people who manage, for a time, to disguise their agendas while keeping one foot firmly in the fringe camp. For instance, Jared Taylor of the white-supremacist *American Renaissance,* is skilled at posing as an academic expert on race relations and is presented on TV as such. John Tanton, the mastermind of various "immigration reform" groups that demonize Latinos, is financed by white supremacists.

In the 1990s, bashing Bill Clinton was a pastime shared by both the mainstream and the extremist Right. Many of the charges laid against Clinton—that he and his wife, Hillary, had conspired to murder White House counsel Vince Foster; that Clinton had a hidden black "love child"; that he was conspiring with the "New World Order" at the United Nations to give away American sovereignty—originally circulated in the militia meeting halls and the gatherings of Montana Freemen. By the latter part of the decade, these claims were being circulated for broad public consumption by leading mouthpieces of the mainstream conservative movement. They culminated in the Clinton impeachment fiasco, which demonstrated the power of an increasingly fanatical movement to foist its political agenda on an unwilling public. Polls consistently showed that the public disapproved far more of the effort to impeach Clinton than it did of Clinton's behavior.

But the baiting did not end when Clinton left office. If anything, it accelerated in the ensuing years, driven particularly by three major issues: the 9/11 attacks and the "war on terror," the invasion of Iraq, and immigration. In all three cases, the demonization of liberals grew sharper and louder, as did the reflexive reliance on conspiracy theories and apocalyptic fearmongering.

Through the 1990s, the mainstream media remained generally leery of conspiracy theories and xenophobic paranoia. It became common, however, in the first decade of the new millennium to find kooky nonsense being broadcast to millions by supposedly respected mainstream news figures. Thus, Lou Dobbs could broadcast maps of a fanciful "Aztlan" (which figures prominently in the Reconquista theories) taken from a white-supremacist Web site;

or he could tell his audience that illegal immigrants are bringing a wave of leprosy to American shores (drawn, once again, from kooky far-right sources whose claims fly in the face of established facts), and it raises scarcely an eyebrow. Glenn Beck can tell his audiences all about a nonexistent "North American Union" conspiracy to turn the continent into a single nation, and those who criticize such balderdash are dismissed as liberals. Bill O'Reilly calls DailyKos readers Nazis and Klansmen, and no one other than his targets appears to notice the outrageousness of the charge.

The thread running throughout this relentless demonization is scapegoating, a thread that brings movement conservatives closest to resembling the far-right extremist and his "quest for whom to blame and whom to eliminate." Indeed, scapegoating lays the groundwork for purging, the impetus not merely to defeat but to eliminate the opposition by whatever means might be at hand.

How is any kind of discourse possible in this environment? How is it possible to be civil to people who are constantly placing you under assault, both verbally and physically? How can there be dialogue when the normative rules of give and take and fair play have been flushed down the drain?

Ironically, the mainstream Right has largely avoided confronting its role in poisoning the public well by accusing liberals of being unconscionably vile in how they respond. It's become a common theme, and not just from the usual quarters. Malkin devoted an entire book, titled *Unhinged: Exposing Liberals Gone Wild,* to the subject. Among the "centrists" of the Beltway Village media, "wise men," like David Broder and Howard Kurtz call on "decent" Democrats to eschew the very kind of ugly hardball politics Republicans have spent the past decade mastering, and to ignore the loud voices of their increasingly irate base.

It's a neat trick. Not only has the village lunatic gained permission to continue wandering the town square poking everyone he dislikes in the eye with a sharp stick, but he gets to claim victimhood when the victims respond angrily. Unfortunately, in the process, the whole village is transformed, and not for the better.

2

The Transmission Belt

I was driving around Billings, Montana, in the middle of a nasty blizzard in 1996, trying to figure out what the hell was going on, when the voice belonging to "The Talent on Loan from God" hit my ears.

There are, I suppose, a few things you have to admire about Rush Limbaugh, and one of them is his voice. It is absolutely distinctive. I can hear it through a rolled-up car window and identify it at once. But that afternoon in early March, his voice on the radio in my little rented car, came as something of an epiphany. There wasn't anything new or remarkable about that day's broadcast. It just answered a question I had been trying to understand.

I was in Billings because a few days before, the FBI had arrested two leaders of the Montana Freemen at their compound near Jordan, Montana. I attended their initial hearings at the federal courthouse, drove up to Jordan for a day, then drove back to Billings for more courtroom action at the arraignments. This was quite a bit of driving, especially with the ice and snow storm that had come through about a week before and was continuing to rage.

Mostly, I was trying to get a handle on the seething, venomous hatred toward the government that was seeping out in the bile of movements like the Freemen, but was also much, much more widespread. Almost anyone you talked to in rural America was embittered by their hatred of the "gummint" in nearly all its forms, particularly the federal one. Certainly it had been on full display in the federal courtroom in Billings, where LeRoy Schweitzer and Dan Petersen had done their best to disrupt the hearings with their insistence that the entire proceedings against them lacked legitimacy.

I was no stranger to feelings of hatred for the government. In my early 20s, I'd witnessed the death of a great-aunt as a result of the 1976 collapse of the Teton Dam in southeastern Idaho—a disaster caused by the arrogance and incompetence of federal bureaucrats. I knew firsthand that government could be lethally stupid. But the kind of ideology being promoted by the Freemen, both in the courtroom and in their pseudo-legal writings, went beyond even that. It was blind, irrational, utterly visceral hatred that surpassed even the worst things I had heard from the mouths of Birchers while I was growing up. In fact, it reminded me of talk I had heard previously in only one other place: the Aryan Nations compound in Hayden Lake. There were the paranoid conspiracy theories, the pseudo-legal "constitutionalism," even the barely concealed race-baiting and anti-Semitism. Only the usual accompaniment of Hitler worship and cross-burning was missing.

The thing about government-bashing out West is that nearly anyone who has lived here for any length of time, particularly if they have deep family roots, has directly benefited from government programs. Such programs are, in fact, responsible for their very presence on this land. That situation has created a complex love/hate relationship between the government and the ranchers and farmers who have been its main beneficiaries, and sometimes its victims.

Most farming and ranching operations in the interior West,

such as those in eastern Montana, originated with homesteading and irrigation projects created by the federal government in the early part of the 20th century. The federal government builds our roads, pays for our schools, constructs our water-supply and irrigation systems and the dams that make them go. We're actually terribly dependent on the "gummint," which chafes rather nastily against Westerners' own deeply mythologized sense of self-reliance and independence.

The sheer venom coming from the Patriot movement, however, was in another universe. Built around strange conspiracy theories and fire-breathing rhetoric, the movement was wildly out of far-right field; for it to be taking root in a place like Montana, where common sense was usually the real coin of the realm, was incongruous. It was disturbing to see how many people with ordinary working-class, agricultural backgrounds, with rock-solid reputations in the community, were being drawn into the Patriot movement and embracing its rhetoric, if not its agenda.

How had this happened? What was encouraging people to make this leap? I was puzzling over this that day in Billings while I was tootling through the snow, listening to Rush on the radio. On that day, I had decided to try listening to him from the viewpoint of someone like the auto-mechanic-turned-Freeman, Dan Petersen, or some other working-class stiff from Jordan—someone not particularly well educated (indeed, innately suspicious of schooling), prone to a visceral kind of patriotism and similar politics, and insistent on his identity as an independent westerner. By doing that, I got an answer, or at least part of one.

Limbaugh was holding forth that day on the subject of federal bureaucrats who, he claimed, were attempting to ignore the will of the people regarding control of federal lands and the tax bureaucracy. At the apex of the rant, Limbaugh began speculating about the motives of these bureaucrats: they didn't care, he said, about "democracy"; they would probably just as soon dispose of it, and any kind of responsiveness to the public altogether if given the opportunity; they would be happier in a dictatorship, which was what they were establishing anyway.[1] Or so Rush told us.

Suddenly, I had a very clear picture of how hatred of the government had reached such illogical and hysterical heights. Americans were being told, relentlessly and repeatedly, that government was not only a bad thing but that it was inherently evil. Government was conspiring to take away their freedom and enslave them. The person telling them this was a mainstream conservative. He was giving them essentially the same message espoused by the Freemen and militias, but this time with the mantle of mainstream legitimacy. Rush was taking people up to the edge of Patriot beliefs, and more or less introducing his listeners to them. And if his listeners were like people in Montana (or anywhere else the Patriot movement set up shop, which was largely every corner of the country), who already had Patriots for neighbors, they would take the next step themselves.

Limbaugh's defenders would, no doubt, depict this kind of talk as simple hyperbole intended to emphasize his point and inject some humor. Such justifications are disingenuous: why say something that incendiary if at some level you don't mean it? We cannot overlook the effect such talk has on audiences, who may not be as sophisticated or as inclined to distinguish the hyperbole from the supposedly reasonable discourse. Indeed, the bulk of "dittoheads" I have met tend to take his every utterance as virtual Gospel.

Limbaugh might claim that he's merely being critical of government, but his rhetoric goes beyond such acceptable (in fact, desirable) robust political speech; it argues for the overthrow and dismantling of the system itself. And this is where one must draw the line, if anywhere, between being a politically active citizen and an extremist, right or left. Limbaugh dangerously straddles that line.

This is the same kind of demagoguery President Clinton referred to in his remarkable address in Minneapolis a few days after the 1995 Oklahoma City bombing:

> In this country we cherish and guard the right of free speech. We know we love it when we put up with people saying things we absolutely deplore. And we must always be willing to defend their right to say things we deplore to the ultimate degree. But we hear so many loud and angry voices in America today whose sole goal seems to be to try to keep some people as paranoid as possible and the rest of us all torn up and upset with each other. They spread hate. They leave the impression that, by their very words, that violence is acceptable. You ought to see—I'm sure you are now seeing the reports of some things that are regularly said over the airwaves in America today.
>
> Well, people like that who want to share our freedoms must know that their bitter words can have consequences and that freedom has endured in this country for more than two centuries because it was coupled with an enormous sense of responsibility on the part of the American people.
>
> If we are to have freedom to speak, freedom to assemble, and, yes, the freedom to bear arms, we must have responsibility as well. And to those of us who do not agree with the purveyors of hatred and division, with the promoters of paranoia, I remind you that we have freedom of speech, too, and we have responsibilities, too. And some of us have not discharged our responsibilities. It is time we all stood up and spoke against that kind of reckless speech and behavior.
>
> If they insist on being irresponsible with our common liberties, then we must be all the more responsible with our liberties.

When they talk of hatred, we must stand against them. When they talk of violence, we must stand against them. When they say things that are irresponsible, that may have egregious consequences, we must call them on it. The exercise of their freedom of speech makes our silence all the more unforgivable. So exercise yours, my fellow Americans. Our country, our future, our way of life is at stake.[2]

Though Clinton certainly never identified Limbaugh as one of those "angry voices," Limbaugh immediately responded with cries of censorship and claims that Clinton was attempting to silence him. Since then, the protests have been so constant that the claim that Clinton blamed Limbaugh for Oklahoma City has now become a stock argument to prove the supposed perfidy of liberals. Ann Coulter repeated this charge in her book *Slander: Liberal Lies About the American Right*: "When impeached former president Bill Clinton identified Rush Limbaugh as the cause of the Oklahoma City bombing, he unleashed all the typical liberal curse words for conservatives. He blamed 'loud and angry voices' heard 'over the airwaves in America' that were making people 'paranoid' and spreading hate."

Clinton did not name anyone. The voices he probably had in mind were those belonging to the likes of G. Gordon Liddy (notorious for describing how to deal with federal agents: "Head shots!") and some of the more vicious Patriot types, like Chuck Harder. Harder constantly hawked Patriot conspiracy theories outright, along with a full dose of rhetoric about violently resisting officials from the federal government. But Clinton used general terms probably because he recognized the fact that characters like Limbaugh and his fellow movement arch-conservatives also have a certain amount of responsibility as transmitters—the people who repackage far-right ideas for mainstream consumption and thereby lend them legitimacy.

The bitter truth is that Clinton was right: words have consequences. When you promote an essentially extremist worldview tailored to fit a mainstream audience, you're spreading poison that can have extremely violent consequences. In the wake of the Oklahoma City bombing, its chief perpetrator, Timothy McVeigh, made clear—through interviews and writings—that his hatred of the government was fanned by both extremist and mainstream voices. Clinton was alluding to *all* these voices.

While Limbaugh cannot be blamed directly for Oklahoma City, neither can he be wholly absolved. Whining does not relieve him of the responsibility for his words. Timothy McVeigh, and the wave of Patriot domestic terrorists who followed him between 1995 and 2000, did not occur in a vacuum. Over 40 incidents of serious right-wing domestic terror in the United States were carried out in those years by people as disparate as antiabortion fanatics like Eric Rudolph and James Kopp to free-range gunmen like Buford Furrow. In the milieu that nurtured such creatures, Limbaugh and other ostensibly "mainstream" media, political, and religious figures helped transmit and reinforce extremist ideas that became extremely volatile when wedded to a personality with a violent predisposition.

Transmitters like Limbaugh make two things happen: they inject extremist ideas into the mainstream, and they bring the two sectors closer together. Mainstream conservatives gain more sympathy for extremist beliefs, and the extremists gain more confidence because they are now within the mainstream. The result is that right-wing extremists wind up exerting a gravitational pull on mainstream conservatism—and by extension, the whole political continuum—that far exceeds their actual size or, for that matter, political viability. That the entire spectrum has shifted steadily rightward in the past 10 years and more could not be more self-evident. The results have, as in Oklahoma City, been devastating.

If nothing else, Oklahoma City should at least have been a warning to Limbaugh that it was time to tone down the rhetoric, to stop demonizing government employees and federal officials. Unfortunately, anti-government bile is still a constant of his radio rants. Certainly it was that day in Billings, which was nearly a year after Oklahoma City.

But then, he has not been alone, either.

"Hitler was more moral than Clinton," intoned the nice-looking, dark-haired man in the three-piece suit. "He had fewer girlfriends."

The audience laughed and applauded, loudly.

A remark like that might hardly have raised an eyebrow in post-Monica America in the 1990s, particularly in the meeting halls of mainstream conservatism. By the end of Bill Clinton's tenure in the White House, no hyperbole seemed too overblown in the campaign to convince the rest of us that he was too grossly immoral to continue to hold the presidency.

As the scandal wore on, the volume, intensity, and downright nastiness of his critics reached impressive levels. It wasn't unusual to hear members of Congress calling him a "scumbag" and a "cancer on the presidency." *Orlando Sentinel* columnist Charley Reese at one point called him "a sociopath, a liar, a sexual predator, a man with recklessly bad judgment and a scofflaw."[3]

But the scene above took place four years before Monica, in 1994, long before Clinton handed his enemies a scandal on a platter that seemingly made such epithets acceptable. It was not at a Republican caucus or Christian Coalition meeting, but at a gathering of right-wing "Patriots" who had come to hear about forming militias and common-law courts and defending their gun rights—indeed, their families—from what they called the New World Order. They numbered only a hundred or so and only half-filled the little convention hall in Bellevue, Washington, but their fervor saturated the room with its own paranoid energy.

And the speaker, who could have passed even then for a local Republican public official (actually, he was nominally a Democrat), was one of the nation's leading Patriot figures: Richard Mack, then sheriff of Arizona's mostly rural Graham County. As a leader in the fight against gun control (his lawsuit eventually went to the Supreme Court, overturning a section of the so-called Brady Law), Mack was in high demand on the right-wing lecture circuit, where he promoted the militia concept to eager acolytes. He usually sprinkled his "constitutional" gun-rights thesis with his theories on church-state separation—a "myth"—and "the New World Order conspiracy."

The similarities between Mack's 1994 sentiments and the hyperbole directed at Clinton in 1998 are not accidental. Rather, they offer a stark example of the way the Far Right's ideas, rhetoric, and issues work their way into the mainstream. For that matter, much of the conservative anti-Clinton paroxysm could be traced directly to some of the smears that first circulated in militia and white-supremacist circles.

How these ideas migrate is also important to understand. Richard Mack, for instance, didn't compare Bill Clinton's morality to Adolf Hitler's at every speaking opportunity. His remark didn't show up, for instance, when he had his moment in the sun speaking before the National Rifle Association's (NRA) national convention in 1994. It did, however, when he was in front of an audience of Patriot believers. That was when he knew it would be most appreciated. It mixed well with the fear of the New World Order he fomented in his quiet, almost sedate speaking tone.

Mack, like Limbaugh, is a transmitter, someone who straddles the boundaries of the various sectors of America's right wing and appears to belong to each of them in turn at various times. Since the 1990s, he has largely faded back into obscurity. But during his heyday, Mack's gun-control message sold well with mainstream, secular NRA audiences. His claims that church-state separation is a myth resonated nicely with the theocratic right-wing crowd as well. And he cultivated a quasi-legitimate image by taking leadership positions in groups like Larry Pratt's Gun Owners of America. But he was most at home in his native base: the populist Right, the world of militias, constitutionalists, and pseudo-libertarians. Mack even occasionally consorted with the hard Right, as when he granted front-page interviews to the Christian Identity newspaper the *Jubilee*.

At the same time he toured the countryside preaching the Patriot message, Mack cut a seemingly mainstream conservative figure. As one of the key players in the effort to overturn the Brady gun-control law—which Mack claimed infringes on his rights as sheriff—he gained his highest public notice. In 1994, the NRA honored him as their Law Enforcement Officer of the Year. The image boost let him tour nationwide, speaking at numerous Patriot gatherings and hawking his books (*From My Cold Dead Fingers* and *Government, God and Freedom*).

Mack's Clinton-bashing was mostly a gratuitous nod to one of the Patriot movement's favorite themes: an almost pathological hatred of the former occupants of the Oval Office. If you had gone to any militia gathering—usually held in small town halls or county fairgrounds, sometimes under the guise of "preparedness expos," "patriotic meetings" or even gun shows—you could always find a wealth of material aimed at proving the Clintons the worst kind of treasonous villains imaginable. Bill and Hillary Clinton, after all, for most of the 1990s, occupied the central position in Patriots' New World Order paranoiac fantasy, and they have continued to feature prominently in these theories well after Clinton's tenure.

"For those in this right-wing conspiracist subculture, Clinton as president represents a constitutional crisis because he is seen as a traitor betraying the country to secret elites plotting a collectivist totalitarian rule through a global New World Order," observed Chip Berlet of the think tank Political Research Associates. "Stories of Clinton's alleged sexual misconduct buttress this notion because they demonstrate symptoms of his liberal secular humanist outlook, which ties him to what is seen as a longstanding conspiracy against God, individual responsibility, and national sovereignty."[4] The Clintons' conspiracy was believed to have its roots in global communism and, ultimately, the "international bankers" (read: Jews) who pull all the world's political and economic strings.

If you had gone to the book table of the Militia of Montana (or MOM, as followers call it) at any Patriot gathering during the 1990s, you could find, alongside army manuals on "Booby Traps" and guerrilla-warfare manuals like *The Road Back,* a healthy selection of books and tapes devoted to Clinton's many perfidies.

> *Black Helicopters over America: Strikeforce for the New World Order.* Jim Keith's militia classic that, besides postulating global preparations for the enslavement of humanity, identified Bill Clinton as an "obvious socialist and possible Soviet agent" whose administration has "ushered in the New World Order."
>
> *Executive Orders for the New World Order.* MOM's popular pamphlet with a list of presidential orders—mostly

related to national emergencies under the aegis of that
X-Files bugaboo, the Federal Emergency Management
Administration (FEMA)—which ostensibly show how
Clinton has prepared for the New World Order takeover.

Big Sister Is Watching You. A supposed expose of Hillary's
secretive claque of "Feminazis," with several suggestions
that a witch's coven might be lurking in the White House.
The MOM catalog describes it thus: "These are the women
who tell Bill Clinton what to do: Lesbians, sex perverts,
child-molester advocates, Christian haters and the most
doctrinaire of Communists, whose goal is to end American
sovereignty and bring about a global Marxist paradise."

Martial Law Rule. An "exposé" by Oregon white supremacist Robert Wangrud of Clinton's continuing imposition
of "martial law" in the United States, which he claims
began under Lincoln and has remained in place since.
Elsewhere, Wangrud has been known to argue that civil-
rights legislation constitutes the treasonous act of "race
betrayal."

The Death of Vince Foster and *The Clinton Chronicles.*
The now-infamous creations of Citizens for Honest
Government, which supposedly laid bare Clinton's
involvement in the murder of his aide as well as a web
of drug-running and murders in rural Arkansas.

Indeed, the militia movement provided most of the early audience for *The Clinton Chronicles.* Large stacks of the books and vid-
eos sold well at Patriot gatherings, and the Arkansas tales continue
to be regarded as articles of faith. The wild and bizarre accusations—easily refuted both in the mainstream media and by a congressional investigation—gained an extended half-life in a milieu
where counterevidence is considered further proof of a conspiracy.

This echo effect resonated long enough that the claims obtained currency in the mainstream.

This is how the Patriot movement of the 1990s, and continuing well into this century, has pulled the national debate toward its own agenda. Regardless of how far-fetched or provably false their claims or beliefs might be, they stay alive in the everything-fits conspiracist mindset of the Far Right. The ideas that have lasting resonance are transmitted to the mainstream, now stripped of their usual racial or religious incendiarism. As the ideas gain more traction in the mainstream, the Far Right's agenda gets realized incrementally.

David Duke knows all about this technique—he has mastered it over the years as one of the nation's leading white-supremacist figures. For years—especially during his Populist Party presidential bid in 1988 and his nearly successful U.S. Senate campaign in 1990—Duke denied being a white racist, despite his background as a KKK leader. Finally, in his unsuccessful 1996 Senate race, Duke abandoned his pretense and began campaigning almost exclusively on the issue of "saving white heritage" and other "racial realities." His campaign literature listed his former Klan leadership, and his Web site contained Duke's favorite theories on racial separation. He noted wryly the similarities between the 1996 GOP platform and his own 1988 presidential platform, running as the candidate of the far-right Populist Party—anti-immigrant, antigay, anti-affirmative action, antiwelfare, antiabortion. "The nation has come to me," he observed.

The Patriot movement works in much the same way. A network of transmitters carry into mainstream settings the Patriots' uniquely reactionary positions in the national debate—whether the topic is gun control, environmental policy, education, or abortion—and the ripples draw the debate in their direction. And deposing the epitome of evil itself—Bill Clinton—was for much of the 1990s near or at the top of the list.

Consider, if you will, the "Clinton Body Count." Probably everyone who had an email account in the 1990s received a version at some time or another. Friends, or friends of friends, passed it along like one of those dreaded chain emails, or the latest Monica Lewinsky joke.

It's gruesome—all those dead people associated somehow with Bill Clinton. (You'd think he was someone famous who came into contact with a lot of people or something.) In some cases, the count is as high as 80. Some of them you know about, like Vincent Foster. But what about that former intern, gunned down in a mysterious Georgetown Starbucks coffee-shop killing? Or those two little boys found dead on the railroad tracks in Arkansas? Why was Commerce Secretary Ron Brown "offed"?

The Clinton Body Count also happens to be one of the Patriot movement's hoariest traditions. It appears to have originated with militia leader Linda Thompson's 1993 essay, which detailed 29 deaths linked to the then-new president. The concept flourished among the movement, showing up at a lot of homemade Web sites. The 1994 version on a Web site called The Patriot had 28 bodies and three "ongoing" cases, some different from Thompson's. Soon the list was growing exponentially, especially when the nonmilitia types who shared a hatred of Clinton joined in the fun. More Clinton-haters linked more conspiracies to the president over the years.

By the early 21st century, even after the end of his term in office, at least 30 sites were keeping track of the Clinton Body Count. One site listed 52 bodies. Another racked up a total of 79. You could read about it at mainstream conservative Web sites, like radio commentator Ken Hamblin's, and The Free Republic, which featured entire sections of its forum devoted to "Suspicious Deaths" and the "Clinton Death Squad." [5] Clinton's supposed onetime paramour, Gennifer Flowers, kept a version of the Clinton Body Count on her Web site, linked alongside copies of her taped conversations with Clinton, a CD of her singing debut, and glamour pix.

The White House tried to draw attention to the flow of what it called "fringe stories" into the mainstream in a 331-page report obliquely titled *The Communication Stream of Conspiracy Commerce.* The report posited that the scandals the Clintons faced were manufactured by his political enemies out of groundless rumors bubbling up from the extreme Right. However, the report suffered from several fatal flaws. On the all-important public-relations front, it cast all this anti-Clinton activity in a conspiratorial light. The fact was that the campaign was fairly open about its desire to end (or at least undermine) Clinton's presidency. It was also sometimes spontaneous and uncoordinated. Conservative commentators had a field day, accusing the White House of finding conspiracies under rocks, comparing the report to Nixon's "enemies" list and offering the Clintons rides in black helicopters. Some even accused the White House of embarking on a conspiracy of its own—attempting to intimidate its enemies by linking them to wackos: conspiracies within conspiracies within conspiracies within conspiracies.

More importantly, the report missed its own target. While it accurately detailed how groundless stories like the Vince Foster suicide/murder got circulated outside of the normal media venues with helpful nudges from well-moneyed enemies like Richard Mellon Scaife, it cast its net only as wide as conservative think tanks and largely mainstream circles. It treated the venues for the false stories as merely "fringe" elements and failed to recognize the interaction of larger segments of conservatism in the stories' spread.

By 1998, the rhetoric once common on the militia front had become nearly indistinguishable from that bandied about on Rush Limbaugh's radio program or, for that matter, on Fox News cable gabfests or MSNBC's *Hardball*. The migration of the accusations against Clinton from the Far Right to the mainstream indicated how deeply conservatives in the 1990s became enmeshed with genuine extremists. In subsequent years, this commingling of ideologies played a role in the presidency of George W. Bush. For most of Bush's tenure, many of these same far-right factions were involved in demonizing liberals who dissented from Bush's Iraq war plans, or demonizing Latinos under the guise of opposing illegal immigration.

Chip Berlet's model of the American Right is a useful way of understanding this transformation. He divides the Right into three sectors:

The secular conservative Right. This comprises mainstream
   Republicans and white-collar professionals, glad to play
   government critic but strong defenders of the social
   status quo.

The theocratic Right. So-called "conservative Christians" and
   their like-minded counterparts among Jews, Mormons,
   and Unification Church followers, as well as Christian
   nationalists. Some of the more powerful elements of
   this faction argue that the United States is a "Christian
   nation," and still others—called "Reconstructionists"—
   argue for remaking the nation as a theocratic state.

The xenophobic Right. These include the ultra-conservatives
   and reactionaries who make broad appeals to working-
   class and blue-collar constituencies, particularly in rural
   areas, with a notable predilection for wrapping themselves
   in the flag. This faction ranges from the relatively mild-

mannered Libertarians—who also have made big inroads into the computer-geek universe—to the more virulent and paranoid militia/Patriot movement, and finally to the hard Right: the neo-Nazis, Klansmen, Posse Comitatus, and various white supremacists. The latter include some of the nastier elements of the Patriot movement, who wish nothing more than to tear down modern democratic America and start over. This is where some of the more insidious ideas (like bizarre tax-protest and monetary "gold standard" theories) and conspiracies (from black helicopters to the anti-Latino Reconquista theory) originate. Thus their appearance in mainstream settings is disturbing.

Transmitters play a central role in the interaction among the Right's competing sectors. Through them, certain extreme ideas gain wider currency until they finally become part of the larger national debate. This is particularly so for mass-media transmitters, like Limbaugh, Bill O'Reilly, or Lou Dobbs. Secondarily, shape-shifters, like Mack, or Jared Taylor of the pseudo-academic racist *American Renaissance* organization, or the leaders of the anti-immigrant Minutemen. These are most closely aligned with the xenophobic Right, but operate within the realm of secular conservatives. They are increasingly important for the former because they lend an aura of legitimacy to ideas, agendas, and organizations that would otherwise be seen as radical or fringe.

Indeed, what fascinates Berlet about the interaction of the sectors is watching

> the transmission belt—how stuff gets essentially a trial run in the Christian right or even the far right, and the messages will get refined, and then they'll be picked up by these intermediary groups and individuals, and refined some more, and then

there'll be a buzz that's created, and then that gets media attention in the mainstream press.

That isn't some conspiracy theory out of the White House. That's how this stuff works, and it's always worked this way. The joke is that it's not a conspiracy—it's the way people organize each other.[6]

3

The Transmitters

The strangest thing about Sen. Trent Lott's slow-motion toppling from his seat as Senate majority leader in 2002 was that the issue that provoked it was not particularly new or unknown. The uproar revolved around his homage to onetime segregationist Strom Thurmond upon his retirement from the Senate. "When Strom Thurmond ran for president, we voted for him. We're proud of it," Lott told a banquet audience. "And if the rest of the country had followed our lead, we wouldn't have had all these problems over all these years, either."[1] Normally such comments would have faded from view once Lott apologized, as he shortly did; they resonated, however, and the story kept percolating because they reflected his deep ties to far-right groups, ties that had been previously reported.

More than anything, these ties reflected Lott's lack of judgment. Like a number of Republicans, he had an open alliance with the Southern variant of extremism, embodied in the neo-Confederate movement. This band of Southern revivalists unabashedly argues for modern-day secession by the former Confederate States. "The central idea that drives our organization is the redemption of our independence as a nation," says the mission statement for the League of the South. And like most right-wing extremists, they pathologically hated Bill Clinton. "Impeach Clintigula Now!"

shouted a typical banner from a neo-Confederate Web site. As with their militia brethren elsewhere in the country, they found that hatred of the former president proved a potent recruiting tool.

Lott contributed a regular column to the neo-Confederate *Citizen Informer* magazine, usually pontificating on mainstream issues. He was joined by other columnists, however, who ranted about "Aracial Whites" and discussed the logistics of secession. The white-supremacist Council of Conservative Citizens (CofCC) and other neo-Confederates have a fondness for Mississippi's senior senator dating back to his efforts to rehabilitate the name and reputation of Jefferson Davis. In return, the senator lent them his ear as well as the air of legitimacy that his name as a columnist gave their magazine. He also told CofCC gatherings that they "stand for the right principles and the right philosophy."[2]

When finally called out on this behavior amid the counter-accusations that flew during the Clinton impeachment, Lott's spokespeople offered a startlingly misleading denial: "This group harbors views which Senator Lott firmly rejects. He has absolutely no involvement with them either now or in the future."[3] The questions were, of course, about his *past*.

Collective amnesia, however, had let Lott slide through until his now-infamous bout of nostalgia. Just as curious was the compartmentalized way the Lott matter eventually played out, with no ramifications for anyone else—including, say, Attorney General John Ashcroft, who has had his own dalliances with neo-Confederates. This containment served the purposes of Republican strategists, who have been hoping in recent years to remake the party's image by finally shaking the shadow of the "Southern Strategy"—the longtime Republican electoral plan built around using race as a wedge issue to appeal to white Southern voters on such matters as desegregation and busing.

These strategists may not be aiming to make significant inroads into the minority communities, though they do pay the notion some lip service and make sure their candidates appear in photo opportunities with black schoolchildren. Instead, their obvious target in remaking their image is moderate white suburban voters, whose reluctance to vote Republican is often associated with the GOP's lily-white, and often openly anti-minority racial image. The harsh reality is that the Republican Party, and mainstream conservatism generally, has for some time now been flirting with extremists across a broad range of issues, and in a number of different sectors and political blocs. Lott was merely the tip of the iceberg.

Lott, and politicians like him, are also transmitters, and they play an important role for right-wing xenophobes. They help lend people like the neo-Confederates a veneer of legitimacy, and they help their ideas, and ultimately their agendas, gain admittance to the mainstream. Transmitters come in a variety of guises: politicians and public officials, media figures, and religious and cultural figures.

Politicians and Public Officials

Lott was by no means the only Republican who maintained ties to neo-Confederates and other Southern racists. Rep. Bob Barr of Georgia, chief sponsor of a 1997 bill to impeach Clinton, also made appearances before the CofCC. Over the years he has also been openly associated with the populist-right John Birch Society and has shown a striking penchant for placing the militias' issues—gun control, tearing down the United Nations, fighting "globalism"—atop his own list. Former Mississippi governor Kirk Fordice maintained open ties with the CofCC and other neo-Confederate factions. And Louisiana governor Mike Foster— who was President Bush's 2004 campaign chair in that state—was caught and fined for buying David Duke's mailing lists, despite his effort at concealment.[4]

The South, however, was only one of many staging grounds for mainstream conservative politicians to commingle with right-wing extremists. In New Hampshire, Republican senator Bob Smith made open alliances with the Patriot/militia-oriented Constitution Party. Indeed, he nearly ran for president on the party's ticket).[5] Former representative Helen Chenoweth of Idaho, who chaired a natural-resources subcommittee and was one of the first to join Barr as an impeachment cosponsor, had long associations with her home district's militiamen—and you can still buy her antienvironmental video, "America in Crisis," from the Militia of Montana. Former Republican representative Steve Stockman of Texas likewise made open alliances with several Texas Patriot groups and defended their agenda in Congress.[6] Republican representative Ron Paul of Texas continues to peddle Patriot-style New World Order conspiracy theories to his constituents and followers even today.[7] In more recent years, figures like Republican representative Tom Tancredo of Colorado and former representative J. D. Hayworth of Arizona have generated a lot of publicity in their open embrace of the anti-immigrant Minutemen.[8]

Probably the most significant transmitter to make a mark on the political scene in recent years is Sarah Palin, the Alaska governor who was John McCain's 2008 running mate on the GOP ticket. During the 1990s, as mayor of Wasilla, Palin formed political alliances with figures from the main Alaska contingent of the Patriot movement, the Alaskan Independence Party, and she continued to court them as the state's Republican governor.[9] This background rose to the surface during the latter phases of the 2008 campaign, when Palin began making accusations—calling Barack Obama a "socialist" who "palled around with terrorists" and attacking him for not being "pro-American"—straight from the right-wing populists' handbook.

Nearly every noteworthy transmitter in politics is a conservative Republican. The exception was former representative James Traficant, an Ohio Democrat who was drummed out of Congress in 2002 in the wake of a set of corruption convictions. Traficant trotted out a broad range of Patriot theories and agenda items during his career, but he was a near-total pariah in his own party. Indeed, before his convictions, Republicans had attempted to persuade him to change aisles.[10]

The spectrum of transmitters also includes a bevy of local and state officials who tread comfortably in multiple universes. Several state legislatures, notably Montana's, have had significant Patriot presences among their ranks, all of them ultraconservative Republicans. And then there was the GOP's 1996 nominee for governor in Washington, Ellen Craswell, a religious conservative who argued for remaking America as a "Christian nation." She also attributed a horrendous January 1993 storm in Seattle on God's wrath for Clinton's inauguration, which had taken place that day. (Oddly enough, the weather in Washington DC, where the ceremony took place, was sunny and calm that day.) Craswell later left the GOP to play a prominent role in the pro-militia U.S. Taxpayers Party and its Washington offshoot, the American Heritage Party (both of which later morphed into the Constitution Party). She reportedly returned to the Republican fold before she passed away in 2008.[11]

Other political organizations also transmit far-right ideas and agendas in mainstream settings. In the 1990s and later, the most notable of these was the Free Congress Foundation, run by right-wing guru Paul Weyrich, one of the architects of the Reagan Revolution, a founder of the Heritage Foundation, and someone who reputedly enjoyed considerable influence in the George W.

Bush White House. Weyrich's transmission of right-wing ideas continued well into this century—as a scathing report from the Southern Poverty Law Center (SPLC) detailed—and did not end until his passing in December 2008.[12]

Other groups who transmit far-right themes into the mainstream include Larry Pratt's Gun Owners of America, whose connections to the extremist Right have been thoroughly documented. Gary Bauer's coproduction with James Dobson, the Family Research Council, spreads numerous antihomosexual memes that originated on the Far Right. The anti–affirmative action group Center for Individual Rights has its origins with the white-supremacist Pioneer Institute but has also been the "driving force" in the campaign against the University of Michigan's affirmative action program. So-called "Wise Use" groups, which organized against federal wildlands protections, spread antienvironmentalist conspiracy theories into the mainstream. And Operation Rescue (now called Rescue America) openly consorted with a number of violent antiabortion extremist groups and sympathized with their calls for the murder of abortion providers. (Some of its leading figures later resurfaced during the 2006 controversy over Terri Schiavo, the Florida woman whose contested "vegetative state" sparked an uproar from the religious Right.)

Religious and Cultural Figures

Among the leaders of America's religious Right, Pat Robertson enjoys a uniquely powerful position, both as overseer of a large broadcasting and evangelical empire and as the first fundamentalist Christian leader in recent times to make a significant run for the presidency. He also has a history of transmitting far-right themes into the mainstream, especially his frequent claims that America is a "Christian nation" and similar advocacy of theocratic government.

His most notorious instance of trafficking extremist material came with the publication of his 1992 tome, *The New World Order*, which enjoyed a considerable audience on the extremist Right. The book is chockablock with conspiracist allegations and references, including his invocation of the well-known Patriot belief that the Freemason conspiracy is "revealed in the great seal adopted at the founding of the United States." Two articles—one by Michael Lind and another by Jacob Heilbrunn—in the *New York Review of Books* demonstrated conclusively that the bulk of the concepts in the book were drawn directly from such notorious anti-Semitic works as Nesta Webster's *Secret Societies and Subversive Movements* and Eustace Mullins's *Secrets of the Federal Reserve*.[13]

Robertson's cohort in right-wing evangelizing, the late Rev. Jerry Falwell, likewise had a history of trotting out far-right themes, including the claim that the Antichrist was a Jewish man currently alive. Falwell likewise was closely involved in promoting the conspiracist *Clinton Chronicles*. In the years before his death in 2007, Falwell caused a national controversy by suggesting that gays, and lesbians and liberals in general, were responsible for the September 11 attacks. He then created an international uproar by proclaiming that Muhammad, Islam's chief prophet, was a "terrorist." He subsequently issued nonapology apologies (of the "I'm sorry if anyone's feelings were hurt" variety) for both statements.

Robertson and Falwell are to the religious Right what Limbaugh is to the army of imitators who fill the ranks in the rest of talk-radio land. They repeat themes and ideas that originally circulated among extremists. By presenting them in mainstream contexts they lend them a facade of legitimacy. Perhaps the most important pastors of this ilk are the Christian Reconstructionists, whose agenda is openly theocratic. Their stated purpose is to install a "Christian" government that draws its legal foundations from

Scripture, not the Constitution. Their radical agenda, however, is endorsed by a broad array of conservative politicians, notably by the powerful Council for National Policy, which boasts a membership from the whole range of mainstream conservatism, and was, in fact, cofounded by R. J. Rushdoony, one of the leading lights of Reconstructionism.[14]

One of the theocratic Right's leading figures, Pastor John Hagee, promotes an apocalyptic vision of Armageddon in the Middle East. He declared that Hurricane Katrina was "the judgment of God against New Orleans," called Catholicism "the Great Whore," and has openly adopted the "New World Order" conspiracy theory. He also enjoys real influence in Washington, DC as the head of a "pro-Israel" lobby, and is reputed to be one of George W. Bush's favorite televangelists. Republican presidential candidate John McCain sought out his endorsement in the 2008 campaign, though McCain later expressed regret for having done so when Hagee's remarks about Catholics and Jews surfaced in the press.[15]

Then there are the conservative figures who transmit far-right religious ideas to the mainstream through the entertainment industry. Filmmaker Mel Gibson is the most obvious example. His film *The Passion of the Christ* was criticized for its anti-Semitic stereotypes and the way it seemed to blame Jews for the death of Christ. Gibson heatedly denied such imputations. However, he belongs to an extremely conservative Catholic sect that rejects modern Vatican reforms of the church (and is noted for blaming Jews for the crucifixion). His father, Hutton Gibson, has a history of promoting anti-Semitic theories such as Holocaust denial, and Gibson has repeatedly refused to disavow his father's activism. This was all underscored by Gibson's subsequent drunken-driving arrest in Los Angeles, when he indulged in a number of anti-

Semitic epithets ("Fucking Jews ... Jews are responsible for all the wars in the world") and asked the arresting officer if he was Jewish (he was).[16] One of Gibson's subsequent films, *Apocalypto,* similarly indulged in ugly racial stereotypes in its depiction of ancient Mayan civilization and seemed to suggest that the genocide that ultimately befell them at the hands of Spanish Conquistadors was richly deserved.[17]

Media Transmitters

As seemingly maladjusted cranks go, Ann Coulter has carved out a nice little career for herself as an obsessive hater of all things liberal, spicing up her television appearances with a frothing, twitchy dyspepsia that seems to infect everyone on the sound stage. Coulter, like many of her media compatriots on the Right, first developed a significant public persona in the '90s while transmitting memes from the extremist Clinton-hating Right into the mainstream of conservatism. Since then, she has expanded into other fields and has been important in bringing the two sectors even closer together.

Coulter has built much of her reputation on being outrageous, as on the occasion when she penned a column about Muslims that concluded, "We should invade their countries, kill their leaders, and convert them to Christianity."[18] Unsurprisingly, she has indulged in a litany of Clinton-hating memes that originated in the extremist Right, ranging from equating him with Hitler to hinting before Y2K that he intended to declare martial law, to indulging in later disproven rumors that he had fathered an illegitimate black child. The quintessential Coulter "transmission" remark, though, came after September 11, in an interview with the *New York Observer*: "My only regret with Timothy McVeigh is he did not go to the New York Times Building."

Most of the subsequent commentary on this remark focused on

its seeming endorsement of terrorist violence, which her defenders, such as those writing on the *Wall Street Journal* op-ed page, dismissed airily as merely lacking in a sense of humor. "Why would anybody even pretend to believe that Ms. Coulter wishes any real harm to the *New York Times* or wishes to convert all Muslims forcibly to Christianity?"[19]

This line of defense is nearly identical to that deployed by Rush Limbaugh when he tries to claim that he's merely an "entertainer": something along the lines of, "Why would you take them seriously in the first place?" A few possible answers could be: because they have audiences of millions who hang on their every word as Received Wisdom; because every major broadcast and cable-news network has presented them, and people like them, as serious thinkers whose words are worthy of the public's consideration. More to the point, exactly which parts of Ann Coulter are we *not* supposed to take seriously, and how, exactly, are we supposed to discern those parts from the rest?

There should never have been any question that this remark was beyond the pale of acceptable public discourse. Coulter should have become a pariah, at least on the public airwaves. Indeed, you'd have expected not merely journalists to denounce her for this remark but fellow conservatives as well. That this never happened—that, in fact, conservatives have defended her vigorously to this day—is significant on its own.

We can discern even more consequential subtexts here. Coulter clearly suggested that the only thing wrong with McVeigh's attack was his choice of targets. Yet all of the postmortems about her remark missed the implied context: that the extremist Right of Timothy McVeigh allied itself with and was indirectly doing the bidding of mainstream conservatives like herself. Coulter's "joke" was an acknowledgement of the relationship. She certainly gained herself even more fans among the Patriot crowd. And that's how the ties grow stronger.

For the past decade or more this uneasy alliance has been gaining ground, as ideological and political traffic between movement conservatives and right-wing extremists becomes increasingly common. Sometimes the exchange happens almost accidentally, often at the intersection between personal ambition and lurking agendas, as when David Horowitz published the views of white supremacist Jared Taylor at his *Frontpage* Webzine.[20] Sometimes, as with Coulter, it is done with apparently full intent.

Yet for all her notoriety, Coulter is a minor player as a media transmitter. Let's look more deeply at the role played by transmitters in the various sectors of the media.

Radio

While many of Rush Limbaugh's critics would like to lump him in with the hard Right, he is mostly a secular conservative who only occasionally dabbles in xenophobic or theocratic dogma. However, Limbaugh artfully presents ideas from the hard Right for legitimate consideration by the mainstream. His transmissions are clearest when he's at his most shrill, decrying bureaucrats in Washington who "would just as soon do away with democracy" and similar hyperbole. "The second violent American revolution is just about—I got my fingers about a quarter of an inch apart—is just about that far away," he said on air, describing the sentiments behind the Patriot movement. "Because these people are sick and tired of a bunch of bureaucrats in Washington driving in to town and telling them what they can and can't do with their land."[21]

At other times, Limbaugh has dabbled in wink-and-nudge racism. On his thankfully short-lived TV program, for instance, Limbaugh promised to show his audience footage of everyday life among "welfare recipients." He then ran a video of the antics of a variety of great apes—mostly orangutans, gorillas, and chimpanzees—lounging about zoos. The audience applauded and laughed. Limbaugh also sounds themes that often are taken whole from stories circulated first among the Patriot Right: Clinton body counts, education conspiracies, phony medical and environmental tales. Perhaps his most important role is as a font of outright misinformation.

Just as significant, perhaps, are the hordes of Limbaugh imitators on the airwaves who appear willing to say anything outrageous in the hope of garnering higher ratings. Foremost among these is Michael Savage, the obnoxiously xenophobic hatemonger who in 2003 was awarded a slot on MSNBC's Saturday cable-TV lineup. He lost that spot after four months when he told a caller who identified himself as gay, "Oh, you're one of the sodomites. You should only get AIDS and die, you pig. How's that? Why don't you see if you can sue me, you pig. You got nothing better than to put me down, you piece of garbage. You have got nothing to do today, go eat a sausage and choke on it."[22]

Savage is particularly gifted at presenting overtly racist appeals in soft wrapping, so that his listeners know what he means, even if he can't be pinned down for it later. At times, however, his racism is nearly naked, such as when he calls for the deportation of all immigrants, and the internment of Muslim-Americans. Likewise, his contempt for common decency is abundantly evident. After a tsunami on December 2004 wiped out more than 200,000 lives in southeastern Asia, Savage told his audience that it "wasn't a tragedy" because the majority of victims were Muslim.[23]

Perhaps just as disturbing is the eliminationist tone of much of Savage's rhetoric aimed not at a racial or ethnic group but at liberals generally: "I say round them up and hang 'em high!" and

"When I hear someone's in the civil rights business, I oil up my AR-15!" Here is a 2007 rant aimed at liberal critics:

> I'm more powerful than you are you little hateful nothings. . . . You say you represent groups, you represent nobody but the perverts that you hang around with and I'm warning you if you try to damage me any further with lies, be aware of something: that which you stoke shall come to burn you, the ashes of the fireplace will come and burn your own house down. . . . If you harm me and I pray that no harm comes to you, but I can't guarantee that it won't.[24]

Another Limbaugh-wannabe with a more modest reach is Chuck Harder, a Florida-based talk-show host whose topics have ranged from United Nations takeovers to the then-looming Y2K apocalypse—as well as the full complement of Clinton scandals. Harder also broadcast daily updates from the Freemen standoff in Montana in 1996, and once featured renowned anti-Semite Eustace Mullins—one of the radical Right's revered figures—as an "expert" on the Federal Reserve.

Cable TV

Among all the transmitters of ideas and pseudo-facts originating in the Far Right, one entity stands in a class all its own: Fox News. The cable-news behemoth touts itself as "fair and balanced," but no one has ever really figured out just who they think they're kidding. Probably the dittoheads who buy up Limbaugh and Coulter books.

An open bias is one thing, but broadcasting far-right conspiracy theories is another. And that's what Fox has done on numerous occasions. The most noteworthy of these, though it received almost no attention at the time, occurred on February 21, 2001, when Brit Hume interviewed a fellow named Bob Schulz of We the People Foundation. Schulz was propounding a tax scheme that is built upon a hash of groundless conspiracy theories that have their origins in the far-right Posse Comitatus and other extremist tax protest schemes. It was, in fact, also remarkably similar to the Montana Freemen's theories. Yet, for the duration of the interview, Hume listened intently and evidenced no skepticism whatsoever about the fantastic claims regarding federal taxes Schulz was making.[25]

This wasn't the only time a Fox pundit interviewed Schultz. When he staged a "hunger strike" (there's no evidence he actually went without food) later that year, Fox's Sean Hannity interviewed him and was only a little less credulous than Hume.[26] Schulz eventually gave up his "hunger strike" after the intervention of Republican representative Roscoe Bartlett of Maryland. He offered to give Schulz's group a briefing on tax laws with IRS officials, but called that off when Schulz announced the meeting would be "putting the IRS on trial." Later that November, he was threatening the federal government with a "final warning" to all branches of government to "obey the Constitution, or else."[27] The courts later issued an injunction preventing Schulz from promoting his tax-theory scams. They concluded that he had not only engaged in illegal activity but he had also exposed a large number of ordinary citizens to criminal liability for misfiling their federal income taxes. When he ignored the injunction, he was cited for contempt of court. Finally, in April 2007, the Justice Department sued to prevent Schulz from marketing his scam.[28]

Then there's Bill O'Reilly, the former tabloid-TV-show host who now poses as a "journalist": the chief talking head at Fox. O'Reilly in particular has a penchant for conspiracy theories, even though he especially prides himself on "no spin" broadcasts, and uniformly bristles at suggestions he's doing otherwise. He even goes so far as to call his critics, particularly liberal Web sites like Media Matters for America, DailyKos, and HuffingtonPost, "Nazis" and "hate groups." Back in 2001, a news story at WorldNetDaily—the conspiracist Web site where O'Reilly's online column originally appeared, and with whom O'Reilly had a long association—credulously described O'Reilly's interview with a Texas reporter touting a theory linking the Oklahoma City bombing to Osama bin Laden.[29] This wasn't the only time O'Reilly promoted this theory; he did so again later that year, when he hosted the original source of all these theories—McVeigh's attorney, Stephen Jones.[30] It has remained one of O'Reilly's favorites.

O'Reilly's record extends well beyond his propensity for right-wing conspiracy theories. Notably, he has throughout the decade sounded an ominous theme popular on the Patriot Right: that liberals who criticize George W. Bush's war efforts are "traitors."

> Americans, and indeed our foreign allies who actively work against our military once the war is underway, will be considered enemies of the state by me.
>
> Just fair warning to you, Barbra Streisand and others who see the world as you do. I don't want to demonize anyone, but anyone who hurts this country in a time like this, well, let's just say you will be spotlighted.[31]

This from the same man who accused Clinton of malfeasance during the Bosnian campaign, and who undermined our position abroad by openly suggesting that Clinton's missile attacks on al Qaeda were an attempt to "wag the dog."

These, of course, are mere samplings. The popular *Hannity and Colmes* program on Fox News is also rife with this kind of rhetoric, largely from cohost Sean Hannity and his guests. And Fox News broadcasts, including the scrolling news feed across the bottom of the screen, are riddled with these underlying themes as well. The result is a steady drip of extremist memes blending into the day's Republican talking points.

Fox News' ratings successes also spawned a host of imitators on other cable channels. Foremost among these were CNN's Lou Dobbs and Glenn Beck. For much of the past several years, Dobbs has reported obsessively about illegal immigration and in the process has transmitted a host of claims and agendas from the far nativist Right. Almost nightly he has carried reports characterizing these immigrants as "stealing" American jobs, claiming falsely that these immigrants are bringing in diseases like leprosy at alarming rates, that they're conspiring to take over the American Southwest, and that they're bringing an increase in criminality to the nation's neighborhoods. Not only have his sources for these tales often been white-supremacist hate groups but he has featured on his program leaders of racist hate groups, such as American Border Patrol, without explaining to his viewers the guest's background. At other times he has touted the xenophobic Minutemen border patrols as a glorified "neighborhood watch."

Glenn Beck, who enjoyed regular airtime and a starring role at CNN Headline News before joining Fox News in January 2009, has similarly indulged in a variety of such transmissions. He harps on a supposed "North American Union" conspiracy intended to overthrow the United States (and along the way, publicly endorsing the John Birch Society); asked Keith Ellison, the nation's first Muslim congressman, to "prove to me that you are not working with our enemies"; and wondered aloud whether or not Barack Obama is the Antichrist. He also has devoted entire broadcasts to religious speculation about the Apocalypse (certain to involve and most likely destroy Israel as the site of Armageddon, he and his guest agreed).

The Internet

Any conservative who surfs the Web—or anyone who watches conservatives—is familiar with the Free Republic Web site, the ultra-conservative site in a class of its own in the transmission of the xenophobic Right's agenda into the mainstream of secular conservatism. Free Republic (like the Patriot movement) avoids wading into racial or religious discussions, and presents itself as purely a "conservative" political forum, but it has become one of the chief breeding grounds for conspiracy theories on the Right. During Bill Clinton's presidency, these included his alleged plans for overthrowing democracy and installing a New World Order dictatorship. Several of its post-9/11 threads blame the entirety of that disaster on Clinton.

The most significant part of the Web site's reach, though, is the kind of following it has created. Self-labeled Freepers—the site's army of contributors, commenters, and avid followers—have become an increasingly organized manifestation of some of the extreme sentiments that circulate at the site, to the point of having serious real-world effects. They played significant roles in several incidents involving thuggery and intimidation during the 2000 post-election Florida debacle, including disrupting an appearance by Jesse Jackson (in concert, as it happens, with white supremacists from Don Black's Stormfront organization) and engaging in noisy, intimidating protests outside of Al Gore's vice-presidential residence. [32]

Not quite as potent are a couple of well-read Webzines: News-Max and WorldNetDaily. Both have, at various times, been connected (though the latter only secondarily) to funding by right-wing guru Richard Mellon Scaife, who has on several occasions displayed his own predilection for extremist beliefs (particularly in his avid promotion of the Vince-Foster-was-murdered theories). Both Webzines, not coincidentally, also carried breathless coverage of Bob Schulz's anti-tax campaign.

WorldNetDaily in particular has been extremely conspiracy-prone over the years. In the run-up to the arrival of the Year 2000, for example, its major theme was the Patriot belief that Clinton intended to use the social chaos certain to proceed from the feared Y2K technological disaster as a pretext for declaring martial law and thereby establishing his dictatorship. One of the chief promoters of this theory was the zine's editor, Joseph Farah, who penned numerous columns on the subject.

NewsMax has similarly been a major conduit of extremist anti-Clinton propaganda, especially since Christopher Ruddy, the Scaife-funded "investigative reporter," took over its reins. Ruddy devoted years to proving Clinton had Vince Foster murdered and pursued dozens of other Clinton conspiracy theories, all equally groundless. Since joining Newsmax (he's currently its CEO) the site shifted its focus to attacks on Muslims and liberals as "traitors," while loudly defending President Bush's war efforts and attacking Democrats, particularly Barack Obama, first as a candidate and then as president-elect.

Finally, there are the blogging hordes of the Right—the movement disciples who propagate right-wing talking points through their personal (or group) Web sites. Not all of these act as transmitters, but a number of the higher-traffic sites do. The most notable of these is Michelle Malkin's blog, which often trades in outlandish conspiracy theories about supposed "jihadists" preying on the unsuspecting American public. She also assiduously promotes the oft-repeated-but-equally-groundless Reconquista theory. Over at

Little Green Footballs, readers are treated to a steady diet of bilious posts about Muslims and liberals, and the results are predictable: the site's comments threads are rife with expressions of hate toward Arabs and other Muslims, as well as threats and general bile directed at "treasonous" Democrats. These are only a couple of the more popular right-wing blogs that indulge in such excesses; a broad spectrum of lesser blogs indulge in even more outright hatemongering.

The Press

Within journalistic circles, the *Wall Street Journal* remains a well-respected paper for its reporting staff, but for the better part of a decade the paper's editorial page has become one of the real scandals of print journalism, particularly its unethical predilection for publishing provably false and thinly disguised smears of various liberals, then refusing to correct the errors. Foremost among these liberal targets was Clinton during his tenure, but in subsequent years, Democratic leaders like Al Gore and John Kerry have fallen victim to similar smears. Not surprisingly, right-wing extremists of various stripes generated many of these false facts, which the *Journal* then endowed with the mantle of respectability.

This propensity had manifested itself well before Clinton was elected president. For example, the *Journal* editorial page championed the work of Charles Murray, coauthor of the now-infamous *The Bell Curve*. The newspaper helped make the book broadly acceptable to mainstream conservatives, many of whom avidly embraced its thesis that blacks were demonstrably less intelligent than whites due to genetic wiring. As Lucy Williams of Public Research Associates explained in her analysis of how conservatives treated Murray, "By articulating a definition of poverty that associated it explicitly with illegitimacy, then associating illegitimacy with race, the Right made it acceptable to express blatantly racist concepts without shame."[33]

Likewise, the *Journal* propagated all kinds of extremist propaganda in its pursuit of Clinton. One of its chief sources was Floyd Brown, a longtime Clinton enemy from the Arkansas days. Brown was responsible for the circulation of much of the early Whitewater dirt on Bill Clinton, most of which was as groundless as it was scurrilous; when reporters looked into his claims, they found them to be uniformly bogus. In the 1990s, his Web site not only contained a host of Monica-related impeachment screeds but you could also find screaming exposés of the Clintons' alleged involvement in the United Nations one-world-government plot. Yet, in 1994, members of the *Journal's* editorial board sat down with Brown and examined his anti-Clinton information, and shortly thereafter nearly half of its editorial page was devoted to reprinting materials obtained from Brown.[34] Moreover, the *Journal* continued to recycle the allegations from that material for much of the following six years.

The other major organ that transmits right-wing memes is the Moonie-owned newspaper, the *Washington Times*, which suffers from a variety of ethical maladies. Most of these are related to spreading extremist memes about Bill Clinton, as well as championing various white-nationalist causes emanating from the neo-Confederate movement (with which, until a recent housecleaning, two senior editors had long associations).[35] But the conspiracy-mongering continued after Clinton left office. For a long period between 1999 and 2003, the paper ran pieces suggesting that Al Qaeda and not white supremacists were really behind the Oklahoma City bombing. More recently, it has touted the Reconquista conspiracy theory as well as the "North American Union" theory.

Pundits

Pundits are the rich orphans of the media business. Some are former reporters, some are former political operatives, and some are just propagandists in the Limbaugh mold. Among them, transmitters are common, many of them picking up far-right memes because of their outrageousness quotient: the best way to make your reputation as a pundit is to say something that makes headlines. No publicity is bad publicity, as they say. And the demand for pushing that "cutting edge" farther rightward becomes insatiable.

Pundit-transmitters range from one-time liberals, like Christopher Hitchens, to barely concealed extremists, like David Horowitz and Michael Savage. In between, it was commonplace to hear the late Barbara Olson repeat a Patriot legend, or for Peggy Noonan to indulge in plainly irresponsible speculations about Muslims, often straight out of the nativist handbook. The most notorious of them, probably, is Ann Coulter.

The effect of all these voices is rarely direct or acute but rather cumulative. The effect on audiences of hearing this ever-more-outrageous hatefulness repeated endlessly and in the guise of mainstream speech can be lasting and profound. But who, exactly, are the audience, who are the receivers of these transmissions?

4

A Black and White World

"Transmitters" of fringe ideas into the mainstream have two audiences. The first (and by far the largest) is made up of the many millions of ordinary mainstream conservatives who tune in and log on to the Right's army of media talking heads and movement leaders. The second includes their xenophobic counterparts on the far Right, where the memes come from in the first place. For the latter, these transmissions signal that their formerly unacceptable beliefs are gaining acceptance; they hear these transmissions as an invitation for them to move into the mainstream without having to change their views. The former hear them as an invitation to think more like the latter without shame.

And so for the past decade and more, and particularly since 2005, the mainstream conservative movement has become a more and more comfortable home to a variety of right-wing xenophobes, who formerly were relegated to the Right's outer fringes. Conservatives, however, uniformly reject this assertion, arguing that their movement is not home to a bunch of wild-eyed lunatics; they say it's the home of tax-paying, churchgoing, job-holding, productive members of society.

In my experience, the average Patriot movement member maintains all the appearances of being a mainstream player in society. Many of them are veterans. Most of the rest are agrarian or blue-collar workers with families. They pay their taxes (unless they've been drawn in deeply by one of the tax-protest schemes), vote, and attend church. Data collected through the 1970s and 1980s demonstrated that "Christian Patriots" on average were better educated than the population at large; many of these groups' members are even highly educated, and some are of better-than-average means. The sociologists who studied them found that the model that best explains them is one called the "new social movements theory," which recognizes that there can be considerable interaction between these groups and the mainstream, and that many of their followers are, in fact, as mainstream-based as can be. This is borne out by the spread of the Patriot movement's agenda via mainstream channels, as we've described in previous chapters.

False stereotypes are beloved among folks on the Left for their value in lampooning right-wingers, and equally cherished on the Right by conservatives loath to admit their influence. Such stereotypes, however, have obscured the extent to which right-wing xenophobes have woven themselves into the fabric of mainstream conservatism. This illusion has especially manifested itself in rural America, where the actual number of extremists is hardly overwhelming, but where they have many sympathizers. I have often heard neighbors, friends, and relatives of Patriots say, "Well, I don't buy everything they say, but I think some of it might be true, and I certainly can understand why they'd feel that way."

The psychological makeup of people drawn to far-right movements helps explain how these True Believers intermingle with people in the larger mainstream. Sociologists Dick Anthony and Thomas Robbins describe the Patriot movement and its millenarian relatives as "exemplary dualist movements": those that appeal to people with an extreme black-and-white, dualist worldview. This worldview is a direct product of the current larger social malaise, namely, alienation from a "sense of belonging" to modern society. Such malaise is further heightened during times of national trauma, when people tend toward psychological "splitting": dividing the world into good and evil. These movements, Anthony and Robbins explain, help provide followers with a substitute sense of belonging. Their appeals essentially "attempt to heal the split self" by projecting all that is negative in their worldviews onto "devalued contrast symbols"—other people, usually objectified, who embody the "evil" in their worldview. These people are "scapegoats designated by the group or, more generally, nonbelievers whose values and behavior allegedly do not attain the exemplary purity and authenticity of that of devotees."[1]

This quite accurately describes, in my experience of knowing such people, how and why people are attracted to such hateful and outlandish beliefs. This black-and-white, Manichean dualism is where the fringe and the mainstream meet. Such thinking has always been pronounced among far-right fanatics and the theocratic Right, but of late it has become a staple of mainstream conservatives as well.

As Anthony and Robbins note, susceptibility to authoritarianism increases during periods of social chaos such as we have had since the 9/11 terrorist attacks. When "mainstream cultural coherence declines, and anomie and identity confusion become more common," it's not unusual for the psychologically traumatized to seek out these kinds of movements as a way to end their "psychic pain."

And in America, the chief meeting ground for right-wing dualism and the authoritarian personalities it attracts is well-known: fundamentalist Christianity.

The fundamentalist Right and the extremist Right have always done a certain amount of commingling. Witness, for example, Pat

Robertson's New World Order skirmish, and the white-hot rhetoric over abortion. Since the early 1980s, conservative Christians have had an explicit alliance with the secular corporatist Right—Ronald Reagan and the first George Bush represented this latter bloc—whose participation was as much tactical as heartfelt.

Not so the presidency of George W. Bush. While secular neoconservatives were running Bush's foreign policy, on domestic policy the Christian Right was almost completely in charge, from the debate over gay marriage to issues involving abortion rights and affirmative action. Most of all, Bush himself gave his own fundamentalist beliefs an extraordinarily high profile—to the point that such beliefs became identified with the president's agenda. This is strange, if you think about the fact that corporatists dominated the roster of the Bush administration, and corporate interests control nearly every aspect of the Bush agenda—from tax policy to "corporate reform" to media ownership to environmental policy to the war in Iraq.

Most disturbing about the Bush administration, however, was not merely its devout corporatism but the way it used religion in the service of the corporatist agenda. It explicitly identified the Bush agenda with God's and suggested that Bush's every step was divinely inspired. Bush asked his followers to stick with him as an act of *faith*. The essential message was: he's a good man with good advisers, he prays, and he's not Clinton, so he must be right.

Indications of a significant confluence of the religious Right and the Bush administration were already apparent when Bush campaigned in 2000, but were not out in the open until 2003. For instance, the reports that came leaking out of the annual Conservative Political Action Conference (CPAC) in Crystal City, Virginia, in late January 2003, made the confluence almost official:

It was like a right-wing version of a Workers World rally, with one crucial difference. Workers World is a fringe group with no political power. CPAC is explicitly endorsed by people running the country. Its attendees are Bush's shock troops, the ones who staged the white-collar riot during the Florida vote count and harassed Al Gore in the vice presidential mansion. Bush may not want to embrace them in public, but they are crucial to his political success and he has let them know, in hundreds of ways, that their mission is his.

. . . Rev. Lou Sheldon, the founder of the Traditional Values Coalition and sworn enemy of homosexuality, put it best. Asked if Bush was in sync with his agenda, he replied, "George Bush *is* our agenda!"[2]

The atmosphere at the CPAC gathering was strikingly like that of a militia meeting 10 years before. The Clinton hatred remained palpable as an important trigger, but the focus had shifted to two other topics. First came the utter demonization of all things liberal, with a rising quota of eliminationist rhetoric.

At a Thursday seminar titled "2002 and Beyond: Are Liberals an Endangered Species?" Paul Rodriguez, managing editor of the conservative magazine *Insight,* warned that the liberal beast wouldn't be vanquished until conservatives learn to be merciless. "One thing Democrats have long known how to do is play hardball," he intoned, urging Republicans to adopt more "bare-knuckle" tactics.[3]

The second topic was an exaltation of all things Bush, with a heavy emphasis on the Christian aspect of his "character" and the clear implication of divine Providence in his presidency.

Gatherings like CPAC give a broad range of extremists, posing as ordinary Joes or Limbaughite loudmouths, the opportunity to spread their radical ideas among the whole sector of mainstream conservatism. Unassuming conservatives go to these gatherings and come away exposed, if not outright converted, to some of these extremist beliefs.

A steady stream of newspaper stories also described Bush's religiosity. The commingling of religion and politics under Bush was noteworthy especially for his predilection for portraying (and indeed, seeing) himself in a messianic light. Former Bush speechwriter David Frum, in his behind-the-scenes book about the early years of the Bush administration, described how fellow Bush staffer Michael Gerson told Bush after his September 20, 2001, televised speech to a traumatized nation, "Mr. President, when I saw you on television, I thought—God wanted you there." According to Frum, Bush replied, "He wants us all here, Gerson."[4] Not only did Bush see himself as a man on a divine mission but he actively cultivated this view of his importance among his staff and throughout his administration. Moreover, the White House similarly promoted this image to the public, particularly among conservative Christians.

By turning the White House into an organ of the religious Right, Bush signaled that he was a full participant in what was rapidly becoming the most important meeting ground for a broad range of right-wing beliefs: evangelical Christianity. Bush's overt political appeals to the fundamentalist views of his audiences— particularly in portraying himself as receiving divine guidance— gave himself immunity from fault and his every step the Lord's imprimatur. He thereby also placed himself in the charismatic position of combined political and religious leadership. The effect was to lead individual followers to identify their religious beliefs with Bush's political agenda and to draw nearly the entire evangelical bloc behind him politically.

Fundamentalist Christianity is among the most clear-cut

expressions of a Manichean dualism in American society. Its world is divided into good and evil, black and white. In turn, this kind of dualism signals a propensity toward authoritarianism, or what Erik Erikson called totalism: the eager embrace of a totalitarian society.

Religiosity has been almost universally recognized as an important element of any manifestation of fascism in the United States. As early as 1935, Sinclair Lewis observed: "When fascism comes to America, it will be wrapped in the flag and carrying the cross."[5] More recently, scholar Robert O. Paxton remarked that "religion ... would certainly play a much larger role in an authentic fascism in the United States than in the first European fascisms."[6]

A brief look at our history seems to substantiate these predictions. Earlier forms of fascism in America were explicitly "Christian" in nature. This is particularly true of the extremists who formed small but widespread societies around neo-Nazi philosophies and admiration for Hitler, most notably those led by the crypto-fascist mystical "philosopher" William Dudley Pelley in the 1930s. Pelley's legions, the Silver Shirts, earned their name by wearing silver uniforms modeled after Hitler's brown ones and marching through the streets on various occasions. Despite the theater (or perhaps because of it), Pelley drew large numbers of former Klansmen and other white supremacists, particularly those attracted to his anti-Semitic rantings (which included the infamous "Franklin Prophecy" hoax—the false claim that Founding Father Benjamin Franklin had made anti-Semitic remarks at the Constitutional Convention of 1787, a legend whose legacy is still with us).[7] Pelley's support was so broad he ran for president in 1936, though he garnered only a tiny portion of the vote. Nonetheless, he maintained some impetus through the later 1930s, especially in working-class and rural districts. A *Life* magazine spread depicted a gathering of Silver Shirts in Chehalis,

Washington, at a private home. The audience and the activity of the meeting closely resembled a militia meeting in the 1990s.[8]

Karen E. Hoppes, a graduate student at Western Oregon State College, wrote extensively about Pelley in the 1980s. She examined the Christian fundamentalism that was a significant feature of Pelley's "philosophy."

> Finally, the link with fundamental Christianity establishes the uniqueness of American fascism. The majority of fascist groups justified their existence by their desire to change the United States into a Christian society. . . . The relationship between the religious identity of these groups and their political demands can be shown by a careful survey of their rhetoric. The Christian fascist does not distinguish between the application of the terms anti-Christ, Jew and Communist. Neither does he distinguish between Gentile and Christian.[9]

Hoppes particularly notes Pelley's sermons arguing that "Christians of the United States must put the issue of conniving Jewry above all other issues and treat with it drastically. This means a pogrom . . . of colossal proportions." Observed Hoppes:

> For the Christian fascist, this up-and-coming war against the Jew would result in the founding of a new moral community—a Christian America. This community would tie itself to Christian ethics and Christian structure, as interpreted by these Christian fascists. Thus, the link with Christianity provided a unifying element for the membership in American fascist organizations. Members not only prayed with their comrades, but fought the "Christian" battle against the anti-Christ Jew. This gave them a surpassing sense of righteousness. Most of the membership came from the evangelical styled churches, with each Christian fascist group claiming to be under the umbrella of Christian thought and action.[10]

This uniquely American Christo-fascism was always limited in its reach, but not entirely short-lived, even though Pelley eventually was convicted (on dubious grounds) of sedition in 1942. By the time he emerged from prison in 1950, his Silver Shirts movement had been long since abandoned and dismantled. However, some of his associates kept the ideological flame alive. The most notable of these was Gerald L. K. Smith, who played a central role in taking over the Christian Identity movement in the 1930s and '40s and remaking it into the proudly racist religion it is today. Likewise, the Posse Comitatus movement, which advocated forming "citizen militias" back in the 1970s, was a product of "Christian fascism." It was cofounded by Identity leader William Potter Gale and Mike Beach, a former Silver Shirt. It, in turn, gave birth to the Patriot/ militia movement of the 1990s.[11]

Through most of the intervening years, these Christian extremists were relegated entirely to the fringe of society. This began to change in the 1990s, thanks to the confluence of two forces: the emergence of the Patriot movement and the growing revolutionary fervor of movement conservatives. The proto-fascist Patriots represented the efforts of Christian fascism to mainstream itself. Conservatives, looking to broaden their appeal and undercut mainstream liberalism, began adopting more ideas and memes that had their origins in the Patriot movement. Fundamentalism was particularly ripe territory for this, especially because conservative Christians organize around so many of the issues that attract both mainstream conservatives and extremists, such as abortion, education, gay rights, taxes.

This trend became apparent, for instance, after the 2003 arrest of Eric Rudolph, the man who bombed the Atlanta Olympics as well as a string of abortion clinics and gay bars in the 1990s. A story in the *New York Times* pondered whether Rudolph should properly be called a "Christian terrorist." It included an interview with one of Rudolph's local sympathizers.

> "He's a Christian and I'm a Christian and he dedicated his life to fighting abortion," said Mrs. Davis, 25, mother of four. "Those are our values. And I don't see what he did as a terrorist act."[12]

Both Mrs. Davis and the reporter's basic question show how the distinction between the Christian Identity movement and mainstream Christianity has been blurred—something that has become increasingly easy to do as Identity rhetoric attunes itself to the mainstream, and conservatism itself becomes increasingly bellicose and intolerant. The more Identity and similar extremist beliefs are identified with fundamentalist Christianity, the greater becomes their ability to influence the agenda of mainstream conservatism. This is why maintaining the delineation is important to contain the forces of fascism that are abroad today.

When the *Washington Post,* in a June 2003 piece, tackled the same question, it interviewed James Aho, who observed that he was reluctant to use the term "Christian terrorist," because it is "sort of an oxymoron. . . . I would prefer to say that Rudolph is a religiously inspired terrorist, because most mainstream Christians consider Christian Identity to be a heresy," Aho said. If Christians take umbrage at the juxtaposition of the words "Christian" and "terrorist," he added, "that may give them some idea of how Muslims feel" when they constantly hear the term "Islamic terrorism," especially since the Sept. 11 attacks.

"Religiously inspired terrorism is a worldwide phenomenon, and every major world religion has people who have appropriated the label of their religion in order to legitimize their violence," Aho said.[13]

Indeed, it is plain now that democratic societies all over the world are up against the many faces of such extremists. Fundamentalism is, after all, an explicitly antimodern movement. Religious scholars, such as Karen Armstrong, in her excellent book *The Battle for God: A History of Fundamentalism*, like to point out that the movement arose as a reaction to modernism, or more specifically, as a reaction against the many failures of modern society.

Both Islamic and Christian fundamentalism have been gaining considerable momentum over the past generation, but the ascendance of the radical segment, which all fundamentalist movements host, has become much more pronounced in Islam. These are popularly referred to as "Islamists" or, more tendentiously, "Islamofascists."

But, as Rudolph and many others like him make frighteningly clear, the "Christo-fascists" (if you will) are equally eager to bring down democratic society and replace it with theocratic authoritarianism. And while they trail the Islamists in influence, their impact on American society has been substantial, although largely unnoticed by the media. Annually, right-wing extremists within our borders are responsible for a sizeable number of crimes. The Southern Poverty Law Center (SPLC) tracked over 60 such cases between 1995 and 2005.[14] As Mark Pitcavage of the Anti-Defamation League points out, these range from "bombings and bombing plots to assassination plots and murders to weapons and explosives violations to hate crimes to massive frauds and scams (amounting in some cases in the hundreds of millions of dollars) to the myriad of lesser crimes." Even if you totaled up several years' worth of criminal activity related to Islamic extremism, it would not come close to that of our own homegrown terrorists. Needless to say, these totals are overwhelmed by the awful extravagance of the 9/11 attacks, but the reality is that an average American in the heartland is much more likely to be harmed by a right-wing domestic terrorist than an Al Qaeda operative.

Indeed, leaders of extremist factions have been fairly explicit in advocating "piggyback" terrorism. Such advocacy seeks to increase the level of chaos, creating an echo effect with international terrorism that exponentially enhances the psychological damage. Consider, for instance, the post–September 11 remarks made by William Pierce, the late leader of the neo-Nazi National Alliance. In a radio address he said, "Things are a bit brittle now. A few dozen more anthrax cases, another truck bomb in a well-chosen location, and substantial changes could take place in a hurry: a stock market panic, martial law measures by the Bush government, and a sharpening of the debate as to how we got ourselves into this mess in the first place." And on his Web site, Pierce declared that "terrorism is not the problem." He went on to write that the current threat is "the price for letting ourselves, our nation, be used by an alien minority to advance their own interests at the expense of ours"— meaning, of course, Jews.

Since then, right-wing extremists have been arrested for anthrax hoax letters sent to abortion clinics, while others have been arrested for sending similar letters to liberal luminaries.[15] Engaging in a clear-cut case of "piggybacking," these violent True Believers have the means as well as probably the desire to amplify any terrorist attack perpetrated by international terrorists.

But the most consequential aspect of their agenda lies in their efforts to mainstream themselves. In the process, they have had a deep and lasting effect on secular and religious conservatism.

5

The Conservative Movement and Its Morph

The line between right-wing extremists and "the conservative movement" has been increasingly blurred in the past 10 years, so blurred, in fact, that at times the two are nearly indistinguishable.

Distinguishing, for instance, between George W. Bush's contempt for the United Nations and the kind that a John Bircher might harbor is difficult. Bush once reportedly waxed nostalgic before a group of visiting Texans about the old "Get Us Out of the U.N.!" billboards that were common in Bircher country.[1] Over the years, Bush made multiple gestures of conciliation to a variety of extreme right-wing groups, but he particularly set the tone during the 2000 election season. That year, the Bush campaign made unmistakable appeals to neo-Confederates in the South Carolina primary, underscored by his speaking appearance at the ultra-conservative Bob Jones University, a school that had long resisted desegregation. Once elected, Bush and his GOP cohorts continued to make a whole host of other gestures to other extremist elements. He attacked affirmative action, kneecapped the United Nations, undermined civil-rights-law enforcement, and gutted bias-crime laws. As a result, white supremacists and other right-wing extremists came to identify politically with George W. Bush more than any other mainstream Republican politician in memory. This was embodied by the endorsement of Bush's 2000 candidacy by a range of white supremacists, including David Duke, Don Black of Stormfront, and Matthew Hale of the World Church of the Creator.[2]

However, the signal event of 2000 that went under most people's radar was Patrick Buchanan's bid for the presidency on the Reform Party ticket. This move drove everyone from the Patriot movement firmly into the arms of George W. Bush and the Republican Party. Right-wing xenophobes make up only a tiny portion of the electorate, at best about 3 to 4 percent of the vote. During the 1990s, these voters gave Ross Perot's Reform Party nearly half its total base. This was critical in the 1992 election, when George H. W. Bush saw much of his conservative base go to Perot. It didn't matter quite so much in 1996—Clinton defeated the GOP's Bob Dole quite handily, with or without Perot's help— but the lesson was clear. That 3 to 4 percent was killing the GOP. So in 2000, Buchanan took over the Reform Party. He managed to do this with a maximum of acrimony, so that the party became split into its Buchananite wing, largely the white-nationalist faction, and its Perotite wing. Buchanan's side won the war and got to carry the party's banner in the national election. Then Buchanan selected a black woman, Ezola Foster, as his running mate.

The white nationalists, who had been Buchanan's foot soldiers, abandoned him immediately. And where did they flee? Largely to the GOP. As David Duke's manager explained it to a reporter: "After Buchanan chose a black woman as his veep [Duke] now thinks that 'Pat is a moron' and 'there is no way we can support him at this point.'" The Democrats—with a Jew on the ticket— had a good chance at the time to win the race outright. The combination of all these factors herded the Far Right handily into the Republican camp.

If someone had intended to sabotage the Reform Party and drive its voters back to the GOP, they couldn't have done a better job than Buchanan did with his choice of running mate. While no one can say Buchanan had this end in mind—it certainly is feasible he believed his own propaganda—neither does it seem beyond the pale for an old Nixon hand to take a political bullet for the home team.

Since 2000, much of the dissipation of the energy in the Patriot movement was directly related to the identification by right-wing extremists with George W. Bush for much of his tenure. The announced reason (according to a report in the *New York Times*) for the disbanding of Norm Olson's Michigan Militia, for instance, was the belief among its members that Bush had the country headed back in the right direction, as it were. "Mr. Olson attributed the dwindling membership to the election of President Bush. Across the nation, there is a satisfaction among patriots with the way things are going," he said.[3]

In the 2000 election, many former Patriots—disillusioned after the failure of the Y2K scare to materialize, but still maintaining their attitudes about government, liberalism, and conspiracies, and disenfranchised by Buchanan's campaign—turned to the politics of the Bush team, which made all the right gestures to make them feel welcome.

The Patriot movement never came close to achieving any kind of actual power, outside of a handful of legislators in a smattering of western states. But the absorption of large numbers of its followers into mainstream conservatism brought a wide range of extremists together under the banner of Republican politics, where they defended the agenda of President Bush and indulged in their hatred of all forms of liberalism.

After the 9/11 terrorist attacks, the rhetorical attacks on liberalism became enmeshed with a virulent strain of jingoism, which at first blamed liberals for the terrorism, then accused them of treason for questioning Bush's war plans. A broad campaign of hatred was waged against liberals—particularly antiwar activists. Its main purpose was to politically consolidate the Right, but it had two other significant consequences: it commingled mainstream pro-Bush forces with a number of people with far-right beliefs, and it gave the xenophobic element of Patriot foot soldiers an increasingly important role within the mainstream Republican Party.

The result: the political center of the conservative movement shifted farther and farther to the right. This brought forth a political creature no one could recognize.

A lot of people call themselves "conservatives" nowadays. But how conservative are they really?

After enduring eight years of ostensibly conservative rule under George W. Bush and a Republican Congress, let's assess the outcome:

- Is it conservative to drive the national economy into the ditch and oversee the collapse of global financial markets through a combination of mismanagement and misguided fiscal philosophy?
- Is it conservative to rack up the largest national deficit in history and have only the vaguest outlines of a plan for putting the national budget back in the black?
- Is it conservative to ignore warnings of imminent terrorist threats merely because a preoccupation with terrorism is seen as too similar to your predecessor's presidency?
- Is it conservative to attack another nation under false pretenses?
- Is it conservative to jettison a half-century's worth of multilateral diplomacy and cooperation to pursue a radical vision

of a unilateralist America— called "the Bush Doctrine"— supposedly capable of imposing its will on the rest of the world?

- Is it conservative to allow the torture, rape, and killing of civilians under the guise of interrogating prisoners in the nation we now occupy as a result of the Bush Doctrine?
- Is it conservative to adopt the legal position that the president's wartime powers allow him to supersede international law and the Geneva Conventions, and to argue before the Supreme Court that those powers allow the government to indefinitely imprison American citizens at will without right to trial?
- Is it conservative to issue hundreds of "signing statements" that place the president outside congressional purview and above the law? To blatantly flout federal surveillance laws and proceed with the wiretapping of thousands of American citizens?

These questions suggest that conservatism and the "conservative movement" are two entirely different things. Conservatism, in its original state, is not a dogmatic philosophy but rather a style of thought, an approach to politics and life in general. This style stresses the status quo and traditional values and is typified by a resistance to change and a view of mankind as innately corrupt and in need of restraint. The conservative movement, however, is a decidedly dogmatic political movement that demands obeisance to its main tenets and a distinctly defined agenda.

Nearly everyone who follows the contours of the political landscape is well aware of the nature of this movement, and how it has managed to rise to power: a 2004 *New York Times* piece by Matt Bai reported on the work of a Democratic operative named Rob Stein, who had carefully examined the structure of the movement and its effectiveness.

The presentation itself, a collection of about 40 slides titled "The Conservative Message Machine's Money Matrix," essentially makes the case that a handful of families—Scaife, Bradley, Olin, Coors and others—laid the foundation for a $300 million network of policy centers, advocacy groups and media outlets that now wield great influence over the national agenda. The network, as Stein diagrams it, includes scores of powerful organizations—most of them with bland names like the State Policy Network and the Leadership Institute—that he says train young leaders and lawmakers and promote policy ideas on the national and local level. These groups are, in turn, linked to a massive message apparatus, into which Stein lumps everything from Fox News and the *Wall Street Journal* op-ed page to Pat Robertson's "700 Club." And all of this, he contends, is underwritten by some 200 "anchor donors." "This is perhaps the most potent, independent institutionalized apparatus ever assembled in a democracy to promote one belief system," he said.[4]

When such a movement takes shape and then obtains real power—as the conservative movement did between 2000 and 2006—it often takes on a real life of its own, mutating into entirely separate entities that often bear little resemblance to their root values and often become travesties of their origins.

Liberals are not the only ones who have observed this transformation of conservativism into a dogmatic movement; many longtime conservatives who remain true to their principles have as well. And although this conservative movement, in the course of this mutation, has become something entirely new, a fresh political entity quite unlike anything we've ever seen before in our history, it seems somehow familiar, as though we *have* seen something like it before.

And the reason the form of the conservative movement in the

21st century is so familiar and disturbing is that its structure has morphed into a not-so-faint hologram of 20th-century fascism. The conservative movement is not genuine fascism, however, for even though it bears many of the basic traits of that movement, it lacks the following key elements:

- Its agenda, under the guise of representing mainstream conservatism, is not openly revolutionary.
- It is not a dictatorship.
- It does not yet rely on physical violence and campaigns of gross intimidation to obtain power and suppress opposition.
- American democracy has not yet reached the stage of genuine crisis required for full-blown fascism to take root.

The traits 20th-century fascism and 21st-century conservativism share include an obsession with action for action's sake; the exaltation of instinct over intellect, and of tradition over progress; the insistence by both that they represent the "true" national identity; and the violent rejection and desire to eliminate both foreign enemies and internal ones, the latter being those deemed toxic to the national body politic. The architectural structure it shares with fascism is its ultranationalism (embodied, perhaps, in John McCain's 2008 campaign slogan, "Country First"), its increasing embrace of a selective right-wing populism, and its authoritarianism.

It is in this sense that I call it *para-fascism*. Unlike the genuine article (or even its nascent form, proto-fascism) it presents itself under a normative, rather than a revolutionary, guise; and rather than openly exult in violence, it pays lip service to law and order. Moreover, even in the areas where it resembles real fascism, the similarities are often more familial than exact. It is, in essence, less virulent and less violent, and thus more likely to gain broad acceptance within a longtime stable democratic system like that of the

United States. Yet, even in the key areas of difference, it is not difficult to discern that those dissimilarities are gradually shrinking, and in danger of disappearing.

The principal danger has always been of a kind of political gravitational pull: the more extremist ideologies creep into the mainstream, the more they transform the nature of the mainstream. An excellent example of this effect is the Southern Strategy initially deployed by Richard Nixon in 1968 and 1972. Its long-term effect was to transform the GOP from the party of Lincoln to the party of Strom Thurmond, from a bastion of progressivity on race to the home of neo-Confederates who argue for modern secession and a return to white supremacy.

The final morph into para-fascism occurred within the dynamic of the conservative movement after it took control of all three branches of American government in 2000. By seizing the presidency through means perceived by nearly half the nation at the time as illegitimate, conservative-movement ideologues had to find a way to govern without a popular mandate. Rather than moderate its approach to governance, the Bush administration instead acted as though it had won in a landslide and proceeded to follow an openly radical course of action by doing the following:

- Instituting a massive transfer of the tax burden from the upper to the middle class
- Formulating, in the wake of the 9/11 attacks, the radical "Bush Doctrine" of unilateralist preemption
- Undermining civil liberties under the Patriot Act and creating a policy of incarcerating citizens indefinitely as "enemy combatants"
- Justifying the invasion of another nation by raising the false specter of the "imminent threat" of weapons of mass destruction

- Violating the Geneva Conventions during prisoner interrogations at Bagram, Guantánamo, and Abu Ghraib
- Ignoring federal wiretapping laws that regulate the surveillance of American citizens
- Erecting massive obstacles to transparency, to make it easier to operate in secrecy whenever possible

The radical course followed by the Bush administration was, in fact, guaranteed to further divide the nation rather than unify it in a time of need. Maintaining power and instituting its agenda in this milieu meant, for the conservative movement, a forced reliance on sheer bluff: projecting "strength and resolve" while simultaneously attacking its political opponents as weak and vacillating. Pulling this bluff off required the assistance of a compliant press eager to appear "patriotic," and it received it in spades. Mostly, the movement has depended on a constant barrage of emotion-driven appeals to the nation's fears in the post-9/11 environment. These began with color-coded terrorism "alert status" reports, which would sometimes rise to "high alert" without any particular explanation from the Bush administration; though this alert system was later dropped, the "war on terror" became a standard White House pretext for any number of policies and actions, including the illegal wiretapping of citizens that began in 2003.

But does all this add up to fascism? Not, as we shall see, in the fullest sense of the word. However, it does replicate, in nearly every regard, the architecture of fascism in its second stage of growth— the stage at which, in the past, it has obtained power.

6

Understanding Fascism

The term *fascism* has come to be nearly useless over the past 30 years or so. In many respects, leftists are most responsible for its degradation; lobbing it at anyone conservative or corporatist in the 1960s and '70s became so common that its original meaning—describing a very distinct political style, if not quite philosophy—became utterly muddled, at least in the public lexicon.

Over the past 30 years or so, *fascism* has come to be loosely used to describe the broader concept of *totalitarianism*, which encompasses communism as well. Liberals are every bit as prone to this particular confusion as conservatives. The difference, perhaps, is that the latter often do so deliberately, as a way of obscuring the genuine fascism that sits at their elbows.

The godfather of this obscurantism is Rush Limbaugh, who for years has been holding forth on the rise of "feminazis" in the ranks of the Left; at various times he has told listeners that because Nazism had "socialism" in its original name (that is, National Socialism) it was actually a left-wing movement. Various other right-wing propagandists have proposed similar readings of history.

But this notion leapt onto the *New York Times* bestseller list in 2008 when Jonah Goldberg of the *National Review* published his book *Liberal Fascism: The Secret History of the American Left, from Mussolini to the Politics of Meaning*. Goldberg's book was essentially an up-is-down-inside-is-out mishmash of history and political philosophy that stipulated, primarily, that "fascism, properly understood, is not a phenomenon of the right at all. Instead, it is, and always has been, a phenomenon of the left."

He bases his argument on the following definition of fascism:

> Fascism is a religion of the state. It assumes the organic unity of the body politic and longs for a national leader attuned to the will of the people. It is totalitarian in that it views everything as political and holds that any action by the state is justified to achieve that common good. It takes responsibility for all aspects of life, including our health and well-being, and seeks to impose uniformity of thought and action, whether by force or through regulation and social pressure. Everything, including the economy and religion, must be aligned with its objectives. Any rival identity is part of the "problem" and therefore defined as the enemy.[1]

There's an obvious problem with this: Goldberg's definition does not fit fascism per se. One could use nearly the same terms and ideas to define a Marxist-Leninist state, or any other kind of totalitarian state. His definition describes totalitarianism (or authoritarianism, if you will) generally, but not fascism specifically.

Fascism is a specific species of totalitarianism, and it is best understood not simply by the things it has in common with other forms of this phenomenon (and there are plenty, complete state control of the individual's mind and life being the most essential) but by what distinguishes it. The academic debate over the "fascist minimum" (that is, what is its ineluctable core) has raged for some years. Goldberg's book did nothing to advance this debate; on the contrary, it muddied the waters of public understanding with illogical nonsense.

Most Americans believe they know what communism is, largely because it is an ideology based on a body of texts and revolving around specific ideas. In contrast, hardly anyone can explain what comprises fascism, mainly because all we really know about it is the regimes that arose under its banner. There are no extant texts, only a litany of dictatorships and atrocities. When we think of fascism, we think of Hitler and perhaps Mussolini, without understanding anything about the conditions that carried them to power.

At the same time, it's important that both liberal and conservative Americans have a clear view of what fascism is, not just as an abstract definition, but as a real-life phenomenon. Fascism is not an extinct political force. Most Americans view Nazism as some kind of strange European virus that afflicted only the Germans and Italians, and only for a brief period—this by way of reassuring ourselves that "it couldn't happen here." But a look at the history of fascism shows this not to be the case, that the Germans and the Italians were ordinary, civilized people like the rest of us. And that what went wrong there could someday go wrong here, too. How, then, are we to know if that is what's happening, as it seems to happen so gradually that the populace scarcely recognizes it?

In its early years, fascism was best understood as an extreme reaction against socialism and communism, as "extremist anti-communism." This view, predictably, was offered up by communists, who saw everything through their own ideological prisms. In reality, fascism was more complex than that, though the fear of communism was no doubt an essential element that fueled its recruitment and ideological appeal. At the time, there were very few attempts to systematize the ideology of fascism, though some existed (see, for example, Giovanni Gentile's 1932 text, "The

Doctrine of Fascism").[2] Its true spirit was best expressed in an inchoate rant like Adolf Hitler's *Mein Kampf.*

Fascism was explicitly antidemocratic, antiliberal, and corporatist, and it endorsed violence as a chief means to its ends. It was "revolutionary" in its fervor, yet sought to defend status-quo institutions, particularly business interests. It was also, obviously, authoritarian; the claim that it was oriented toward "socialism" is crudely ahistorical, if not outrageously revisionist. Lest we forget, socialists were among the first people targeted by Mussolini's black-shirted thugs, and they were among the first people imprisoned and "liquidated" by the Nazi regime.

However, it's important not to confuse fascism as a movement on the rise with fascism as a power. If we can only identify fascism in its mature form—the goose-stepping brownshirts, the full-fledged use of violence and intimidation tactics, the mass rallies—then it will be far too late to stop it. Fascism arose as a much more atomized phenomenon, at first mostly in rural areas; then it spread to the cities, and if we look at those origins, it becomes clear that similar forms already exist in America.

Fascism springs from very ancient sources; its antecedents have appeared all throughout history. It adapts to changing conditions. As the French specialist on the extreme Right, Pierre-André Taguieff, puts it:

> Neither "fascism" nor "racism" will do us the favour of returning in such a way that we can recognise them easily. If vigilance was only a game of recognising something already well-known, then it would only be a question of remembering. Vigilance would be reduced to a social game using reminiscence and identification by recognition, a consoling illusion of an immobile history peopled with events which accord with our expectations or our fears.[3]

Assessing the genuine potential for fascism in America requires identifying the core components of fascism itself: its ancient wellsprings that remain with us today. Then, we need to ask ourselves what we are doing to keep those forces in check.

One of the problems nowadays with loosely attaching the term *fascist* to figures who are merely conservative—including Rush Limbaugh and George W. Bush—is that the actual mechanism by which genuine fascism manifests itself gets obscured. Such bandying of the term lends itself to hysterical assessments, when clarity and focus are what are really needed.

Let's take a hard look today at the actual nature of fascism, by way of understanding not just what trends really fit the description in today's world but how much danger in the post-9/11 environment they actually represent.

The first attempts to study fascism were largely conducted from a Marxist point of view, which predictably explained it primarily as a reaction against the "communist revolution." In many ways, that's what it was, though as stated above, it was also a great deal more. Many of these early studies, not surprisingly, reduced fascism to an aggressive form of capitalism. In the years after World War II, when fascism had largely been eradicated as a form of governance, studies of it expanded the definition considerably, leading to a far more realistic, nuanced, and accurate understanding.

The bulk of these studies essentially defined fascism by describing a series of traits that were found to be pervasive among fascist systems. The best-known example of this approach is Stanley Payne's work, which offers a "typological definition" of fascism, focused on the "fascist negations": antiliberalism, anticommunism, and anticonservatism (though with the understanding that fascist groups were willing to undertake temporary alliances with groups from any other sector, most commonly with the Right).[4]

Payne's approach, similar to that of many scholars of fascism, is useful; it offers important descriptive information that helps us get a sense of the multifaceted phenomenon of fascism. But these approaches share a similar flaw: a number of the traits described in these systems can also describe communism—which is by its nature apposite to fascism—as well as other political ideologies. In that sense, it's clear these traits tend to be endemic to totalitarianism broadly. In other words, they will be woven into fascism but won't be unique to it.

The consensus (and debate) since the early 1990s over fascism has tended to revolve around the work of Oxford Brookes University professor of history Roger Griffin. His 1991 text, *The Nature of Fascism*, is considered by many to be the definitive work on the subject. Griffin has essentially managed to boil fascism down to a basic core he calls "palingenetic ultranationalist populism." (*Palingenesis* is the concept of mythic rebirth from the ashes, embodied by the phoenix.) Griffin offers this boiled-down definition:

> *Fascism*: modern political ideology that seeks to regenerate the
> social, economic, and cultural life of a country by basing it on
> a heightened sense of national belonging or ethnic identity.
> Fascism rejects liberal ideas such as freedom and individual
> rights, and often presses for the destruction of elections, legis-
> latures, and other elements of democracy. Despite the idealistic
> goals of fascism, attempts to build fascist societies have led
> to wars and persecutions that caused millions of deaths. As a
> result, fascism is strongly associated with right-wing fanaticism,
> racism, totalitarianism, and violence.[5]

Griffin explains that if we look for fascism using the Payne or Marxist models, we'll mostly be looking for a mature phenomenon.

However, if we think of it as "a core ideology of ultranationalism that aspires to bring about the renewal of a nation's entire political culture, then the picture changes." The fascist core that emerges is "its only permanent feature: the war against the decadence of society and the struggle for national rebirth."

If we think of fascism in these terms, we can recognize its antecedents throughout history, and moreover, get a much clearer picture of the presence of latent fascistic forces at work around the world. Griffin's definition tends to confirm the characterization of Islamic fundamentalists as "Islamofascists," but makes clear that there is at least one important difference: while fascism has typically sought to achieve "national rebirth" by fusing a mythologized notion of "traditional values" with modernist idealism, Islamists are irrevocably antimodern in their worldview. Antimodernism could be, as it is among far-right Christian Identity extremists, more a pose to recruit and discipline the faithful than a core principle, and thus may get discarded when no longer convenient. (Another key difference is that fascism historically has arisen in the context of democracies in a state of decay—a condition that does not exist in Middle Eastern nations where radical Islam is most popular.)

This way of viewing fascism also confirms that such forces are at work in the United States today, though not directly, as one might suppose, in the form of such mainstream GOP figures as Rush Limbaugh and George W. Bush. We may hear Republican luminaries from time to time refer to the theme of national rebirth, but not frequently enough for it to become a major theme (yet). And although their nationalistic and populist tendencies are well-known, both are mitigated to a great extent by their general refusal to partake of the conspiracy theories, anti-Semitism, and other forms of irrational, fringe thinking common to right-wing populists.

However, the similarities between these figures and the behavior of historical fascists are plentiful enough to throw up a warning sign. And as we'll see, they do, indeed, play an important role in the potential for a resurgence of genuine fascism in America.

Robert O. Paxton, in his landmark 2005 study *The Anatomy of Fascism*, neatly sums up the place of fascism in the history of politics as the emergence of a "dictatorship against the Left amidst popular enthusiasm."[6] But what are its guiding principles?

Fascism, according to some who have studied it, is a kind of "political religion"—that is, it coalesces around a "sacralization of politics" that acts as a substitute faith for its followers. Italian political theorist Emilio Gentile, who studied the totalitarian movements of interwar Europe, writes that this sacralization takes place when

> more or less elaborately and dogmatically, a political movement confers a sacred status on an earthly entity (the nation, the country, the state, humanity, society, race, proletariat, history, liberty, or revolution) and renders it an absolute principle of collective existence, considers it the main source of values for individual and mass behaviour, and exalts it as the supreme ethical precept of public life.[7]

This imparts to fascism a particular trait that Paxton describes as one of the real telltale signs of its presence:

> Each national variant of fascism draws its legitimacy, as we shall see, not from some universal scripture but from what it considers the most authentic elements of its own community identity. Religion, for example, would certainly play a much larger role in an authentic fascism in the United States than in the first European fascisms, which were pagan for contingent historical reasons.[8]

Can fascism still happen in America? Paxton leaves little doubt that the answer to this must be affirmative.

> Fascism can appear wherever democracy is sufficiently implanted to have aroused disillusion. That suggests its spatial and temporal limits: no authentic fascism before the emergence of a massively enfranchised and politically active citizenry. In order to give birth to fascism, a society must have known political liberty—for better or for worse.[9]

Fascism is not a single, readily identifiable principle but rather a political pathology, best understood (as in psychology) as a constellation of traits. Taken individually, many of these traits seem innocuous enough, even readily familiar, part of the traditional American political hurly-burly. A few of them, definitely not all, are present throughout the political spectrum. Only when taken together does the constellation become clear, and then it is fated to take on a life of its own.

What sets fascism apart from nearly all other kinds of politics is that, at its core, it is not about thought. It's all a matter of the gut. Milton Mayer describes this in his book *They Thought They Were Free: The Germans 1933–1945*:

> Because the mass movement of Nazism was nonintellectual in the beginning, when it was only practice, it had to be anti-intellectual before it could be theoretical. What Mussolini's official philosopher, Giovanni Gentile, said of Fascism could have been better said of Nazi theory: "We think with our blood."[10]

However, Paxton's study is the one that draws out this point in the greatest detail. Indeed, he describes the centrality of emotion—and not any intellectual forebears—as forming the basic structure on which the fascist argument rests, because fascism is built not on ideas but, as he puts it, on "subterranean passions and emotions." Fascism is passionate nationalism, allied to a conspiratorial dualism and a crude Social Darwinism, voiced with resentment toward the forces, or conditions, that restrain "the chosen people."

Paxton breaks these forces down into nine "mobilizing passions" that "form the emotional lava that set fascism's foundations."[11]

We can use these nine "mobilizing passions" to assess how close the para-fascism practiced by movement conservatism comes to re-creating the components of genuine fascism.

1. *A sense of overwhelming crisis beyond the reach of any traditional solutions.* This condition has been especially rampant as one of the clarion calls of movement conservatives since the terrorist attacks of 9/11. It has been enhanced by incessant Republican fearmongering about the "threat of terrorism," particularly when conservatives are faced with potential political defeat. And it has, as we've seen, played a significant role in the movement's success in appealing to the dualist impulses of a traumatized public. September 11 was "the day that changed everything," indeed.

The main difference between para-fascist appeals of this nature and their more virulent cousins is that the solutions posed for confronting this crisis have not, so far, been open calls for disposing with democratic institutions outright. Instead, democratic institutions are seen as presenting obstacles to the effective defense of the nation that may be overlooked in times of crisis as a crude necessity of self-defense.

What we have seen has been more in the fashion of gradual erosion of these institutions: a chewing away at civil liberties through the Patriot Act; the emergence of the executive power to detain citizens under "enemy combatant" designations; and the White House's flagrant flouting of federal wiretapping laws that regulate the surveillance of American citizens. There also have been antidemocratic campaigns to erode Americans' voter rights. One such campaign involved a White House effort to politicize the nation's U.S. Attorneys offices under the Justice Department in a transparent effort to push "voter fraud" prosecutions of minority voters. Conservative-movement operatives are thought to be associated with such efforts. Finally, and perhaps most horrifyingly, the U.S. government has legalized the torture of prisoners held as "terror suspects," justified by authorities as high-ranking as Supreme Court Justice Antonin Scalia with the rationale that the imminent threat of potential nuclear attack (as in the popular TV show *24*) justifies the use of such measures.

As long as the para-fascists continue to operate, at least outwardly, on the basis of a respect for democracy, this cannot be said to be a genuinely fascist trait on the part of movement conservatism. However, the more movement conservatism undermines these institutions by appealing to the threat of imminent terrorist attack, the less this can be claimed.

2. *The primacy of the group, toward which one has duties superior to every right, both universal and personal, and the subordination of the individual to it.* As we've noted, conservatives have continually stressed the primacy of Americanness. We are obligated, as "patriots," to subordinate all kinds of civil rights and free speech to this group identity. We saw this most recently during John McCain's Republican presidential campaign, which overtly sought to inflame the nation's culture wars by building its campaign around the slogan "Country First."

This emphasis on the group or the nation has been an ongoing theme since 9/11. The movement's bandwagon jingoes have quickly and fiercely denounced anyone who had the audacity to wonder how American policy might have contributed to the root causes of terrorism. They have argued that privacy rights, racial profiling, and normative prohibitions against torture should be willingly sacrificed in the pursuit of national security, even without a scintilla of evidence that such measures would actually enhance security. It is also a dominant theme in right-wing anti-immigration agitation, where figures like Patrick Buchanan, Bill O'Reilly, and Lou Dobbs warn against the Latino and third-world "avalanche" that they fear will overwhelm "white culture" in America.

These modes of thought are not altogether absent elsewhere in the political sphere, but are quite pronounced among movement conservatives.

3. *The belief that the group one belongs to is victimized, which justifies any action without legal or moral limits against the group's enemies, both internal and external.* Again, this is a pronounced tendency among conservatives. They have consistently emphasized the nation's victimhood in the 9/11 attacks, and have attacked any suggestion of a more nuanced view as "unpatriotic." They have further argued consistently that the 9/11 attacks justify nearly any action, regardless of legal or moral limits—for example, Abu Ghraib and Guantánamo Bay—against America's enemies.

This tendency is almost utterly absent elsewhere along the political spectrum. While many liberals also gladly participate in the belief that America is primarily a victim in the war on terror, a common charge against liberals is that they are "anti-American" for even suggesting that the nation ought to operate within the larger framework of the international community.

4. *Dread of the group's decline under the corrosive effect of individualistic liberalism, class conflict, and alien influences.* A favorite conservative theme is a dread of national decline under the corrosive effects of liberalism, which is often identified with equally dreaded alien influences. Sean Hannity's bestselling screed, *Deliver Us from*

Evil: Defeating Terrorism, Despotism, and Liberalism, is the most blatant example. There have been many other iterations of this meme as well, such as Dinesh D'Souza's *The Enemy at Home: The Cultural Left and Its Responsibility for 9/11*; Michael Savage's *The Threat Within*, which argues that the nation's real enemy is liberalism; or Rush Limbaugh's incessant harangues blaming liberals for everything wrong with the country. Pundits like Savage, Michelle Malkin, and Lou Dobbs have built careers out of denouncing the threat posed by illegal immigration and have connected it frequently to the terrorist threat.

This motivating passion became especially pronounced during the 2008 presidential campaign by Barack Obama's political opponents—both the official Republican campaign and its "independent" smear-artist surrogates. The latter were more explicit in spreading the lie that Obama was Muslim (and therefore a nefarious agent working on behalf of the nation's enemies), while the former simply amplified these claims by emphasizing Obama's "alienness" as a man of mixed racial descent and a complex religious background.

Obviously, this meme does not appear among liberals in any shape or form, nor for that matter among any nonmovement conservatives, except for the extremists of the racist and Patriot Far Right. Indeed, it's difficult to even find a liberal equivalent to the conservative argument, to wit, that conservatives are at the root of all the nation's ills.

5. *The need for closer integration of a purer community, by consent if possible, or by exclusionary violence if necessary.* Movement conservatives clearly have made use of this meme. They have consistently argued for a closer integration of a purer American community under the aegis of "national unity." However, this unity is not a natural one reached by compromise; rather, it can only be achieved

by a complete subsuming of American politics by the conservative movement, the creation of essentially a one-party state. Citizens can join by consent if they like, or they can face exclusion as a consequence. There is also a pronounced tendency to see national identity in racial terms (for example, "white"), particularly when immigration is the topic of debate.

This motivating passion is not entirely absent from liberalism or centrism; the speeches by Democrats such as Barack Obama and Hillary Clinton at their 2008 national convention likewise stressed themes of national unity. But their argument was clearly an inclusive one—saying, in essence, that everyone across the political spectrum was an American, and that all of us need to pull together as a nation. The conservative-movement argument, in stark contrast, is not inclusive in the least; the kind of "unity" it promotes is one in which Americans can come together only under the banner of their ideology; otherwise, they will face exclusion. In many instances, this exclusion is cast in terms that explicitly threaten violence or even arrest. Attendees wearing antiwar or anti-Bush T-shirts or adorning their cars with liberal bumper stickers not only were refused entry to Bush's public appearances on the campaign trail in 2004, they were threatened with arrest for merely having tried. The same has been true of any Bush or Cheney public appearance in the years since.

In this regard, the fascist propensities of the conservative movement are particularly clear and unmistakable. However, the levels of violence being threatened remain (at this writing) relatively low-level, and no arrests of lasting consequence have resulted from the threats.

6. *The need for authority by natural leaders (always male), culminating in a national chief who alone is capable of incarnating the*

group's destiny. While denouncing their opponents as "weak on terror," conservatives have consistently portrayed themselves— and particularly the leaders, George W. Bush and John McCain, respectively—as the only persons capable of making the nation secure from terrorists in its role as the dominant global superpower, the "beacon of democracy."

This motivating passion is, however, less clear in certain regards, particularly gender roles. The conservative movement not only has highly placed women in media roles (see, for example, Coulter and Malkin) but it also has had women in key positions in Republican campaigns and high office—most notably 2008 vice-presidential nominee Sarah Palin, as well as Bush administration officials Condoleezza Rice, Karen Hughes, and Christine Todd Whitman. But the tendency here, too, is toward a strongly male hierarchy; the movement's female pundits have a notable propensity for attacking women's rights (Coulter has even suggested they not be allowed to vote), while those in key positions are either eventually moved out—Hughes and Whitman—or given primarily roles as spokespersons for policies largely determined by the men in charge of the show (see Rice). Meanwhile, derision of the opposition often deploys rhetoric that expresses an overt hostility to a "feminine" approach, and this hostility is encouraged at every turn. When one of his supporters referred to Hillary Clinton as a "bitch" on the campaign trail, John McCain simply laughed along.

The claims of their ideology's exclusive ability to "lead America to its destiny," however, have become striking in recent years, especially as Bush—and in his footsteps, McCain—has defended his approach to the "war on terror" and the invasion of Iraq within the framework of the "new American century." In this vision, formulated by his top policy advisers, the United States will continue to dominate global affairs for the foreseeable future. Bush called this "a calling from beyond the stars." The innate similarity of this style of leadership to the fascist vision of "national destiny" could not be more clear.

7. *The superiority of the leader's instincts over abstract and universal reason.* This aspect of the fascist appeal was particularly pronounced during the 2004 Bush presidential campaign, and continued during McCain's 2008 presidential campaign. Bush's defenders and supporters continually stressed his superiority as a president because of his reliance on his instincts and "resolve" and his marked refusal to engage in abstract reasoning. In 2004, John Kerry, in contrast, was consistently portrayed as a morally confused, "flip-flopping" intellectual, and much the same critique was directed against Obama in 2008, though to notably less effect.

The same was true of conservatives' reluctant and belated embrace of John McCain in the 2008 campaign. McCain's Vietnam War heroism and his status as a onetime POW were given as the essential reasons to vote for the man. And although he had betrayed nearly all the positions that once earned him renown as a congressional "maverick," and despite surrounding himself in his campaign by the same lobbyists he claimed independence from, his character was considered by his supporters as well as his sycophantic chorus in the mainstream press to be unimpeachable. In contrast, Obama was consistently portrayed as an Ivy-League elitist and a "presumptuous" climber; the racial dog-whistle aspects of this meme were made explicit when Republican representative Lynn Westmoreland of Mississippi called Obama "uppity."[12]

Of all the overlapping of movement conservatism and the motivating passions of fascism, this instance is the most pronounced and unmistakable.

8. *The beauty of violence and the efficacy of will, when they are devoted to the group's success.* Over the past decade, conservatives have

trod frequently into arguing in favor of a war ethos. Certainly the armchair generals who rhapsodized over the use of "shock and awe" tactics in the invasion of Iraq gave voice to this, at times suggesting there is a kind of beauty to violence, especially at the service of the imposition of American will.

However, this motif as a motivating passion is not particularly pronounced when it comes to the conservative movement in general. There is little open promotion of an ethos of violence, except when conservative pundits talk reflexively about nuking the enemy or doing away with them altogether. And the Bush administration sometimes paid lip service to the pain and sorrow associated with war, though, interestingly enough, that concern was only expressed about American servicemen, not Iraqi civilians.

Genuine fascism, in contrast, positively gloried in violence as a *domestic* solution as well as an international one, advocating the thuggish tactics of SA brownshirts in silencing the Left. So far, only hints of this tendency have appeared in the conservative movement. Until they become more explicit, this particular fascist passion cannot be said to concretely exist in the current setting.

At the same time, it must be observed that right-wing rhetoric—particularly the eliminationist kind—is so innately violent, and moreover permissive about the use of violence, that it has the effect of promoting a general environment in which violence is accepted and even glorified.

9. *The right of the "chosen people" to dominate others without restraint from any human or divine law, "right" being decided solely by the group's prowess in a Darwinian struggle.* One can find some evidence of this tendency among conservatives. In defending the Bush administration's actions—particularly the invasion of Iraq under the pretense of a nonexistent "imminent threat," and the conditions that led to international-law violations at Abu Ghraib

and Guantánamo—many conservatives simply dismissed their critics by invoking 9/11 and our larger "right," by sheer virtue of our national military power, to dominate other nations and individuals without restraint. There are other ways this trait manifests itself as well. The Bush administration's hostility to the international criminal courts was well established even before 9/11, and became pronounced in the ensuing years. Its contemptuous treatment of the United Nations was consonant with this as well.

It's important to observe, however, that in the case of the conservative movement, "Darwinian" (or more correctly, "Social Darwinian") does not accurately describe their view of the natural world order. Theirs is more of a religious view akin to Manifest Destiny, a belief in American exceptionalism viewed through a prism of apocalyptic fundamentalist Christianity. In the end, the outcome is not remarkably different; their view still describes the world in competitive instead of cooperative terms, and the destructive outcome of putting it into practice is at least as great.

Nonetheless, the conservative movement exhibits many of the attributes of this passion, particularly in its assertion of the right to operate without restraint, in this case justified by the horrors of 9/11. Otherwise, how could we have invaded another nation under false pretenses and in violation of international law?

All nine of these "motivating passions" are present, at least in rough form or outline, in the post-2000 conservative movement. Five are present in a strong and clear way, two of which show no mitigating factors. The presence of two others is mixed and somewhat mitigated, and the remaining two show up in only very mild form.

There are other less important, possibly merely stylistic, similarities between fascism and the conservative movement:

- A propensity to view the weak with contempt, to associate weakness with femininity, and to excoriate the feminine and glorify the masculine. "Girlie men" was only the tip of the rhetorical iceberg in this regard.

- A fondness for depicting enemies and the opposition as animals—typically either vermin or vicious killers.
- An excess of eliminationist rhetoric advocating the utter exclusion of entire blocs of the nation's population.

All told, we see that the conservative movement has become a kind of precursor to fascism even when the differences are significant enough to preclude it being accurately described as the real thing. Other aspects of the historical framework of fascism, identified by people like Paxton and Griffin, reveal even more significant differences. I briefly mentioned these differences in chapter 5, but here is a more detailed exploration of them.

The agenda of the conservative movement, under the guise of representing mainstream conservatism, is not openly revolutionary. This is in large part due to the origins of a movement that has traditionally been a defender of the status quo. A noteworthy aspect of the conservative movement, though, is that beneath the conservative mask lies a deeply radical, mostly reactionary, agenda. This is especially the case in its approach to foreign policy, which embarked the nation for the first time in its history on a unilateralist campaign of world domination.

George W. Bush and his conservative wrecking crew pushed for a radical makeover of policy and the approach to governance from the start of his administration. This effort was not a consequence of 9/11; instead, 9/11 provided Bush cover for an agenda he intended to implement from his first day in office.

It is not yet a dictatorship. Always in the past, fascism appeared as a discrete movement that rose to power from the ground up. In contrast, the mechanics in this instance involve a subtle yet unmistakable transformation from within an already established force in the political system—namely, the conservative movement. However, this movement, unlike fascism, has never openly espoused the virtues of authoritarian dictatorship (though there *was* Bush's onetime joke that "If this were a dictatorship, it would be a heck of a lot easier, just so long as I'm the dictator"). Conservatism continues to operate within the framework of a democratic republic.

At the same time, the movement's growing hostility to democratic institutions has been noteworthy, as manifested in incidents ranging from the *Bush v. Gore* decision, which undermined individual voting rights, to former House majority leader Tom DeLay's Texas redistricting program, to the recall of California governor Gray Davis, to the ongoing vote-suppression tactics used in the 2004 election and afterward. This hostility has theoretical underpinnings in the conservative movement, particularly noteworthy in Supreme Court Justice Antonin Scalia's discussions of the "tendency of democracy to obscure the divine authority behind government" and the need "to combat [this tendency] as effectively as possible."[13]

The conservative movement does not yet rely on physical violence and campaigns of gross intimidation to obtain power and suppress opposition. There have been hints of such inclinations, ranging from the intimidation of voters in 2000 in Florida to minor incidents of violence and intimidation, which were especially common in the 2004 campaign. However, none of this has received explicit encouragement from the movement. Instead, an environment has emerged in which these kinds of thuggish tactics are considered everyday expressions of heated political views. In this same environment, liberals and other opponents of the movement are responding in kind, which only stokes the flames higher and justifies in the minds of movement followers their own innately violent responses.

American democracy has not yet reached the stage of genuine crisis required for full-blown fascism to take root.

Paxton emphasizes that fascism is almost exclusively a result of the failure of democracy, and for this reason, only appears in formerly democratic states. Nearly every scholar of fascism agrees that it has successfully seized power only when these democratic states are in crisis.

Para-fascism has not arisen because of some conspiracy of closet fascists lurking in the conservative movement, but rather because of the inexorable pull of the forces latent in the American body politic, combined with an unchecked lust for power and certain historical events of politically earthshaking moment. Yet, in part because of the seeming familiarity of so many of its traits, the appearance of a fascist architecture on the political scene does not appear to be immediately threatening—especially in the hollow, not fully fleshed-out form it has taken in the American conservative movement. It's only when we stand back and assess the emerging shape that the danger becomes clear.

Para-fascism, as it exists now, remains a political pathology, but a manageable one.

Americans put flesh on the fascist bones to the extent that we find ourselves in the throes of a real crisis of governance; demand utter fealty to the national identity, even at the expense of democratic institutions or democracy itself; identify liberalism as the root of all evil in America, as a domestic enemy little distinguishable from those from abroad; justify monstrous acts by pointing to our own victimhood; rely on the "strength" and instincts of our leaders instead of their wisdom and powers of reason; allow violence to become part of the political landscape; and pursue an insane apocalyptic vision of world domination.

Can it happen in America? As Paxton says, America is one of the nations where fascism may yet manifest itself in this era of mass politics. Indeed, he identifies the possible origins of fascism in America:

> It may be that the earliest phenomenon that can be functionally related to fascism is American: the Ku Klux Klan. Just after the Civil War, some Confederate officers, fearing the vote given to African Americans by the Radical Reconstructionists in 1867, set up a militia to restore an overturned social order. The Klan constituted an alternate civic authority, parallel to the legal state, which, in its founders' eyes, no longer defended their community's legitimate interests. In its adoption of a uniform (white robe and hood), as well as its techniques of intimidation and its conviction that violence was justified in the cause of the group's destiny, the first version of the Klan in the defeated American South was a remarkable preview of the way fascist movements were to function in interwar Europe.[14]

History corroborates Paxton's thesis as well as its expansion. The Klan of the early 20th century was even more pronouncedly fascist than the original one, particularly in its claim to represent the true national character: "100 percent Americanism" was the organization's chief catchphrase. Its origins—its first members were the mob that lynched Leo Frank, a Jewish Atlantan wrongly convicted of murdering a young white girl—were openly violent. David Chalmers, in his book *Hooded Americanism: The History of the Ku Klux Klan*, is unequivocal in placing the Klan firmly on the right of the political spectrum and well into the proto-fascist camp:

Throughout its history, the Klan has been a conservative, not revolutionary, organization. As a vigilante, it has sought to uphold "law and order," white dominance, and traditional morality. To do this it has threatened, flogged, mutilated, and on occasion, murdered. The main purpose of the Klansmen, Kligrapps, Kludds, and Night Hawks, Cyclopses, Titans, Dragons, and Wizards assembled in their Dens, Klaverns, and Klonvokations, rallying in rented cow pastures, and marching in solemn procession through city streets, has been to defend and restore what they conceived as traditional social values. *The Klan has basically been a revitalization movement.*[15]

The Klan was about much more than mere racism. It wished to enforce—through violence, threats, and intimidation—what it called "traditional values" and "100 percent Americanism." It was essentially populist, but there was no mistaking it for anything "progressive." The latter, in fact, was its sworn enemy.

Chalmers describes how Col. William J. Simmons, the man most responsible for the revival of the Klan in the 1915–20 period, and the leader of the group that burned a cross atop Stone Mountain in honor of the mob that lynched Frank, shifted the Klan's focus from merely attacking blacks to a broad range of targets:

Upon being introduced to an audience of Georgia Klansmen, Colonel Simmons silently took a Colt automatic from his pocket and placed it on the table in front of him. Then he took a revolver from another pocket and put it on the table too. Then he unbuckled a cartridge belt and draped it in a crescent shape between the two weapons. Next, without having uttered a word, he drew out a bowie knife and plunged it in the center of the things on the table. "Now let the Niggers, Catholics, Jews, and all the others who disdain my imperial wizardry, come on," he said. . . . Simmons explained that the Japanese were but a superior colored race. Never in the history of the world, the Klan believed, had a "mongrel civilization" survived. The major theme, however, was the rich vein of anti-Catholicism, which the Klan was to mine avidly during the 1920s, and it was this more than anything else which made the Klan.

To the Negro, Jew, Oriental, Roman Catholic, and alien, were added dope, bootlegging, graft, night clubs and road houses, violation of the Sabbath, unfair business dealings, sex, marital "goings-on," and scandalous behavior, as the proper concern of the one-hundred-percent American. The Klan organizer was told to find out what was worrying a community and to offer the Klan as a solution.[16]

The Klan's leaders conceived of the organization as a kind of "special secret service bustling about spying on radicalism and questionable patriotism," which gradually became an unofficial form of community vigilance.[17] Philip Dray, in his book about the history of the lynching era, *At the Hands of Persons Unknown*, describes this opportunism on the part of the Klan as well:

> Marketed like any other business or lodge association, the Klan was eventually franchised in twenty-seven states and varied its purpose to confront a wide palette of enemies. To a town inundated with unemployed blacks, one historian has pointed out, it was the Klan of the Griffith film; if bootleggers ran amok, the Klan was an auxiliary police outfit; in the face of labor activism, Klan members became corporate thugs and enforcers; where immigrants threatened to overwhelm a city, the Klan stood ready to publicize 100 percent Americanism. As the organization served as a kind of enforcement group for godly values, many clergymen became Klan members or boosters. Jesus Christ himself, it was said, would have been a Klansman.[18]

The "community values" agenda became, in short order, a justification for all kinds of violence. Accompanying the Klan's "social calendar" were a variety of lynchings, shootings, and whippings. Usually the victims were blacks, Jews, Catholics, and various immigrants, but at times they could be white, Protestant, and female—depending on how "immoral" they had been. According to Sara Bullard:

> In Alabama, for example, a divorcee with two children was flogged for the crime of remarrying, and then given a jar of Vaseline for her wounds. In Georgia a woman was given 60 lashes for a vague charge of "immorality and failure to go to church"; when her 15-year-old son ran to her rescue, he received the same treatment. In both cases ministers led the Klansmen responsible for the violence.[19]

For a while the Klan was immensely popular, bolstered particularly by D. W. Griffith's film *Birth of a Nation,* which was an homage to the Klan and helped inspire Simmons. It briefly became a nationwide organization with chapters in all 48 states, and a political powerhouse in several, including Oregon, Indiana, Tennessee, Oklahoma, and Maine, where the Klan played a critical role in the 1924 election of Owen Brewster to the governorship. That same year, the Klan made waves at the Democratic convention when the Klan-backed candidate, William Gibbs McAdoo of Georgia, declined to denounce Klan activities. Al Smith of New York managed to block his nomination, largely on these grounds, and West Virginia's John Davis emerged as the compromise selection. He lost to Calvin Coolidge.

As Chalmers writes:

> In 1922, the Klan helped elect governors in Georgia, Alabama, California, and Oregon, and came close to knocking Missouri's Jim Reed out of the U.S. Senate. It was reported that perhaps as many as seventy-five members of the lower house had received help from Klan votes. An undetermined, and unguessable,

number of congressmen, veterans, and newcomers, had actually joined the hooded order, and E.Y. Clarke was asking the local chapters to suggest likely candidates for the future. The next year, the Klan continued to expand, with its greatest strength developing in the upper Mississippi Valley and in the Great Lakes kingdom of D.C. Stephenson.[20]

During the prewar period, the Klan's brand of politics meshed naturally with that of open fascists, even if uneasily at first. This initial unease reflects a historical fact about fascism: congenitally nationalistic it expressed bigotry against other "foreign" nationalities in its every iteration, creating a certain level of hostility between Klansmen and Italian and German fascists. But ideological affinities always eventually won out. Chalmers describes the operational associations that eventually formed between European fascists and the Klan, which included a number of Nazi "front" organizations that had leaders with Klan backgrounds. George Deatherage, founder of the Knights of the White Camellia, claimed proudly that the Nazis had copied both their infamous salute as well as their anti-Jewish policy from the Klan.[21] And on August 18, 1940, several hundred robed Klansmen gathered near Andover, Maryland, on the grounds of the German-American Bund's Camp Nordlund with a contingent of uniformed Bundsmen, at which one of the Bund officials proclaimed: "The principles of the Bund and the principles of the Klan are the same." As it happened, the Bund at the time was being funded and operated by Hitler's Nazi party.[22]

All this time, the Klan's propensity for violence became its trademark. In Tulsa, where the Klan was such a prominent and active presence that it kept a public "whipping field" where it publicly humiliated various miscreants, the violence eventually erupted into the massive Tulsa Race Riot of 1921. The resulting death toll of African Americans is estimated to have been between 300 and 3,000. Klan violence was not relegated strictly to the South, but it was particularly intense there, especially the use of cross burnings to threaten and intimidate blacks. This became notably the case in the 1930s and '40s, when the Klan attempted to stem the oncoming tide of the civil rights movement. In the early 1950s, the *Brown v. Board of Education* ruling ordering the desegregation of Southern schools actually produced a second revival of the Klan, all of it focused on the "traditional values" of white supremacy and its fruits: Jim Crow, segregation, and lynchings.

And it is not as if the Klan has since gone away. In the ensuing years, it has remained the implacable enemy of civil rights not merely for blacks but for any minority, including gays and lesbians. Its activities have remained associated with violence of various kinds, including a broad gamut of hate crimes committed against every kind of nonwhite, or non-Christian, or for that matter non conservative. In the recent past, it has revived its nativist roots by becoming vociferously active in the immigration debate, openly sponsoring anti-immigrant rallies at which Klan robes have been seen.

But fascism, as the Klan's example demonstrates, has always previously failed in America, and Paxton's analysis points with some precision to exactly why. Fascism is an essentially mutative impulse in the pursuit of power; that is, it abandons positions as fresh opportunities for acquiring power present themselves. This is particularly true as it moves from its ideological roots into the halls of government. In the end, the resulting political power is often, as Griffin puts it, a "travesty" of its original ideology. Paxton describes it thus:

> In power, what seems to count is less the faithful application of the party's initial ideology than the integrating function that

espousing one official ideology performs, to the exclusion of any ideas deemed alien or divisive.[23]

Paxton identifies five stages in fascism's arc of flight:

(1) The creation of the movements; (2) their rooting in the political system; (3) their seizure of power; (4) the exercise of power; (5) and finally, the long duration, during which the fascist regime chooses either radicalization or entropy.[24]

In the United States, as in France and elsewhere, fascism typically failed in the second stage, because it failed to become a cohesive political entity, one capable of acquiring power. As Paxton observes, "The ascendant liberalism of FDR effectively squeezed the life out of the nascent fascist elements in the U.S.," in no small part because Roosevelt effectively shared power with the Right, which thus had no incentive to form a coalition with fascists. Moreover, Roosevelt's New Deal program made significant inroads for liberal politics in rural America.

Significantly, Paxton points out that fascism in Europe took root in a neglected agricultural sector—something that did not happen in the United States in the 1930s. Indeed, it gained its second-stage power in the crucible of organized thuggery against liberals and leftists in Germany and Italy:

The German strikes were broken by vigilantes, armed and abetted by the local army authorities, in cases in which the regular authorities were too conciliatory to suit the landowners. The Italian ones were broken by Mussolini's famous blackshirted squadristi, whose vigilantism filled the void left by the apparent inability of the liberal Italian state to enforce order. It was precisely in this direct action against farm-worker unions that second-stage fascism was born in Italy, and even launched on the path to power, to the dismay of the first Fascists, intellectual dissidents from national syndicalism.[25]

Fascism as a political force suffered from the same sort of bad timing in the United States when it arose in the 1920s: there was no great social crisis, and the conservatives in power didn't need to form an alliance with fascism. When it arose again in the 1930s, the ascendance of power-sharing liberalism, popular in rural and urban areas, again left fascism little breathing room.

And in the 1990s, when proto-fascism reemerged as a popular movement in the form of the Patriots, conservatives once again enjoyed a considerable power base (they were in control of Congress) and had little incentive to share power. Moreover, the economy was booming—except in rural America.

Unsurprisingly, that is where the Patriots built their popular base. And importantly, much of that base building revolved around a motif that created a significant area of common interest with mainstream conservatives: hatred of Bill Clinton and a fear of all things liberal. There is where the alliance between right-wing extremists and mainstream conservatives first took root and flowered. But since then, it has taken on a life of its own.

7

Proto-Fascism, Para-Fascism, and the Real Thing

Conservatives, and the mainstream media to some extent as well, have airbrushed the bombing of the Murrah Federal Building in Oklahoma City on April 19, 1995—in which 168 people died and over 800 were injured—so it appears as the act of a single maniac (or two).

This image distorts the reality in the national memory: Oklahoma City was the signature event of a wave of right-wing terrorism that struck America in the 1990s, derived wholly from an ideological stew of venomous hate that has since been seeping into mainstream conservatism. Indeed, since 1995, the Southern Poverty Law Center (SPLC) has identified over 60 cases of domestic terrorism—either actual attacks or planned violence that was nipped in the bud by effective law enforcement. These range from well-publicized cases, such as Olympics bomber Eric Rudolph's rampage of terror and Buford Furrow's gun attack on a Los Angeles day-care center, to lesser-known cases, such as the plot to blow up a Sacramento propane facility or the cyanide bomb built by a man named William Krar.[1]

The Patriot movement that inspired Tim McVeigh and his cohorts, as well as the other would-be right-wing terrorists who followed him, derives almost directly from overtly fascist elements in American politics. As previously described (see chapter 1), much of its political and "legal" philosophy comes from the Posse Comitatus movement of the 1970s and '80s, which itself originated (in the 1960s) from the teachings of renowned anti-Semite William Potter Gale, and was further propagated by Mike Beach, a former Silver Shirt follower of the neo-Nazi ideologue William Dudley Pelley.

Fascism, as we've seen, grows out of an impulse that appears throughout history and in many different cultures. This impulse is, as Roger Griffin puts it, "ultra-nationalism that aspires to bring about the renewal of a nation's entire political culture." Griffin, moreover, argues that current-day fascism is "groupuscular" in nature; that is, it is made up of smallish but virulent, potentially lethal, and certainly problematic "organisms." As Griffin suggests, this groupuscular form appears to pose little threat, but it remains latent and is capable of wreaking serious havoc. It is, he writes, "ideally suited to breeding lone wolf terrorists and self-styled 'political soldiers' in trainers and bomber-jackets dedicated to a tactic of subversion known in Italian as 'spontaneism.'" In the United States, this manifestation of fascism has been embodied in the person of McVeigh and more broadly in the Patriot movement.[2]

Though the Patriot movement is fairly multifaceted, most Americans view it through media images that focus on a single facet: the often-pathetic collection of bunglers and fantasists known as the militia movement. Moreover, they've been told that the militia movement is dead. And, in its 1990s form, it is, more or less. But it lives on in a dozen or more offshoots, many of them widely portrayed as mainstream organizations—the most notable being the anti-immigrant Minuteman movement, which provides a case study of how proto-fascism, through mainstreaming, becomes para-fascism.

The militia movement was only one strategy of the broad coalition of right-wing extremists who call themselves the "Patriot" movement, which also included an array of tax protesters, "constitutionalists," antiabortion extremists, antienvironmentalists, various conspiracy theorists, and the movement's core of religious white nationalists. The strategy of forming militias was aimed at recruiting from the mainstream, particularly among gun owners. It eventually fell prey to disrepute and entropy, for reasons mostly related to financial mismanagement and competing egos and agendas, as well as the failure of its dire warnings of a New World Order apocalypse around the supposed Y2K problem in late 1999. Other Patriot strategies have proved to have greater endurance. One of the most important of these is "common law courts" and their various permutations, which revolve around the idea of "sovereign citizenship," and conceive of every white Christian male American, essentially, as a king unto himself. The movement is always mutable.

This fundamental strategy also includes forming vigilante citizen militias to perform necessary "community-security" functions, giving rise to perhaps the most famous of these offshoots: the Minuteman movement, which to this day organizes "border watches" along the U.S.-Mexico border in California, Arizona, and Texas (as well as other states, including Washington along its border with Canada). When Minuteman Project cofounder Chris Simcox began organizing border-watch patrols in early 2003 in his hometown of Tombstone, he called his outfit the Tombstone Militia (though he changed it in relatively short order to the Civil Homeland Defense Corps). Simcox's campaign was attracting press attention as early as January 2003, when he was inviting media members to observe the group's patrols. Typical of both the supporters and the offshoots of the Minuteman Project, they have consistently identified themselves with the militia (or Patriot) movement, and they call themselves "militias" unhesitatingly. Likewise, prior to the announcement of the Minuteman Project, press coverage of the border-militia movement referred consistently to the participants as "militiamen."[3]

The Minutemen have similarly spouted both Patriot-style New World Order conspiracy theories and their own special brand of xenophobic conspiracism—notably, the claim that Latino immigrants are part of a grand "reconquista" plot by Mexico to reclaim the southwestern United States. And when cofounder Jim Gilchrist—who actually concocted the original Minuteman Project scheme in October 2004 and linked up with Simcox the following spring to make it happen—ran for Congress in 2006, he did so on the ticket of the American Independent Party, which happens to be the California chapter of the Patriot-oriented Constitution Party. Gilchrist later indicated he would like to run for president under its banner.

Since 2007, however, the Minutemen have fallen on hard times, crumbling under the weight of financial mismanagement and leadership disputes. In that respect, they continue to trace the career arc of most right-wing populist movements: the further they fall into disarray, the more groupuscular they become. In the wake of the decline of the major Minuteman organizations, dozens of smaller, localized entities—some already displaying a tolerance for white-supremacist ideology and a taste for violence—have sprung up on their own.

Yet the Patriot movement and its offshoots, like the Minutemen, cannot be properly described as full-fledged fascism. In fact, they do not resemble mature fascism in the least. However, it's important to keep in mind Paxton's key insight here: *Fascism, by nature, is essentially mutative.* What we see of nascent forms of fascism bears only a familial resemblance to their mature forms.

The Patriot movement on its own has been in a down cycle since the end of the 1990s. Its recruitment numbers have dropped. Its visibility and level of activity are in stasis, if not decline. During these down periods, the remaining True Believers tend to become even more radicalized. There is already a spiral of violent behavior associated with Patriot beliefs, particularly among the more unstable hard-core adherents—reflected, certainly, in the rampages of Eric Rudolph, Buford Furrow, and perhaps Jim David Adkisson. As Griffin suggests, we can probably expect to see an increase in these "lone wolf" kind of attacks in coming years.

But there is a more significant aspect to the apparent decline of the Patriot movement: its believers, its thousands of foot soldiers, and its agenda, never went away. They didn't stop believing that Clinton was the Antichrist or that he intended to enslave us all under the New World Order. They didn't stop believing it was appropriate to preemptively murder "baby killers" or that Jews secretly conspire to control the world.

They're still with us, but they're not active much in militias anymore. They've largely been absorbed by the Republican Party. Indeed, in the past decade the movement has been fantastically successful in mainstreaming itself—especially through the media (and general public) embrace of its anti-immigrant wing, as well as the spread of classical Patriot monetary and taxation theories reflected in the populist Republican presidential campaign of Rep. Ron Paul. And it is important to remember that right-wing populism has always gone in cycles. It never goes away—it only becomes latent and resurrects itself when the conditions are right.

So, what makes movement conservatism para-fascist?

At times it seems, when dealing with the movement, as if we've entered a funhouse mirror maze. Or more to the point, a dark and labyrinthine cavern, twisting through an endless maze, whose architecture we can only vaguely discern if we hold up our torches.

Every now and then, though, someone within the movement hierarchy—often one at the very top—will flash a little light on the metastatic architecture of the conservative movement. When this happens, it can be a little like the scene in *Aliens* when Ripley's flamethrower lights up the interior of the lair into which she has wandered.

The mutability of truth is what has made confronting the conservative movement feel so maze-like, because factuality in its hands is like clay: you never know what bizarre argument they're going to come up with next. They even sometimes turn established historical consensus on its head. First, we had Ann Coulter penning a defense of McCarthyism in her book *Treason*; then there was Michelle Malkin, justifying the forced incarceration of 122,000 Japanese Americans with *In Defense of Internment*. The coup de grâce came when Jonah Goldberg devoted nearly 500 pages in his book *Liberal Fascism* to selling the up-is-down notion that fascism is "a phenomenon of the left."

The problem is not isolated merely to right-wing pundits; it implicates right-wing politicians themselves, most notably George W. Bush and his administration. Ron Suskind, in a 2004 *New York Times* piece describing Bush's faith-based approach to the presidency, outlined the operative mindset within the White House. A senior adviser to Bush told him that "guys like me [Suskind] were 'in what we call the reality-based community,' which he defined as people who "believe that solutions emerge from your judicious study of discernible reality." He continued: "We're an empire now, and when we act, we create our own reality. And while you're studying that reality—judiciously, as you will—we'll act again, creating other new realities, which you can study too, and that's how things will sort out. We're history's actors ... and you, all of you, will be left to just study what we do."

The conservative movement's agenda is inclined to shift rapidly according to its need to acquire power by "creating new realities." But this "created" reality more often than not has only a passing resemblance to factual reality, which has unmoored the movement from real-world principles, including the historically conservative kind. As we have seen, movement conservatism has come to resemble nothing genuinely conservative at all but rather something starkly radical: profligate spending and economic recklessness; incautious and expansionary wars, pursued unilaterally; exaltation of religious fervor and assaults on science; and the undermining of the civil rights of minorities. The neo-Confederate-laden GOP no longer has even a passing resemblance to the party of Lincoln. Even at the micropolitical level, during debate, the famous conservative carefulness, politeness, and reserve has vanished.

The conservative movement, as such, is an ever-shifting beast. Its drive is power, and in that drive it has gradually adopted the familiar architecture of another power-mad right-wing phenomenon of modern mass politics: fascism. Robert O. Paxton explains how fascism similarly picked up and dropped ideologies at will, according to its power needs, in *The Anatomy of Fascism*. Unlike the usual "isms," he explains, fascism is not dependent on any written truths, but is "true" only "insofar as it helps fulfill the destiny of a chosen race or people or blood." He quotes an Italian fascist writing in 1930:

> We [Fascists] don't think ideology is a problem that is resolved
> in such a way that truth is seated on a throne.... The truth of
> an ideology lies in its capacity to set in motion our capacity for
> ideals and action.[4]

Indeed, fascist leaders exulted in the fact that they had no rational policy program. As Mussolini was culminating his climb to power in Italy in 1920, his retort to a left-wing critic made this plain: "The democrats of *Il Mondo* want to know our program? It is to break the bones of the democrats of *Il Mondo*."[5]

This fist-shaking style of political discourse, in fact, was one of the real hallmarks of fascism. It signaled, above all else, the rightness of power by virtue of it being used to intimidate and silence dissenters. To the fascist leader, diplomacy is a parlor game for the weak; what counts is the raw will of the man of action. Whether he is right is moot; his strength and resolve in the exercise of power are what count. This harsh authoritarianism, indeed, has been a significant aspect of right-wing populist movements throughout American history, particularly the Klan and the Posse Comitatus, as well as their various racist-right offshoots, including today's Patriots and modern neo-Nazi skinheads.

As we have seen, this same style of discourse has become endemic to the American Right this decade, riddled as it is with eliminationist rhetoric and venomous contempt. Vice President Dick Cheney's infamous "Go fuck yourself" retort to Sen. Patrick Leahy in 2004 was only the highest-level expression of it. Right-wing talkers have grown even more virulent in hurling eliminationist rhetoric at liberals and minorities. The debate over illegal immigration, in particular, has been riddled with it. And conservative politicians have increasingly resorted to eliminationist appeals as their hold on power has been slipping away.

In the 2008 presidential campaign, we were treated to a steady diet of these appeals, built around a racially charged depiction of Barack Obama as a "dangerous" brown-skinned man with a radical ideology, and his supporters as besotted tools of the Enemy. Conservative emails and mailers, often from anonymous sources or "independent" groups, attempted to portray Barack Obama as a Muslim and a "terrorist sympathizer," and frequently emphasized his race. The GOP's vice-presidential nominee, Sarah Palin, attacked Obama on the stump for "palling around with terrorists," and issued appeals to "real Americans" in rural areas. John McCain called Obama a "socialist." The right-wing pundits went even more overboard, calling him "anti-American" and a "Marxist." At Fox News' online forum, conservative talking head James Pinkerton told readers that Obama was linked to a man who admired Lucifer.[6]

For the first time this decade, however, such rhetoric fell flat with the voting public. Polls taken in the wake of the McCain campaign's incendiary appeals made clear that, while such talk clearly energized his Republican base, it turned off independent and undecided voters. What particularly bothered voters was not just the rhetoric and its failure to address the serious issues before them (particularly the faltering economy), but the ugly behavior that emanated from it: the threats and shouts of "terrorist" during Republican rallies, the open expressions of racism outside them.

The McCain campaign scaled back its rhetoric; but the forces unleashed were not so easy to put back in a bottle. News reports rolled in of ugly incidents of vandalism, threats, and other acts of intimidation directed at Obama supporters. One McCain campaign worker even tried to claim she had been robbed and assaulted by a black Obama supporter who carved a "B" into her cheek with a knife, and campaign officials ran to promote this racially incendiary tale to the press; a day later, she admitted that it was all a hoax.

This is the real danger of para-fascism: once certain forces are unleashed, they often take on a life of their own and prove impossible to contain. If enough of the natural barriers that keep fascism at bay in a democratic society break down, then the half-formed hologram of fascism takes on substance and becomes the real thing. This is the danger movement conservatism has unleashed on America.

As America moves forward amid the reality of a President Obama, it may want to brace itself for a spate of domestic terrorism and homegrown violence. Because even before Obama's election, it was clear that some of the more violence-prone sectors of the Far Right were winding themselves up for just such an eventuality.

The prospect of an Obama presidency sent the racist Right into a frenzy as early as June 2007, when a Klan leader from Indiana named Ray Larsen promised that he would be assassinated before taking office.[7] Things reached a fever pitch by the summer of 2008. On the Web, white supremacists were speculating wildly about what it meant to their movement.

Three white supremacists, reportedly plotting to assassinate Obama at the Democratic National Convention in Denver in August, were caught a week before (though they were not charged with engaging in the plot). A week before the election, two neo-Nazi skinheads were arrested in Tennessee, charged with plotting to assassinate Obama at the culmination of a killing spree in which 102 black people were to be killed.

Earlier that summer, a 60-year-old militiaman named Bradley T. Kahle of Troutville, Pennsylvania, was arrested along with four other Patriots for plotting to attack local government buildings. The FBI confiscated hundreds of weapons, including hunting rifles, cannons, homemade bombs, and rudimentary rockets. Before the bust, Kahle told undercover agents "words to the effect of, that 'if Hillary Clinton, or Barack Obama, get elected, hopefully they will get assassinated, if not they will disarm the country and we will have a civil war,'" according to their arrest affidavit.

Kahle also told authorities he planned to visit Pittsburgh so he could get on top of a high-rise and start shooting black people.[8]

Some white supremacists welcomed Obama's ascendancy because they saw it as likely to fulfill their fantasies of unleashing an open race war in America. "I hope Obama wins because in four years, white people just might be pissed off enough to actually do something," said a Virginia Klan leader named Ron Doggett. "White people aren't going to do a thing until their toys are taken away from them. So things have to be worse for things to be better."[9]

Web forums devoted to white supremacists held similar views. "He will make things so bad for white people that hopefully they will finally realize how stupid they were for admiring these jigaboos all these years," wrote a poster named "Darthvader" at the neo-Nazi Vanguard News Network. "I believe in the motto 'Worse is Better' and Obama certainly fits that description."

At the white nationalist forum Stormfront, this view was echoed over and over:

> "Oh man. I am gleefully, sadistically looking forward to Obama as president. . . . It will be a beautiful day when the masses look at the paper and truly realize they have lost their own country."

> "To the average white man and woman, they could look at Obama and see plain as day that whites are not in control."

> "Could it be that the nomination of Obama finally sparks a sense of unity in white voters? I would propose that this threat of black, muslim [sic] rule may very well be the thing that finally scares some sense back into complacent whites throughout the nation."[10]

This language makes clear that they expect a Democratic president to enact policies (particularly regarding gun control) that will provoke "civil war." And no doubt, regardless of how cautious and centrist a course Obama charts as president, they will find those provocations. After all, consider how they reacted to the presidency of Bill Clinton, a cautious and centrist Democrat, not to mention a white Southerner. In other words, they are looking for excuses to act out, and were finding them even before the election (the uproar over ACORN and supposed voter fraud, for instance, seemed posed to produce an endless array of conspiracy theories explaining how Obama cheated to win and undermining his legitimacy).

The extremist Right largely went into remission with the election of George W. Bush; militias disbanded because their followers believed the threat of an oppressive, gun-grabbing, baby-killing "New World Order" had passed. They bided their time by forming Minuteman brigades. Now they can see that their "safe" era is coming to an end. Throughout this time, they've been hankering for an excuse to start acting out violently, and any Democratic presidency can provide it. An Obama presidency, however, will do so in a significant way.

Ironically, the gradual end of the war in Iraq, which Obama has promised, will make this tendency particularly potent. Some veterans returning home from that conflict will be primed and ready to take part in the action.

Since early in the conflict, the Iraq war showed signs of proving to be the Timothy McVeigh Memorial Finishing School: the extreme stresses under which we are now placing these soldiers, especially in the form of multiple tours of duty and forced reenlistment, is eventually going to produce a bumper crop of traumatized citizens, some of whom are going to be extremely vulnerable to the "stab in the back" meme that's become a major note in the right-wing drumbeat on the war. A March 2007 *Journal of the American Medical Association* (JAMA) report revealed that nearly a third of all returning Iraq veterans were diagnosed with some kind of mental disorder. There were particularly high rates of Post Traumatic Stress Disorder (PTSD), as well as substance abuse and other mental conditions. Findings showed a high correlation between these problems and the multiple tours of duty being inflicted on large numbers of troops.[11]

People with traumatized psyches often act out violently. And the violence can be directed at oneself, as in suicide, or at others—especially when they have been led to think of their fellow citizens as the Enemy.

And this mindset, as it happens, is precisely what right-wing pundits and politicians have been pushing on them for the duration of the war. Particularly pernicious in this respect has been Rush Limbaugh, who almost daily for the past eight years and longer has informed his audiences, in various ways, that Democrats are unpatriotic and "terrorist sympathizers." Limbaugh's show is carried daily on Armed Services Radio, which means that our troops in Iraq are among his listeners. Indeed, an article of faith on the Right has become that liberals not only have been undermining the war effort but are now "waving the white flag of surrender" (as Sarah Palin put it in the 2008 vice-presidential debate) in Iraq. They have, in sum, "stabbed our soldiers in the back."[12]

The danger of this kind of incendiary rhetoric is underscored by the reality that hate groups and other extremists, including neo-Nazis, have been making actual inroads into the ranks of the military. A July 2006 report by the SPLC found this infiltration occurring at an alarming rate. Neo-Nazis "stretch across all branches of service, they are linking up across the branches once they're inside, and they are hard-core," Department of Defense gang detective Scott Barfield told the SPLC. "We've got Aryan Nations graffiti in Baghdad," he added. "That's a problem."[13]

The source of the problem, as the report explained, was the extreme pressure military recruiters were under to fill their recruitment quotas. "Recruiters are knowingly allowing neo-Nazis and white supremacists to join the armed forces," said Barfield, "and commanders don't remove them ... even after we positively identify them as extremists or gang members." The military downplayed a neo-Nazi presence in the ranks, Barfield added, "because then parents who are already worried about their kids signing up and dying in Iraq are going to be even more reluctant about their kids enlisting if they feel they'll be exposed to gangs and white supremacists."

One of the noteworthy aspects of this phenomenon is the increasingly military style of the Far Right in recent years, particularly the militias in the 1990s, who openly recruited veterans and current military members. The two cultures have become enmeshed, as embodied by Steven Barry's recruitment plan for neo-Nazis considering a military career as a way to sharpen their "warrior" skills. A July 2008 assessment of the situation by the FBI (titled "White Supremacist Recruitment of Military Personnel Since 9/11") found that the numbers of identifiable neo-Nazis within the ranks was quite small (only a little over 200), but warned:

> Military experience—ranging from failure at basic training to
> success in special operations forces—is found throughout the
> white supremacist extremist movement. FBI reporting indicates
> extremist leaders have historically favored recruiting active
> and former military personnel for their knowledge of firearms,
> explosives, and tactical skills and their access to weapons and
> intelligence in preparation for an anticipated war against the
> federal government, Jews, and people of color.
>
> ... The prestige which the extremist movement bestows
> upon members with military experience grants them the

potential for influence beyond their numbers. Most extremist groups have some members with military experience, and
those with military experience often hold positions of authority
within the groups to which they belong.

... Military experience—often regardless of its length or
type—distinguishes one within the extremist movement. While
those with military backgrounds constitute a small percentage
of white supremacist extremists, FBI investigations indicate
they frequently have higher profiles within the movement,
including recruitment and leadership roles.

... New groups led or significantly populated by military
veterans could very likely pursue more operationally minded
agendas with greater tactical confidence. In addition, the
military training veterans bring to the movement and their
potential to pass this training on to others can increase the ability of lone offenders to carry out violence from the movement's
fringes.[14]

This problem doesn't involve only the neo-Nazis, gang-bangers,
and other violent personalities worming their way into the military. It also affects the many more formerly normal, nonracist
recruits who have been dragged into multiple tours of duty in Iraq,
regardless of the psychological dangers of such treatment. This
includes many people whose evaluations have recommended they
not be returned for duty but have been sent back regardless. Thus
the Timothy McVeigh Memorial Finishing School that is Iraq
continues to operate.

This has the deadly potential to become a significant component
of the predictable surge in far-right activity likely to manifest itself
in the United States in the coming months and years, especially as
Democrats and liberals expand their hold on power. We run the
risk of re-creating the conditions that arose in Germany and Italy

after World War I: the presence of scores of angry, disaffected, and psychologically damaged war veterans poised to organize into a political force aimed at "rebirthing" the nation and its heritage. In our situation, these veterans will likely be faced with unemployment and a wrecked economy, eager for someone to blame and fully trained and capable of violent action.

And their thirst for eliminationism, as was the case in the 1920s, will be deep.

8

Eliminationism in America: A Brief History

Is the desire to eliminate one's adversaries, to purge from our midst the people we deem our enemies, a natural impulse buried deep in our psyches—irresistible, ineluctable, inevitable? Certainly, Glenn Beck seems to think so.

In the summer of 2006, Beck argued on his daily *CNN Headline News* show that if there were further terrorist attacks by Muslims on American soil, concentration camps were all but a fait accompli, and that "Muslims will see the West through razor wire if things don't change":

> All you Muslims who have sat on your frickin' hands the whole time and have not been marching in the streets and have not been saying, 'Hey, you know what? There are good Muslims and bad Muslims. We need to be the first ones in the recruitment office lining up to shoot the bad Muslims in the head.' *I'm telling you, with God as my witness . . . human beings are not strong enough, unfortunately, to restrain themselves from putting up razor wire and putting you on one side of it.* When things—when people become hungry, when people see that their way of life is on the edge of being over, they will put razor wire up and just based on the way you look or just based on your religion, they will round you up. Is that wrong? Oh my gosh, it is Nazi, World

War II wrong, but society has proved it time and time again: It will happen.[1]

Though Beck seems to look forward to such an outcome, he could be right.

In November 2006, Jerry Klein, a DC-area radio talk-show host, decided to scrape below the surface of the right-wing brou-haha over the so-called flying Imams—six Muslim clerics asked to deplane from a U.S. Airways flight, a case touted by a broad range of conservative pundits and bloggers. Klein took the next logical step; that is, on his radio show he called for requiring all Muslims to wear crescent-moon armbands, or perhaps even being tattooed or branded. The response was disturbing, to say the least.

The second caller congratulated Klein and commented, "Not only do you tattoo them in the middle of their forehead but you ship them out of this country . . . they are here to kill us." Another suggested that identifying markers such as crescent marks on driv-er's licenses, passports, and birth certificates did not go far enough. "What good is identifying them?" he asked. "You have to set up encampments like during World War Two with the Japanese and Germans." In all, the sentiments ran strongly in favor of Klein's modest proposal.

Eventually, Klein revealed that it was a hoax. "I can't believe any of you are sick enough to have agreed for one second with anything I said," he told his audience.[2]

These kinds of sentiments, as we have seen, have been bubbling up repeatedly in various circumstances over the past decade. And while it may seem as though this rising drumbeat of elimination-ism proceeding from the American Right is something new and uniquely dangerous, a look at our history actually reveals that it is embedded in our national psyche.

In fact, it is deeply woven into our very makeup, deep strands twisting and turning through our history: the genocide against the Indians, the lynching era and the Ku Klux Klan, the internment of Japanese Americans, the continuing shameful legacy of hate crimes in modern America.

Eliminationism began long before there was even an America. The roots of America's history are bathed in the blood of an eliminationist impulse imported from Europe—and we have never quite outgrown that legacy.

Although life in pre-Columbian America was not exactly nonviolent or idyllic, most Amerindian societies were relatively healthy. This good health was precisely what made them so vulnerable to conquest. Though disease almost certainly was present in Mesoamerica, there is no evidence in the surviving records (which admittedly are scant) that plagues or "contact epidemics" were ever common in these societies.

Europe, in stark contrast, had been convulsed with devastating plagues and epidemics for centuries—cholera, the bubonic plague, smallpox, and tuberculosis all had ravaged the populations of Europe for ages, and by the 16th century were common facets of life. The extant surviving populations had built up some immunity to these diseases. Even as ships were departing for the New World, Europe itself was being ravaged by fresh outbreaks of smallpox, cholera, and bubonic plague, which in some locales produced mortality rates as high as 60 percent (40,000 died in Lisbon alone in the early 1560s).

But these figures paled in comparison to the effect these plagues had as they spread to the New World. Native populations were remarkably susceptible to the Black Plague, and the effects of smallpox beggared description, turning human beings into walking, bleeding pustules from whom the rotting flesh would peel off in chunks. Moreover, once the diseases had run their course, thousands more (particularly children and the elderly) died of starvation and dehydration because so many able-bodied adults who kept them in food and water had perished.

This pattern repeated itself throughout the New World as the plagues, particularly smallpox, spread, first through Mexico, Central America, and South America, then through the rest of North America. Frequently, the epidemics raged ahead of actual contact with Europeans; English explorers along the Atlantic Coast described coming upon villages wiped out by disease, with skeletons so thick on the ground they crunched under the white men's feet.

In a 1992 piece for *Discover*, Jared Diamond estimated that at the time of Columbus's arrival, the native population of North America was some 20 million. Within a century or two, it had declined by 95 percent. "The main killers were European germs, to which the Indians had never been exposed and against which they therefore had neither immunologic nor genetic resistance."[3]

The most commonly articulated European response to these scourges was not one of dismay but of delight. Indeed, the plagues were seen as a sign from God that they were in the right, that the Divine hand of Providence was sweeping the unclean savages from the lands the Europeans were destined to inhabit. Unfortunately, straggling remnants were left behind, and so the Europeans set about finishing the work begun by God. The native tribes—who tended to societies built on good-faith exchanges—were utterly unprepared and incapable of coping with this mindset or the behavior that followed.

In some cases, the English deliberately spread smallpox. E. R. G. Robertson, in his book *Rotting Face: Smallpox and the American*

Indian, describes how Lord Jeffrey Amherst, in 1763, urged the "seeding" of smallpox among local natives who had sided with the French during the French-Indian War. Whether the plan was ever enacted or not is unknown, though it is recorded that those tribes were, indeed, later stricken by the plague.[4]

The English callousness about the spread of the disease reflected the European eliminationist impulse, which had already manifested itself over the preceding centuries in various Jewish pogroms, particularly during the Crusades. It was embodied at the outset by the view of the Native Americans as subhuman. This view was promoted by such "humanists" as Juan Ginés de Sepúlveda, who argued for Spanish colonists in the famed "Debate of Valladolid" of 1550–51, in which a council of 14 church leaders discussed how to deal with the natives of the New World. Sepúlveda had argued that the natives were "barbaric and inhumane people" in whom one could "scarcely find any vestige of humanness." These attitudes about the Indians came to hold sway throughout Europe and were gradually expanded upon. By the time the English began colonizing North America, the belief in the nonhumanity of the natives was commingled with the belief that the plagues were divinely ordained, part of God's design for the New World: in other words, Manifest Destiny.[5]

Thus the British colonists were all too happy to get rid of the straggling remnants of native peoples they encountered as they spread along the Eastern Seaboard. These were heathen savages, the existence of whose souls was an open question at best and, in fact, widely denied. After the massacre of the Pequots in Mystic, Connecticut, in 1637, the commander of the British troops, John Mason, described the outcome, which included the immolation of scores of women and children: "Thus did the Lord judge among the Heathen, filling the Place with dead Bodies!"[6]

Another tendency emerged at this time. Largely in response to various depredations, Indians did offer violent resistance, often at considerable loss of life for the colonists. Such resistance provoked a disproportionate response in which all natives in the vicinity of such acts, and not only those responsible, were targeted for retribution. And so it continued, from colony to colony, Indian war to Indian war, from New England to Virginia to the Carolinas and Georgia and Florida, and thence to Ohio and Tennessee and Kentucky, as the colonists gradually gnawed their way westward. When George Washington waged war on the Iroquois in 1779, it was nothing less than a war of extermination in which, according to Richard Drinnon, the Indians "were hunted like wild beasts." Washington himself approved this approach, later observing that the Indians were little different than wolves, "both being beasts of prey, tho' they differ in shape."[7]

Thus the eliminationist impulse was transmitted almost seamlessly from Europe to the Americas, where it actually grew in a more virulent form, which went hand in hand with an expansionist impulse. Indeed, white Americans generally displayed a wanton disregard for the humanity of the native peoples that only intensified as they marched farther westward.

Thomas Jefferson—who at least saw the Indians as "equal to the white man . . . in an uncultivated state"—nevertheless concluded that the best Indian policy was to remove them from contact with white men. Part of his thinking in pursuing the Louisiana Purchase of 1803 was that the new territory would provide a place for the tribes east of the Mississippi River to resettle, at least until such time as they could reconcile themselves to civilization.[8]

Jefferson took George Washington's idea of creating a "permanent Indian frontier," where the "savages" could live without interference from white men, and vice versa, and began implementing it. In 1803–4, in a series of White House meetings, Jefferson informed the chiefs of the so-called Five Civilized Tribes—the Chickasaws, Choctaws, Creeks, Seminoles, and the largest, the Cherokees—that he intended to resettle them west of the Mississippi, though the program was to be a "voluntary" one. As it happened, the lands he intended to resettle them on were at the time claimed by other tribes, most notably the Osage Nation, a Siouxan tribe whose prowess in war was already legendary among Native Americans. Predictably, many of the Cherokees who attempted to resettle on Osage lands wound up dead, and the resettlement of Indians west of the Mississippi continued to stall over the succeeding years. James Monroe's 1817 treaty with the Osage—brought about by the massacre of 83 Osage encamped on the Arkansas River, mostly women and children, by an Indian war party constituted mostly of Cherokees—forced the tribe to cede some 1.8 million acres in Missouri and Arkansas, leaving them only a small bit of land in Arkansas and Oklahoma.

Nonetheless, many of the straggling remnants of Indians east of the Mississippi resisted relocation. In response, eliminationism became official government policy and led to the passage in 1830 of the Indian Removal Act, which finally realized the concept of the permanent Indian frontier. It was Andrew Jackson, an old Indian fighter from the First Seminole War, who made it a reality. The act empowered Jackson to make treaties with all tribes east of the Mississippi to give up their lands in exchange for lands on the other side of that "permanent" frontier. It was strongly supported in the South, where state officials were engaged in an ongoing fight to gain jurisdiction over Indian lands, particularly in Georgia. Originally the treaties were intended as voluntary, but tremendous pressure was placed on the tribes to sign, and the act's passage made their eventual removal inevitable.

The debate over Indian removal became a turning point in Americans' relations with the Indians—and perhaps more importantly, it was a precursor—in its North-South division and the pitting of human rights against states' right—to the debate over slavery that eventually precipitated civil war. With the bill's passage in 1830, and Jackson's landslide reelection in 1832, Indian removal began to be carried out in earnest. The result, as removal critics had warned, was the effective extinction of numerous tribes, as well as hundreds and even thousands of deaths in nearly every relocation effort. The culmination of these efforts was the notorious Trail of Tears in 1838, in which the Cherokee Nation—some 17,000 people—was forcibly relocated to those former Osage lands in Oklahoma. Something between 2,000 and 8,000 people (the figures are in dispute) died on the Trail of Tears.

The entire program of Indian relocation, which affected not just the relocatees but also such displaced tribes as the Osages, was fraught with bad faith throughout. The Americans, both local government officials and the citizen settlers, elevated deceptiveness to a form of murderous high art: they encouraged the Indians to believe they were dealing with them in good faith, then proceeded to unilaterally abrogate the terms of whatever treaties they signed. And they did all this with remarkable impunity. In many cases, the very authors of the treaties encouraged other whites to break them. In their view, the Indians had no rights worth respecting.

And the federal government, at every turn, accommodated this view—turning a blind eye to the resulting depredations, and facilitating their ability to grab land and resources at every turn. The outline of both official and unofficial U.S. government policy regarding the Indians for the duration of the 19th century was relatively simple: any act that benefited whites was found to be legal.

Red Cloud, the famed Sioux chief, was later to remark, "They made us many promises, more than I can remember, but they never kept but one; they promised to take our land, and they took it."[9]

The ease with which Europeans dispensed with the lives and well-being of the Native Americans reflected a larger aspect of their worldview: for centuries, they saw the outside world as a wasteland of wilderness inhabited by beasts who could be tamed only by elimination. For much of their early history on the American continent, white Europeans saw its endlessly wild landscape as the Enemy: the implacable, alien, deadly swamp it was their mission to subjugate. The wilderness was the embodiment of sinfulness and evil—and so were its inhabitants.

This was true not merely of the human inhabitants, but the animals as well. Settlers hunted predators and other threats—cougars, bears, and wolves especially—to near extinction. Even wild food sources, such as salmon, were wantonly harvested and their habitat destroyed, especially as settlers erected dams on every river on the Eastern Seaboard where they established villages and towns. Stocks were not only depleted but also intentionally wasted.

Lt. Campbell Hardy, an officer of the Royal Artillery in New Brunswick, observed the mentality in action in Nova Scotia in 1837, where once-plentiful salmon stocks were already plummeting:

> The spirit of wanton extermination is rife; and it has been well remarked, it really seems as though the man would be loudly applauded who was discovered to have killed the last salmon.[10]

Perhaps even more symbolic was the fate of the grizzly bear, which at one time ruled both the Plains and the mountain ranges of the West. Between 1850 and 1920, grizzlies were systematically and ruthlessly exterminated everywhere white Europeans came into contact with them. They were effectively eliminated from 95 percent of their traditional range.

The same was true of the native peoples who dwelt in this wilderness. It was common for colonists to view the wilderness as capable of overwhelming civilized men, even from within, turning them into "savages" and "wild men," while the people who had lived there for centuries were commonly viewed as no less than vile beasts themselves. This was not uniformly the case, of course. There were white Europeans who believed fully in the Indians' humanity. Some of them even defended them as cultural equals—though not many. Even among the natives' defenders, it was not uncommon—while acknowledging that they were intelligent humans with souls—to still consider them savages whose capacity for redemption was an open question. Some humanitarian whites may have had sympathy for the natives, but they were utterly ineffectual in stopping the wave of murderous bigotry that swept away all their good intentions along with the Indians themselves, bigotry fueled by the prevailing view of Indians that equated them with the beasts they encountered in this wilderness.

As the Americans' thirst for land and gold grew, the borders of the frontier, that "permanent Indian frontier," continued to shift westward. Treaty after treaty turned out to be mere ruses for outright land theft. A promise made to an Indian was innately nonbinding. The murder of an Indian was considered, if not a nonevent, cause for celebration.

Missionaries were often the forerunners of this push westward, establishing trails and outposts that became way stations and provided a kind of social foundation for the pioneer travelers. Fresh on the missionaries' heels came waves of settlers, many of them in search of free land, others trying to strike it rich by finding gold. The Oregon Trail and California Trail were especially popular after the discovery of gold in California in 1848. Fairly typical of the settlers' views were those voiced by Robert A. Anderson, a California rancher who lived in northern California in the 1860s. Like most of them, he equated the "savages" with the wild beasts they encountered. Theodora Kroeber describes him in her account of the Yana people in her book *Ishi: In Two Worlds*:

> He matched wits and physical prowess with Indians and griz-
> zlies alike; both, in his opinion, "infested" the region and
> should be cleared out. He and Good, Anderson says, used to
> argue at length about how the clearing out was to be done.
> Good was for leaving the women and children alone; Anderson
> believed that immolation was the only effective way to be rid of
> Indians, and grizzlies too, no doubt.[11]

Anderson, together with his longtime companion Hiram Good, organized a systematic program of extermination of the Yanas from 1863 to 1865. Some bands of the Yana, finding their traditional food sources destroyed by invading settlers, had attacked whites in force in 1862; they had continued carrying out lesser attacks, such as the murders of several ranchers and their wives and children.

In response, the ranchers, led by Anderson and Good, who had become expert trackers, embarked on a program of complete extermination. A paid bounty was offered for Yana scalps, and these were then obtained by self-proclaimed "guards" who were essentially local riffraff hired to hunt down and kill any Yana they could find. As Kroeber details, within five months in 1864, three-quarters of the Yana population was exterminated by these men. Women and children were slain as ruthlessly as men. The extermination continued unabated until the last surviving Yana bands were tracked down and massacred. The final massacre occurred late in 1864, when a party of four vaqueros stumbled upon an Indian encampment and proceeded to slaughter most of its 30 or so inhabitants.[12]

This pattern was repeated over and over across the West. Rather than endure any contact with "savages" settlers fully expected would turn against them and murder them, settlers moving westward always chose to act preemptively and slaughter Indians as they found them. This was particularly the case wherever gold entered the picture.

And always these spasms of eliminationist violence were preceded by eliminationist rhetoric. Before there was action, there was talk. And the talk not only rationalized the violence that proceeded, but actually had the function of *creating permission for it.*

The same year the Yana were exterminated, settlers in Colorado, where gold had been discovered in 1858, embarked on a similar program. In this case, the tribes against whom they were arrayed, particularly the Cheyenne and Sioux, were considerably larger and more warlike than the Yana. Nevertheless, the pattern remained similar: depredations by whites provoked violent, often murderous retaliation from Indians, which in turn sparked wanton slaughter of any Indian in the vicinity.

The *Rocky Mountain News* in Denver led the campaign to wipe out local Indians, editorializing in March 1863, "They are a dissolute, vagabondish, brutal, and ungrateful race, and ought to be wiped from the face of the earth." After a series of skirmishes and killings, the *News*, in August 1864, proclaimed that settlers and troops must "go for them, their lodges, squaws and all." Enter John Chivington, a Methodist minister and self-proclaimed Indian hater, who helped Colorado governor John Evans organize a volunteer militia made up of "concerned citizens," whose characters were formed more by saloons than by churches. Chivington made a public speech in Denver in which he "advocated the killing and scalping of all Indians, even infants: 'Nits make lice!' he declared." With his volunteer army in place, Chivington set out "on the warpath," as he put it, ordering his men to, "kill all the Indians you come across." When Indians attempted to negotiate, he was implacable, saying that he was not instructed to make peace, only war.[13]

On November 29, 1864, Chivington set out with a force of some 700 volunteers from their encampment at Fort Lyon, eager to engage in a battle before their 100-day enlistment expired. "Damn any man that sympathizes with Indians," Chivington had told officers who advised against attacking a peaceable Indian camp. "I have come to kill Indians and believe it right and honorable to use any means under God's heaven. . . ." So, at dawn, Chivington and his militia rode to the Sioux camp of Black Kettle (who had been promised safety), where Chivington instructed them: "Kill and scalp all, big and little; nits make lice." Two hours later, everyone in the camp of several hundred people was either dead (the final tally was 98 dead, nearly all of them women and children) or scattered into the nearby woods and plains.[14]

Chivington and his men rode back to Denver triumphant and claiming to have slain 500 warriors; the massacre had been "a brilliant feat of arms," declared the *Rocky Mountain News*. A few weeks later, Chivington put a hundred scalps on display during an intermission at the Denver Opera House, to broad applause.

However, as word of these atrocities got out, there was a predictable outcry from white Americans who had retained some vestige of human decency; but their outrage, as always, had no effect. The killers were downright gleeful about their "victory." The *Rocky Mountain News* declared that "Cheyenne scalps are getting as thick here now as toads in Egypt. Everybody has got one and is anxious to get another to send east." Still, there was an outcry in Congress, and a Senate report eventually declared Chivington's "battle" for what it really was: "a foul and dastardly massacre which would have disgraced the veriest savage among those who were the victims of his cruelty." But whatever a bunch of pointy-headed politicians from back East thought of them didn't bother the locals in the least. As Stannard observes:

> One of them, a senator who visited the site of the massacre and "picked up the skulls of infants whose milk-teeth had not yet been shed," later reported that the concerned men of Congress had decided to confront Colorado's governor and Colonel Chivington openly on the matter, and so assembled their committee and the invited general public in the Denver Opera House. During the course of discussion and debate, someone raised a question: Would it be best, henceforward, to try to "civilize" the Indians or simply to exterminate them? Whereupon, the senator wrote in a letter to a friend, "there suddenly arose such a shout as is never heard unless upon some battlefield—a shout almost loud enough to raise the roof of the opera house— 'EXTERMINATE THEM! EXTERMINATE THEM!'"
>
> The committee, apparently, was impressed. Nothing was ever done to Chivington, who took his fame and exploits on the road as an after-dinner speaker. After all, as President Theodore Roosevelt said later, the Sand Creek massacre was "as righteous and beneficial a deed as ever took place on the frontier."[15]

Other massacres followed: several hundred Sioux (including Black Kettle, who had survived the Sand Creek Massacre) were wiped out four years later, in 1868, by cavalrymen led by a Civil War hero named George Armstrong Custer at the Washita River in Oklahoma. In Montana, 200 Blackfeet were massacred in a similar manner in 1870 in the so-called Battle of Marias River, in which soldiers once again descended upon an unsuspecting camp of mostly women and children, the warriors once again away at the hunting grounds, and fired upon them mercilessly. The massacre was widely reviled in the eastern press (the *Chicago Tribune* called it "the most disgraceful butchery in the annals of our dealings with the Indians"), though the local press widely celebrated it for its "salutary effect on the other tribes." This effect included an eagerness on the part of most Indians to attempt to make peace, often in the form of abject surrender. But this only invited more contempt from whites, which was often voiced as a wish to simply exterminate.[16]

After the Washita massacre, as Dee Brown describes, many of the warring tribes completely submitted to Gen. Phil Sheridan, the Civil War hero who had been charged with overseeing the Indian Wars. His response became famous:

> Yellow Bear of the Arapahos also agreed to bring his people to Fort Cobb. A few days later, Tosawi brought in the first band of Comanches to surrender. When he was presented to Sheridan, Tosawi's eyes brightened. He spoke his own name and added two words of broken English. "Tosawi, good Indian," he said.
>
> It was then that General Sheridan uttered the immortal words: "The only good Indians I ever saw were dead." Lieutenant Charles Nordstrom, who was present, remembered the words and passed them on, until in time they were honed into an American aphorism: *The only good Indian is a dead Indian.*[17]

This implacable racial hatred, combined with a dim view of the Indians' intelligence and skill at battle, led to further tragedies for both sides. George Armstrong Custer, who returned to fight Indian wars in 1874 after gold was discovered in the Black Hills of the Dakotas, also happened to believe—given his experience in such "battles" as the Washita massacre—that Indians could not withstand a charging cavalry and would retreat under such an attack every time. So it was with such hubris that, in 1876, he charged the largest encampment in the history of the Plains Indians—over a thousand strong—with a force of only about 600 men, including his own detachment of about 200, in what was to be the most famous of all the Indian battles, the Little Bighorn. Custer and his men were entirely wiped out.[18]

The defeat only further inflamed the whites, who over the course of the next year tracked down and defeated or captured nearly all the Indians who had been involved in the battle, including the chiefs Sitting Bull and Crazy Horse. Yet trying to accommodate the whites, as Black Kettle and many others found out, was no guarantee of safety. Even the most famous peacekeeper among the Indian chiefs, Chief Joseph of the Nez Perce, whose tribe had aided Lewis and Clark, and who had a long history of cooperation with whites, found himself on the wrong end of settlers' ambitions. In 1877, the Nez Perce found themselves at war with the U.S. Army, and Joseph led his band of some 800 Nez Perce on a remarkable retreat that nearly succeeded before they were caught just short of the Canadian border.[19]

The coup de grâce was finally delivered some 11 years later. The mounting misery of the scattered remnants of tribes produced among them a last, dying spate of messianic movements promising some hope of redemption for their people and their heritage. One of the most prominent of these, involving the ritual of the Ghost Dance, spread widely among the Siouxan peoples living at Wounded Knee on the Pine Ridge Reservation in South Dakota. But reservation officials feared the movement could become grounds for a last-gasp Indian uprising, and they undertook to suppress it with arrests. The resulting discord culminated in the assassination of Sitting Bull, who had taken up residence at Pine Ridge. Soon, the reservation faced outright unrest, and so the soldiers, with four Hotchkiss guns in tow, were called in.

On the morning of December 29, 1890, troops were in the process of culling the men from the women and children when a gun was discharged. Immediately, the four Hotchkiss guns opened fire, mowing down all the men at first, then turning to the milling women and children. Within a matter of minutes, some 200 people were dead. Some of the women were able to escape across the frozen plains, but these, too, were tracked down and shot. Another hundred or so managed to find temporary safety in the hills, but within a matter of days all of them had frozen to death.[20]

After this final, terrible blow, the remnants of American Indians spread in reservations across the West were reduced to virtual nonentities. Their children were forcibly shipped off to boarding schools whose main purpose was to eradicate any vestige of their "savage" heritage and completely "civilize" them; most of these schools eventually descended into horror, leaving behind generations of damaged Indians who had been stripped of their heritage. Even those who had managed to find ways to thrive, such as the Osages—whose oil rights from their treaty lands in Oklahoma led to tremendous economic riches in the 20th century—had their wealth taken from them. Beginning in the early 1920s, a handful of scheming whites successfully undertook to steal land rights away from the Osages by murdering them. The scheme, which became known as the "Osage Reign of Terror," typically involved white men marrying women who held the rights, then having them killed and their murders officially covered up.[21]

At every step of this systematic extermination, whites justified their brutality with eliminationist rhetoric. This rhetoric always recalled the savagery of the Indians, who, indeed, were not hesitant to shed blood and to do so in a brutal fashion that was, as it often was with whites, intended to send a message. Yet, even the most avid of the eliminationists often recognized that the original fault nearly always lay with the invading whites. Kroeber notes that Robert A. Anderson, who led the extermination of the Yana, observed retrospectively in his memoirs the following:

> It is but just that I should mention the circumstances which raised the hand of the Mill Creeks against the whites. As in almost every similar instance in American History, the first act of injustice, the first spilling of blood, must be laid at the white man's door.[22]

Such reflection, however, rarely led the perpetrators to wonder if their murderousness had been anything more than an unpleasant necessity. Regardless of fault, in their view the Indians were still savage beasts for whom the only means of "civilization" was elimination.

At the turn of the century, the Indians were no longer a threat to white Americans, and so the eliminationist rhetoric was gradually replaced with romantic "noble savage" mythology, which made them seem distant and harmless, as they had become. By then, anyway, they had found a new "threat" and a fresh object for elimination: black people.

Slavery and war are the human institutions most closely related to eliminationism as it was practiced historically. All issued from the same dark, violent corner of the human psyche. In that same corner lives the impulse to dominate our fellow humans and reduce them to objects.

Thus, the lion's share of eliminationism practiced by the European colonists in the Americas went hand in hand with making war and enslaving other human beings. For the most part, the violent eradication of the native population—particularly the extermination of the straggling remnants of Indians in North America after 1800—had occurred under the pretense of waging war, which itself was merely a pretext for taking land. And in the early years, at least, when the Spanish took many hundreds of thousands of Mesoamericans as slave labor for their mines—a death sentence in itself—slavery played a significant role in the extermination, both physically and culturally, of the native peoples; those who survived were usually forced *conversos* for whom observing any of their traditional rites or ceremonies was punishable by death.[23]

The natives, however, were seen quite differently than the Africans captured as slaves and brought to American shores by the colonists. The former were identified with the wilderness and were seen as equivalent to untamable beasts. But African slaves were considered completely subservient and thus a negligible threat.

This may explain why, during the years leading up to the Civil War, blacks in the South were rarely the victims of lynchings. Killing someone else's slave was considered an act of theft. The main exception to this was directly related to those occasions when slaves actually became threats, namely, when they revolted. The fear of black insurrection (and there were a handful of real slave revolts, notably Nat Turner's 1831 Virginia rebellion, in which some 60 whites were killed) was so pervasive among Southerners that any rumor that one might occur could bring swift death to the alleged conspirators, even if, as was often the case, it later turned out no such plans existed. In any event, when lynching did occur in the years before the Civil War, the victims predominantly were whites. Many of these were in the antebellum South, where lynch-mob treatment was often administered to abolitionists and other "meddlers."

If the status of black slaves largely protected them from racial violence before the Civil War, the abolition of slavery left them remarkably vulnerable to such assaults after the South's defeat. Once emancipated, they came to be seen as a real threat to whites, and particularly to whites' dominant economic and cultural status. This change of perception became immediately manifest, during Reconstruction, when black freedmen were subjected to a litany of attacks at the hands of their former owners, attacks that went wholly unpunished. As documented by Philip Dray in his definitive study, *At the Hands of Persons Unknown: The Lynching of Black America,* accounts of these crimes turned up in hospital records and field reports from the federal Freedmen's Bureau, all of which described a variety of clubbings, scalpings, mutilations, hangings, and even immolations of former slaves, all within the first year after Appomattox.

In 1866, the violence became discernibly more organized with the emergence of the Ku Klux Klan, which originated with a clique of Confederate veterans in Pulaski, Tennessee, and spread like wildfire throughout the South. Initially, much of the Klan night-riders' activities were relegated to whippings, a punishment intended to remind ex-slaves of their former status. But as the assaults on blacks increased, so did the intensity of the violence visited on them, culminating in a steady stream of Klan lynchings between 1868 and 1871 (when the Klan was officially outlawed by the Grant administration); at least one study puts the number at 20,000 blacks killed by the Klan in that period. In the ensuing years, the violence increased, despite the Klan's official banishment.[24]

The Klan's violence, however, was not broadly eliminationist but rather carefully channeled. Its clear intent was not to drive out blacks generally—they were, after all, a valuable source of labor—but to keep them under the thumb of their white "superiors." The chief means of doing this, however, entailed eliminating anyone who might pose even the slightest hint of a threat to the status of whites, particularly "interlopers" and "outsiders" who arrived after the war to help the freed slaves get on their feet. Francis Butler Simkins's 1927 study of the South Carolina Klan pointed out that the Klan's campaign was "against the Negro as a citizen—one attempting to be a voter and at times, the social equal of other men—rather than against the Negro as a violator of law or the infringer upon the rights of other men." So, to rationalize away their own wanton criminality, the Klan and its supporters relied on rhetoric aimed to convince the public of the criminality of the black population.[25]

The chief purpose of the Klan, as Exalted Cyclops Ryland Randolph of South Carolina explained in 1867 in his newspaper, the *Independent Monitor,* was to stop what they saw as an insidious Northern plan "to degrade the white man by the establishment of Negro supremacy." Needless to say, the Klan's purpose was to degrade the black man by the establishment of white supremacy. This kind of precisely mirrored projection was present in nearly every aspect of white racial hatred toward blacks, particularly in the most common defense for the wave of lynching that was to follow—namely, that lynching was the natural reaction of a community defending itself against savagely lascivious black men and their wanton desire to rape white women.[26]

Sexual paranoia—rooted in long-held Christian European notions about sexuality that associated it with sinfulness, with the "muck" of nature and the wilderness—was central to the lynching phenomenon. In the years following black emancipation, when a previously tiny group of black criminals was joined by the ranks of impoverished former slaves—a vast mythology arose surrounding black men's supposed voracious lust for white women. "The Negro race," after all, was still closely associated with the jungles of Africa, the "heart of darkness" in the European mind; and sexual voraciousness was assumed in such folk. Though they might be tame, they were still scarcely a step removed from wild men of the jungle, still scarcely human. Yet, this was a legend backed up by scant evidence, and one that stands in stark contrast to (and perhaps has its psychological roots in) the reality of white men's longtime sexual domination of black women, particularly during the slavery era.

The omnipresence of the threat of rape of white women by black men came to be almost universally believed by American whites. Likewise, conventional wisdom held that lynchings were a natural response to this threat. The cries of rape, for many whites in both South and North, raised fears not merely of sexual violence but of racial mixing, known commonly as "miscegenation," which was specifically outlawed in some 30 states. White supremacy was not only commonplace, it was, in fact, the dominant worldview in the United States in the 19th and early 20th centuries. Many Caucasians believed they were nature's premier creation. This attitude was supported by a broad range of social scientists of the period, whose views eventually coalesced into the popular pseudo-science known as eugenics, which saw careful racial breeding as the source of social and personal good health and any "dilution" of those strains as representing a gross violation of the natural order. Thus, it was not surprising that a number of lynching incidents actually resulted from the discovery of consensual relations between a black man and a white woman.[27]

Underlying the stated fear of rape, moreover, was a broader

fear of economic and cultural domination of white Americans by blacks and various other "outsiders," including Jews. These fears were acute in the South, where blacks became a convenient scapegoat for the poverty that lingered in the decades following the Civil War. Lynchings were frequently inspired not by criminality but rather by any signs of economic and social advancement by blacks. Such blacks, in the view of whites, had become too "uppity."

There were other components of black suppression: segregation in the schools, disenfranchisement of the black vote, and the attendant Jim Crow laws that were common throughout the South. But lynching was the linchpin because as a form of state-supported terrorism its stated intent was to suppress blacks and other minorities by eliminating them as economic competitors. These combined to give lynching a symbolic value as a manifestation of white supremacy. The lynch mob was not merely condoned but also celebrated as an expression of the white community's will to keep African Americans in their thrall. As a phrase common in the South expressed it, lynching was a highly effective means of "keeping the niggers down."

Moreover, in addition to the night-riding type of terrorist attacks, mass-spectacle lynchings soon began. These were ritualistic mob scenes in which prisoners or even men merely suspected of crimes were torn from the hands of the authorities (if not captured beforehand) by large crowds and treated to beatings and torture before being put to death, frequently in the most horrifying fashion possible: people were flayed alive, their eyes were gouged out with corkscrews, and their bodies mutilated before being doused in oil and burned at the stake. Black men were sometimes forced to eat their own hacked-off genitals. No atrocity was considered too horrible to visit on a black person. (When whites, by contrast, were lynched, the act almost always was restricted to simple hanging.)

Between 1882 and 1942, according to statistics compiled by the Tuskegee Institute, there were 4,713 lynchings in the United States, of which 3,420 involved black victims. Mississippi topped the list, with 520 blacks lynched during that time period, while Georgia was a close second with 480; Texas ranked third with 339. Most scholars acknowledge that these numbers probably are well short of the actual total; many lynchings (particularly in the early years of the phenomenon) were often backwoods affairs that went unrecorded. In that era, it was not at all uncommon for a black man to simply disappear; sometimes his body would wash up in one of the local rivers, and sometimes not.

The violence reached a fever pitch in the years 1890–1902, when 1,322 lynchings of blacks (out of 1,785 total lynchings) were recorded at Tuskegee, which translates into an average of over 110 lynchings a year. The trend began to decline thereafter but continued well into the 1930s, leading some historians to refer to the years 1880–1930 as the "lynching period" of American culture.[28]

Lynchings in their heyday seemed to be cause for outright celebration in the community. Residents would dress up to come watch the proceedings, and the crowds of spectators frequently grew into the thousands. Afterward, memento-seekers would take home parts of the corpse or the rope with which the victim was hung. Sometimes body parts—knuckles, or genitals, or the like—would be preserved and put on public display as a warning to would-be black criminals.

This was the purported purpose of these acts, at least in the South: to wipe out any black person even accused of a crime against whites in a fashion that warned off future perpetrators. This purpose was reflected in contemporary press accounts: lynchings were described in almost uniformly laudatory terms, the victim's guilt went unquestioned, and the mob was identified only as "determined men." Not surprisingly, local officials (especially local police forces) not only were complicit in many cases but they acted in concert to keep the mob leaders anonymous; thousands of coroners' reports from lynchings merely described the victims' deaths occurring "at the hands of persons unknown." Lynchings were broadly viewed as simply a crude, but understandable and even necessary, expression of community will. This was particularly true in the South, where blacks were viewed as symbolic of the region's continuing economic and cultural oppression by the North. As an 1899 editorial in the Newnan, Georgia, *Herald and Advertiser* explained it: "It would be as easy to check the rise and fall of the ocean's tide as to stem the wrath of Southern men when the sacredness of our firesides and the virtue of our women are ruthlessly trodden under foot."[29]

Thus the numbers of deaths produced by the lynching phenomenon only hint at their deeper impact, which affected literally millions of Americans by keeping them in the thrall of terror that their white neighbors might, with the least provocation, murder them with total impunity. As always, the violence was predicated on a fear of future violence; lynching was excused as a preemptive act. Yet, in reality, a black person could be lynched for literally no reason at all, in some cases simply for defending himself from physical assault, or for being in the wrong place at the wrong time. Lynching laughed at the notion of blacks advancing through hard work; moderately prosperous blacks who managed to do so were often the first targets of angry lynch mobs intent on dealing with "uppity" blacks.

Lynchings unquestionably had the short-term desired effect of suppressing blacks' civil rights; the majority of African Americans in the South during that era led lives of quiet submission in the hope of escaping that horrific fate, and relatively few aspired beyond their established station in life. Those who did often migrated northward—where lynchings, as we shall see, were hardly unknown.

Although lynchings eventually declined under increasing public revulsion at their violence and brutality (by the 1930s, mass spectacle lynchings had largely subsided, and by the 1950s, the annual numbers had declined dramatically), they did not disappear altogether, by any means. Certainly, the deep racial animus that had always inspired them was still alive and well, particularly in the South. They continued to occur periodically, but instead of being treated as commonplace, they became the subject of intensive international news coverage. The 1955 lynching of a Chicago teenager named Emmett Till, on vacation in Mississippi, for being "fresh" with a white woman, became a national cause célèbre, playing a prominent role in the claims of civil-rights advocates that justice for black people did not exist in the South.

For those Southerners still dedicated to the tenets of white supremacy, and who permanently opposed the substantial gains made during the 1950s and '60s for African Americans' civil rights—in particular, the desegregation of schools and other facilities that began with the Supreme Court's landmark *Brown v. Board of Education* ruling in 1950—lynching continued to hold its longtime value as a tool for terrorizing the black community and reaffirming white supremacy. But without the cover of public sanction, lynching and racial violence became a surreptitious crime that was strategically deployed in a vain attempt to stem the tide of the Civil Rights movement. As such, lynchers frequently targeted the persons they saw as the source of the agitation. The 1964 slayings of three civil-rights workers in Mississippi, which became a landmark in changing national attitudes toward the movement, was in most respects a classic lynching. But now the lynchers turned to other kinds of violence: burning and bombing African American churches, attacking civil-rights marchers, and assassinating the leaders in the movement.

All these events were largely playing out in the South, which had its own special history as the place where the Klan and lynching had originated. Yet, that focus obscured a broader reality: just as the Klan, by the 1920s, had become a genuinely national phenomenon (with national headquarters located in Indiana), so, too, the lynching of black Americans was widely practiced throughout America. In fact, a quick look at the Tuskegee Institute's state-by-state numbers for the so-called lynching era (1880–1930) reveal that lynchings occurred in nearly every state in the Union, particularly in the Midwest, though not as prolifically as in the South. Likewise, a survey of "race riots" during the same period reveals they occurred in a number of places well outside the South.

During the "Red Summer" of 1919, 76 blacks were lynched, Even more horrifying were the race riots that broke out in 26 cities, including Chicago, Illinois; Washington DC; Omaha, Nebraska; Tulsa, Oklahoma; Charleston, South Carolina; and Knoxville, Tennessee. These insurrections were actually massive assaults by whites upon local black populations, often sparked by an imagined offense. In Tulsa, where a prosperous black population was literally bombed out of existence over two days of complete lawlessness, the rioting was set off by a black youth's alleged assault on a local white girl, which later turned out to have been harmless consensual contact. Nonetheless, a Tulsa newspaper publicly called for the young man's lynching, and when a group of local blacks attempted to ward off a lynch mob, the fighting broke out. By the time the violence had subsided, as many as 300 black people were believed killed, many of them buried in a mass grave, and 35 city blocks lay charred.[30]

The raw numbers of lynched blacks outside the South, however, were smaller for a simple reason: their purpose was different. Lynchings in the Midwest, the Northeast, and the West occurred for an explicitly, and broadly, eliminationist purpose. Unlike their Southern brethren, whites elsewhere simply chose not to let blacks live among them: they violently drove them out of their communities en masse and forbade them to return thereafter. Thus, the fight over *Brown v. Board of Education* and school desegregation took place largely in the South for a very simple reason: school districts outside the South largely did not have to desegregate because blacks had not been permitted to live within their borders for generations. They had simply been driven out.

In the South, whites chose to deal with blacks by oppressing them; in much of the rest of the country, white communities simply eliminated their presence altogether. And by making the South the nation's racial scapegoat, it allowed those communities to smugly pretend that *they* had no such strife to face, and thus were not part of the problem. As a consequence, there has never been an adequate accounting of the long-term effects of the widespread exclusion of African Americans, and resulting demographic segregation, enforced by whites nationally. And thus the unsettled legacy of racism, in the South and elsewhere, continues to be a wound in the national psyche that refuses to heal.

I used to wonder why there weren't more black people in places such as Seattle—which, as urban places go, is pretty damned white—or Idaho, where I grew up, or Montana, where I lived for several years (both of which make Seattle look positively chocolate in comparison). Like almost everyone else, I just chalked it up to the climate and the preexisting lack of colored folks: they didn't live here, I assumed, because they'd naturally feel isolated. It was just one of those accidents of history and demographics.

I also would sometimes hear black leaders and community members in Seattle talk about the somewhat hidden, institutionalized nature of racism in places like the Pacific Northwest, where people can be nice to your face and not so nice in action. And they would sometimes phrase it in stark terms, usually something along these lines: "I would rather deal with Southerners, where the racism is up front and in your face, than people in places like this, where it's all nice and hidden."

Now, granted that hidden racism is buried in our culture everywhere, and that the mask of civility that people in the Pacific Northwest call "politeness" is often just a cover for ugly personal beliefs and cold-heartedness. Still, this always seemed slightly illogical to me: even if you can identify the racism in the culture, isn't a civil mask at least less intimidating, or frightening, than the ugliness of open racism?

James Loewen's 2005 study, *Sundown Towns: A Hidden Dimension of American Racism,* offers a different answer altogether. And it is not a comforting one.[31]

The American landscape *Sundown Towns* reveals is not the one we have created in our own minds, in which the bulk of racial bigotry resides south of the Mason-Dixon line, and in which the enlightened Northern states have, comparatively speaking at least, provided both a racial refuge and social justice. Rather, it shows a landscape in which racism is woven throughout the nation's social fabric, where the brand of bigotry practiced throughout much of the North was even more noxious than that in the South.

Specifically, while the South actively oppressed its nonwhite population, Americans in most of the rest of the country chose not to even tolerate their presence and actively engaged in an ongoing campaign of eliminationist violence to drive them out, forcing them to cluster in large urban areas for their own self-protection

and survival. Loewen reveals the benign, polite, white face of suburban and rural America outside the South as both deeply decep-
tive and ultimately lethal.

What exactly is a "sundown town"? This is how Loewen defines
the term:

> A sundown town is any organized jurisdiction that for decades
> kept African Americans or other groups from living in it and
> was thus "all white" on purpose.
>   ... Beginning in about 1890 and continuing until 1968,
> white Americans established thousands of towns across the
> United States for whites only. Many towns drove out their black
> populations, then posted sundown signs.... Other towns passed
> ordinances barring African Americans after dark or prohibiting
> them from owning or renting property; still others established
> such policies by informal means, harassing and even killing those
> who violated the rule. Some sundown towns similarly kept out
> Jews, Chinese, Mexicans, Native Americans, or other groups.
>   Independent sundown towns range from tiny hamlets such
> as DeLand, Illinois (population 500) to substantial cities such
> as Appleton, Wisconsin (57,000 in 1970). Sometimes entire
> counties went sundown, usually when their county seat did.
> Independent sundown towns were soon joined by "sundown
> suburbs," which could be even larger: Levittown, on Long
> Island, had 82,000 residents in 1970, while Livonia, Michigan,
> and Parma, Ohio, had more than 100,000. Warren, a suburb of
> Detroit, had a population of 180,000 including just 28 minority
> families, most of whom lived on a U.S. Army facility.
>   Outside the traditional South ... probably a majority of all
> incorporated places kept out African Americans.[32]

Moreover, he goes on to explain, the appearance of sundown
towns occurred in every region and in every state. "There is reason

to believe that more than half of all towns in Oregon, Indiana, Ohio, the Cumberlands, the Ozarks, and diverse other areas were also all-white on purpose. Sundown suburbs are found from Darien, Connecticut, to La Jolla, California, and are even more prevalent; indeed, most suburbs began life as sundown towns."[33]

These towns formed neither naturally nor accidentally, but emerged well after the Civil War as the embodiment of emerging white supremacist beliefs, particularly eugenicist notions about the evils of "race mixing" and the innate inferiority of nonwhite races. As Loewen explains, in the first quarter-century after the Civil War, African Americans actually fanned out across the country to resettle and start new lives with their newly won freedom. Outside the South, they lived in rural areas and small towns as well as big cities, filling all kinds of occupations. But this heyday was short-lived, and by 1890, the beginning of what is known as "the Nadir of race relations"—which was to last another 40 years, until 1930—set in. It was the period "when African Americans were forced back into noncitizenship," as Loewen puts it, and it produced what he calls the "Great Retreat"—the forcible elimination of blacks from rural and suburban communities, from which they fled to larger black communities within a handful of urban centers:

> Unfortunately, "the new order of things" was destined to last only six more years. In 1890, trying to get the federal government to intervene against violence and fraud in southern elections, the Republican senator from Massachusetts, Henry Cabot Lodge, introduced his Federal Elections Bill. It lost by just one vote in the Senate. After its defeat, when Democrats again tarred Republicans [as they had before the Civil War, and since] as "nigger lovers," now the Republicans replied in a new way. Instead of assailing Democrats for denying equal rights

to African Americans, they backed away from the subject. The Democrats had worn them down. Thus the springtime of race relations during Reconstruction was short, and it was followed not by summer blooms but by the Nadir winter, and not just in the South but throughout the country.[34]

The Republicans' capitulation on race marked the beginning of a long era of overt racial oppression in America. Although Dixie politics did play a special role, particularly in passing Jim Crow laws and establishing segregation as the law of the South, this occurred nationally. From then on, African Americans were effectively disenfranchised in American politics. The Supreme Court's 1907 *Plessy v. Ferguson* ruling legalized segregation, giving it official imprimatur in the South and effectively legitimizing it elsewhere; 12 non-Southern states passed their own segregation statutes in the years following. The deterioration of the status of African Americans was widespread throughout every aspect of society, especially occupationally, where former bricklayers, carpenters, and postal carriers found themselves out of work or relegated to menial labor.

The models for driving out the "unwanted" blacks from their communities, like the core attitudes themselves, probably originated in the South, where Indian massacres had eventually given way to lynching as the main expression of the eliminationist impulse. However, these attitudes came to prevail not just in the South but also throughout the country. As Loewen explains, it was clear that by the 1890s most white Americans had convinced themselves that blacks themselves were "the problem":

> How were northern whites to explain to themselves their acquiescence in the white South's obliteration of the political and civil rights of African Americans in places such as Harrison?

How could they defend their own increasing occupational and social discrimination against African Americans?

The easiest way would be to declare that African Americans had never deserved equal rights in the first place. After all, went this line of thought, conditions had significantly improved for African Americans. Slavery was over. Now a new generation of African Americans had come of age, never tainted by the "peculiar institution." Why were they still at the bottom? African Americans themselves must be the problem. *They* must not work hard enough, think as well, or have as much drive, compared to whites. The Reconstruction amendments (Thirteenth, Fourteenth, and Fifteenth) provided African Americans with a roughly equal footing in America, most whites felt. If they were still at the bottom, it must be their own fault.

Ironically, the worse the Nadir got, the more whites blamed blacks for it. The increasing segregation and exclusion led whites to demonize African Americans and their segregated enclaves. African Americans earned less money than whites, had lower standing in society, and no longer held public office or even voted in much of the nation. Again, no longer could this obvious inequality be laid at slavery's doorstep, for slavery had ended around 1865. Now "white Northerners came to view blacks as disaffected, lazy, and dangerous rabble," according to Heather Richardson. "By the 1890s, white Americans in the North concurred that not only was disfranchisement justified for the 'Un-American Negro,' but that he was by nature confined to a state of 'permanent semi-barbarism.'"[35]

The chief means of driving out nonwhites was what Donald Horowitz calls "the deadly ethnic riot," wherein one racial or ethnic group takes up arms en masse and attacks another group systematically and thoroughly with the intent of eliminating their presence.[36] Racial cleansings occurred in every corner of the nation, including some larger cities: Denver (of Chinese) in 1880; Seattle (of Chinese) in 1886; Akron in 1900; Evansville, Indiana, and Joplin, Missouri, in 1903; Springfield, Ohio, in 1904, 1906, and again in 1908; Springfield, Missouri, in 1906; Springfield, Illinois, in 1908; Youngstown, Ohio, and East St. Louis, Illinois, in 1917; Omaha and Knoxville in 1919; Tulsa in 1921; Johnstown, Pennsylvania, in 1923; and Lincoln, Nebraska, in 1929.

These race riots often occurred whenever any black community tried to stand up to lynching violence. When this happened, the race riot actually comprised wholesale lethal assaults on black communities by whites, such as the Tulsa riot. The Ku Klux Klan, which had played a formative role in the lynching phenomenon generally, was closely connected with the formation of sundown towns, especially in the Klan's second incarnation as a national organization after 1916. Eventually, the Klan stumbled nationally and fell apart, in large part due to the chaotic personalities and paranoid egos it tended to attract as leaders. But its continuing appeal in the Midwest and elsewhere is reflected in the fact that one of its eventual offshoots, the Independent Klan of America, had its national headquarters in Muncie, Indiana; and even today, the National Knights of the Ku Klux Klan is based in South Bend.

The epicenter of the sundown mentality shifted over the years from small rural towns to the suburbs, particularly because the latter were so often specifically designed to facilitate white flight away from minorities. As Loewen explains, suburbs became "defended communities" where incursion by nonwhites was not permitted. In their early years, many even advertised themselves as "all white" and included covenants that precluded sales of homes to nonwhites. Indeed, Loewen reports that every single planned community he examined specifically excluded nonwhites from its beginning.[37]

The insularity of suburban life also allowed the whites living within them to rationalize away the absence of nonwhites. They had a variety of explanations, including climate and the lack of jobs, but most especially that blacks didn't *want* to live in the suburbs. An absurd notion, it was most recently debunked by historian Andrew Wiese, who demonstrated definitively that African Americans have aspired to achieve the ideal suburban lifestyle as ardently as whites, though with remarkably less success.[38]

Much of this has to do with the persistent myth that the demographic exclusion of minorities from suburbs and other mostly all-white communities is somehow "natural." As Loewen observes:

> Indeed, blaming the whiteness of elite sundown suburbs on their wealth actually reverses the causality of race and class. It is mostly the other way around: racial and religious exclusion came first, not class. Suburbs that kept out blacks and Jews became more prestigious, so they attracted the very rich. The absence of African Americans itself became a selling point, which in turn helped these suburbs become so affluent because houses there commanded higher prices.

The continuing legacy of sundown towns reinforces, generationally, the false stereotypes that originally created them a century ago. They have also had a profound psychological impact on blacks, including the internalization of low expectations and the exclusion of blacks from cultural capital.

Sundown towns enjoyed their heyday in the early 20th century, particularly in the American Midwest; however, one of the first such towns was way out West, in the little coal town of Rock Springs, Wyoming. And it wasn't African Americans who were being driven out, but Chinese immigrants.

The 1885 incident that brought about this situation was known as the Rock Springs Massacre. A mob of 150 white workers, led by union activists, descended on the Chinese section of town, where some 700 people lived, and burned it to the ground, with many of the occupants still inside. The survivors fled to the surrounding frozen landscape, where scores more died from exposure. The incident gave birth to the expression "He doesn't have a Chinaman's chance."[39]

The early Chinese in America were already in something of a limbo-land. Though there were no limitations on their immigration to America, they were forbidden by law from becoming U.S. citizens. When they first arrived as part of the California Gold Rush of 1849, they were welcomed as a significant part of the labor force, especially because they tended to avoid direct competition with white miners and instead provided services, such as laundry and eateries, as well as general labor. But as the gold ran out and the numbers of gold-seekers kept rising, their presence ceased to be welcome.

The situation became intense as the labor pool tightened. Completion of the Central Pacific Railroad in 1869—celebrated by the driving of the Golden Spike—also meant thousands of Chinese laborers were being dumped onto an already crowded labor market, fueling resentment among white laborers. Anti-coolie clubs formed in San Francisco as early as 1862 and quickly spread to every ward in the city, and the agitation grew. In 1870, the first of many large "anti-Oriental" mass meetings was held in San Francisco, and anti-Chinese legislation bolstered many a political career. Eventually, the issue became a national one, and in 1882 Congress passed the Chinese Exclusion Act, which barred any further immigration from China.

The 1790 Immigration Act specified that naturalization was

available only to "free white persons." The language was originally intended to ensure that African Americans and Native Americans were excluded from citizenship (in 1870, Congress updated the naturalization statutes to include Africans), but the law was applied with equal vigor to Asians. Under the 14th Amendment, however, any children of those immigrants born on American soil were entitled to full citizenship, though their parents might be barred. This birthright would play a major role in later anti-Asian agitation.[40]

A belief in the supremacy of the white race—and the need for racial segregation—was an often explicit, and always implicit, feature of the inflamed rhetoric aimed at excluding the Chinese. Speakers at rallies appealed to "racial purity" and "Western civilization" and described Asians in subhuman terms, simultaneously posing the most dire of threats with none-too-subtle sexual undertones. Moreover, agitators claimed, they were innately treacherous, a stereotype that came to play a major role in what followed.

As with all other manifestations of the eliminationist impulse, the rhetoric begat both the lawmaking and the violence that followed. Roger Daniels, in his book *The Politics of Prejudice,* describes this process:

> The anti-Chinese movement did not confine itself to making speeches and holding torchlight parades. No one will ever know how many Chinese were murdered in California; in the best-known outrage, about twenty Chinese were shot and hanged in the sleepy village of Los Angeles one night in 1871. For many years Chinese, like slaves in the South, could not under any circumstances testify against white men in a California court. Congressional enactments during Reconstruction unintentionally improved their legal status, but Western juries were usually convinced that all Chinese were "born liars." Incidental

brutality and casual assault were "John Chinaman's" daily lot;
cutting of his queue was a favorite pastime for the larger bullies,
and a shower of rocks was apt to greet him at any time. Little,
if any, legal punishment was meted out for any crime against
a Chinese. . . . Indignity and insult were not reserved for the
laborer and the living; when a Chinese professor at Harvard
died of pneumonia, the headline in the *Los Angeles Times* was
"A Good Chinaman."[41]

Most of this violence was scattered and periodic until the Rock
Springs Massacre in 1885, which seems to have sparked a wildfire
of violence throughout the West. The effect was especially notable
in California, where the largest numbers of Chinese lived. Elmer
Clarence Sandmeyer similarly describes the aftermath of Rock
Springs:

> Shortly afterward the entire west coast became inflamed almost
> simultaneously. Tacoma burned its Chinese quarter, and
> Seattle, Olympia, and Portland might have done the same but
> for quick official action. In California developments ranged
> from new ordinances of regulation to the burning of Chinese
> quarters and the expulsion of the inhabitants. Among the locali-
> ties where these actions occurred were Pasadena, Santa Barbara,
> Santa Cruz, San Jose, Oakland, Cloverdale, Healdsburg,
> Red Bluff, Hollister, Merced, Yuba City, Petaluma, Redding,
> Anderson, Truckee, Lincoln, Sacramento, San Buenaventura,
> Napa, Gold Run, Sonoma, Vallejo, Placerville, Santa Rosa,
> Chico, Wheatland, Carson, Auburn, Nevada City, Dixon, and
> Los Angeles.[42]

The Pacific Northwest, which had also seen significant Chinese
immigration, was hardly immune. Three Chinese hops workers
were murdered in their tents in the town of Saak (now Issaquah)

near Seattle shortly after the Rock Springs event in 1879. The following year, on February 7, a mob of local whites—mostly labor activists and utopians whose eugenicist beliefs prompted their desire to remove the Chinese—rounded up all 350 or so Chinese in the city and attempted to force them out of town. Eventually, the local police fired upon this mob; four people were wounded, and one man died. The passions cooled, as all but a few Chinese left Seattle within the ensuing weeks. And the city's nascent Chinese community nearly disappeared, at least for the time being.

Chinese immigration gradually ground to a trickle, and the remaining Chinese in America were forced to cluster into a handful of urban areas where they could be relatively safe, notably San Francisco, Los Angeles, and eventually Seattle again. But the demand for their labor never fully recovered, and the industries that formerly employed them—particularly railroad, logging, and canning companies—soon began recruiting Japanese laborers to America in their place.

Rather predictably, the same kind of racial agitation arose in short order against the Japanese. In 1892, Dennis Kearney, an Irish firebrand who had helped lead the fight for Chinese exclusion, warned a San Francisco crowd about "the foreign Shylocks" who were bringing a fresh threat from Asia:

> Japs . . . are being brought here now in countless numbers to demoralize and discourage our labor market and to be educated . . . at our expense. . . . We are paying out money [to allow] fully developed men who know no morals but vice to sit beside our . . . daughters [and] to debauch [and] demoralize them.[43]

Fearmongering and bigotry seemed to follow the Japanese immigrants wherever they set foot. In Washington State, the local newspaper in the White River Valley—where a workforce of about 400 Japanese laborers had established a presence—began agitating for their removal in 1893. An editorial headlined "Stop the Japs" observed that "the sight is distasteful to the working men of this region." A year later, the paper published another editorial declaring that "The Japs Must Go." Eventually, a "citizens committee" passed a resolution demanding that the valley's white farmers discharge their Japanese help; evidently, most complied, though eventually, the Japanese eviction in the valley proved very short-lived. The anti-Japanese bigotry, however, had a much longer life.[44]

Anti-Japanese agitation began occurring up and down the Pacific Coast, wherever immigrant communities appeared, in Washington, Oregon, and particularly in California. The mayor of San Francisco, James Phelan, made a career out of attacking the "Japanese problem." A 1900 speech he gave before a group of laborers laid out the themes that would be repeated by the like-minded many times over the following years:

> The Japanese are starting the same tide of immigration which we thought we had checked twenty years ago. . . . The Chinese and the Japanese are not bona fide citizens. They are not the stuff of which American citizens can be made. . . . Personally we have nothing against the Japanese, but as they will not assimilate with us and their social life is so different from ours, let them keep at a respectful distance.[45]

The Asiatic Exclusion League, established in San Francisco in 1905, was dedicated to repelling all elements of Japanese society from the state. Its statement of principles noted that "no large community of foreigners, so cocky, with such racial, social and religious prejudices, can abide long in this country without serious friction." And the racial animus was plain: "As long as California is white man's country, it will remain one of the grandest and best states in the union, but the moment the Golden State is subjected to an unlimited Asiatic coolie invasion there will be no more California," declared a League newsletter. As one speaker at a League meeting put it, "An eternal law of nature has decreed that the white cannot assimilate the blood of another without corrupting the very springs of civilization."[46]

The ugliness came to a head first in 1907, when San Francisco city officials announced a plan to force Japanese children into segregated Chinese schools; when the Japanese government threatened a diplomatic uproar (backed by Japan's recently established military might) over such actions, President Theodore Roosevelt stepped in and negotiated what was called the "Gentlemen's Agreement": Japan would agree to stop allowing its citizens to emigrate to the United States, and San Francisco officials would back away from their plan.

There was, however, a large loophole in this agreement: Japanese men who were already here were permitted to send for their wives and families to join them. This meant, within a few short years, that the demand for Japanese "picture brides"—women who became spouses through marriages arranged by familial "go-betweens" in Japan, in which pictures of the bride and groom were exchanged before the marriage became final—expanded exponentially among Japanese workers. Soon these brides were arriving in large numbers—and worse still, they soon began bearing children. *Citizen* children.

This set the nativists aflame, and by 1910 they had leapt into action to try to stop what they saw as the inevitable consequences of such a population in their midst. They were fueled by hysterical newspaper reportage on the "Yellow Peril"—a conspiracy theory promoted by the Hearst and McClatchy chains. This theory was premised on the notion that the Japanese emperor intended to invade the Pacific Coast and was sending immigrant laborers as part of a secret "fifth column" that would rise up and wreak havoc when given the signal. Nativists began a campaign to strip away citizenship rights for Japanese children born on American soil, as well as to end property-ownership rights for Japanese immigrants generally.

By 1912 fresh anti-Japanese legislation was bubbling along again in the California legislature. The first of the "alien land laws," which stripped Japanese immigrants of the right to own property, passed in Sacramento in 1913, and so angered people in Japan that "a crowd of some 20,000 Japanese in Tokyo cheered wildly as a member of the Diet [legislature] demanded the sending of the Imperial Fleet to California to protect Japanese subjects and maintain the nation's dignity," and the Japanese government protested angrily to the Wilson administration, to little avail.[47] Indeed, similar legislation soon began bubbling up in other states, particularly those on the Pacific Coast.

The spousal exception to the Gentleman's Agreement was the major focus of the agitation. In 1919 in Seattle, a campaign against Japanese farmers was spearheaded by a man named Miller Freeman, who had been agitating against them since 1907, and had even formed a state "naval militia" to help defend Puget Sound waters in the event of a Japanese invasion. The pretext in 1919 was the return of World War I veterans to the job market, where they were having difficulty finding work; as chairman of the state's Veterans Welfare Commission, Freeman quickly determined that the Japanese were at the root of this problem, as they were of so many others, in Freeman's view.

A July speech before a group of 170 businessmen—titled "This Is a White Man's Country"—kicked off the campaign and created a local uproar. The speech was loudly promoted with a banner headline on the front page of one of the three local dailies, the *Seattle Star*. Declaring that Japanese mothers bore five times as many children as white women, Freeman warned that if the trend were not countered, the entire Pacific Coast would soon be over-run with Japanese. Even then, he declared, they now owned and controlled large amounts of property in the state.

As a result of this travesty, Freeman claimed, World War I veterans returning home from Europe were being shut out of the labor market. "By gaining control of business, the Japanese is crowding our returning veterans out of a chance to get a new start." And if the trend continued, he warned, the result would be inevitable:

> In the face of the flow of Japanese to the Pacific Coast, white people are ceasing to move here from the East. Eventually the whites will be forced to go elsewhere to make a living. . . . Thus, the Japanese will eventually hold the balance of power in politics on the Pacific Coast. They will vote solid, and will control political affairs. Japan retains control of her people everywhere, notwithstanding that they may be accepted as citizens by the countries of their adoption.[48]

As Freeman would make clear on numerous other occasions, even American-born Japanese were not racial equals and could never mix with white society. They were Japanese through and through, and thus their citizenship was of dubious validity at best. Despite later contentions that he had no prejudice against the Japanese, this racial separatism was a cornerstone of Freeman's argument as he presented it in the pages of the *Seattle Star*. He voiced it largely by sprinkling his writing and speeches (including his remarks to the *Star*) with popular aphorisms: "The Japanese cannot be assimilated. Once a Japanese, always a Japanese. Our mixed marriages—failures all—prove this. 'East is East, and West is West, and ne'er the twain shall meet.' Oil and water do not mix."[49]

And his conclusion became a political benchmark:

> It is my personal view, as a citizen, that the time has arrived for plain speech on this question. I am for a white man's Pacific coast. I am for the Japanese on their own side of the fence. I not only favor stopping all further immigration, but believe this government should approach Japan with the view to working out a gradual system of deportation of old Japanese now here.[50]

Freeman's campaign was accompanied by a spate of newspaper stories with blaring headlines, such as "Is This to Remain a White Man's Land?" The stories varied slightly in topic, but their underlying narrative was the same: that neither the Japanese immigrants nor their citizen children could ever become "real Americans." "There is no hope now or in the future for their assimilation," Freeman declared, and so their growing presence could have no other outcome than to drive off Caucasians.

Eventually Freeman's campaign produced a congressional hearing in Seattle, at which the leader of the local chapter of the American Legion declared, "This is the zero hour of Americanism, and we should stand for 100 percent Americanism. The republic was founded for Americans, and not for Japanese, who are un-American."[51]

The next year, 1920, Freeman successfully pushed for passage of a state Alien Land Law in the Washington State legislature. Freeman outlined his reasoning in a speech. "Certainly I did not start out with any prejudice against the Japanese," he said. "And the more I observe of them, the more I admire their perseverance and efficiency."

They are not inferior to us; in fact, they constantly demonstrate their ability to beat the white man at his own game in
farming, fishing and business. They will work harder, deprive
themselves of every comfort and luxury, make beasts of burden
of their women and stick together, making a combination that
Americans cannot defeat.[52]

This was a common refrain among the anti-Japanese agitators,
and it was modeled on arguments that appeared nationally in
popular literature (particularly such books as Madison Grant's *The
Passing of the Great Race,* which warned that "Asiatics" were about
to swamp American culture through immigration and invasion)
and advocated by self-proclaimed scientists who used the questionable methodology of the day to lend an academic veneer to longstanding racial prejudices. Ultimately the issue was couched, like
many racial issues of the preceding century, in the terminology of
eugenics. Thus, many of the campaigns against nonwhites cast the
race in question as not merely subhuman, but pernicious vermin
who posed a serious threat to the "health" of the white race. As
James Phelan, arguing for exclusion in California, put it, "The rats
are in the granary. They have gotten in under the door and they are
breeding with alarming rapidity. We must get rid of them or lose
the granary."[53]

The eugenicists uniformly accorded Asians an advanced position in the sciences and arts and acknowledged their intellectual
capacities but considered them lacking a moral dimension, which
ultimately rendered them an inferior race. As Grant put it: "These
races vary intellectually and morally just as they do physically.
Moral, intellectual, and spiritual attributes are as persistent as physical characters, and are transmitted unchanged from generation to
generation." The assumption that there was a lack of a moral sense

inherent in the "Asiatic" race made them potentially dangerous as economic or military competitors, according to this assessment, because they lacked the normal restraints that "decent" white folk took for granted as part of the fabric of a healthy society.

When the Washington legislature passed the Alien Land Law in 1920, Miller Freeman could not resist a parting kick in the Japanese gut after the victory. In an article addressed to the Japanese community, he offered this blunt assessment: "The people of this country never invited you here. You came into this country of your own responsibility, large numbers after our citizens supposed that Japanese immigration had been suppressed. You came notwithstanding you knew you were not welcome. You have created an abnormal situation in our midst for which you are to blame."[54]

More defeats came in succession for the Japanese. More states throughout the West passed alien land laws in the ensuing years. The Supreme Court upheld the legality of the laws, and in the meantime, another Supreme Court ruling affirmed the exclusion of any Asian immigrant from naturalizing as a citizen. Finally, in 1924, the agitation reached its zenith when Congress passed the Immigration Act of 1924; it was also known as the Asian Exclusion Act because it completely prohibited any further immigration from Asian nations. In Japan, the public had been closely watching the passage of the alien land laws with mounting outrage. And when news of the passage of the Asian Exclusion Act was announced, mass riots broke out in Tokyo and other cities.

The 1924 Asian Exclusion Act was a landmark in many other respects as well. Previously, immigration to America had been largely an open affair: anyone who could prove a "sponsor" was allowed to come (even if citizenship was a restricted matter). Now, largely because of nakedly racist agitation aimed at keeping out the "unassimilable" and "alien" Asian races, the borders were closed for the first time, and the entire concept of an "illegal immigrant" sprang into being.

With Japanese immigration effectively halted altogether, the remaining community settled in, the majority of them employed in farming. Most of them had families and citizen children, many of whom were just coming of age when America went to war with Japan after the attack on Pearl Harbor on December 7, 1941.

The agitation against them had largely subsided, but the mythology that had arisen 20 years before—particularly the widespread "Yellow Peril" conspiracy theories—was still very much alive. And after Pearl Harbor, it flamed fully back to life.

There was a great deal of hysteria along the Pacific Coast in the weeks and months after Pearl Harbor, including sightings of phantom warplanes over Los Angeles and reports of "arrows of fire" near Seattle pointing the way to defense installations. Soon, the need to "lock up" the "dirty Japs" in their midst was a popular topic and was on the tongues of most of the coast's politicians and on the pages of its newspapers.

Such a removal would not be without problems, warned some. "Approximately 95 percent of the vegetables grown here are raised by the Japanese," noted J. R. Davidson, market master for the Pike Place Public Market in Seattle. "About 35 percent of the sellers in the market are Japanese. Many white persons are leaving the produce business to take defense jobs, which are not open to the Japanese."[55] Letter writers to the local newspapers raised the same concerns. However, their concerns were quickly derided as so much hand-wringing from "Jap lovers."

Meanwhile, Senator Tom Stewart of Tennessee proposed stripping citizenship from anyone of Japanese descent. The Japanese, charged Stewart on the Senate floor, "are among our worst enemies. They are cowardly and immoral. They are different from Americans in every conceivable way, and no Japanese who ever lived anywhere should have a right to claim American citizenship. A Jap is a Jap anywhere you find him, and his taking an oath of allegiance to this country would not help, even if he should be permitted to do so. They do not believe in God and have no respect for an oath. They have been plotting for years against the Americas and their democracies."[56]

The press became the chief cheerleaders for removing the Japanese. The *Seattle Times* ran a news story alerting its readers: "Hundreds of alien and American-born Japanese are living near strategic defense units, a police survey showed today.... There are Japanese in the neighborhood of every reservoir, bridge and defense project." The *Times* also ran columns by the well-known conservative Henry McLemore, who frequently attacked the presence of Japanese descendants on the West Coast. In one column, McLemore raged:

> I am for the immediate removal of every Japanese on the West Coast to a point deep in the interior. I don't mean a nice part of the interior, either. Herd 'em up, pack 'em off and give 'em the inside room of the badlands. Let 'em be pinched, hurt, hungry and dead up against it.... Personally, I hate the Japanese. And that goes for all of them.[57]

Pearl Harbor also served as a pretext for the traditional voices of white supremacy to rise to the fore. "This is a race war," proclaimed Mississippi congressman John Rankin on the House floor.

> The white man's civilization has come into conflict with Japanese barbarism....
> Once a Jap always a Jap. You cannot change him. You cannot

make a silk purse out of a sow's ear. . . . I say it is of vital importance that we get rid of every Japanese, whether in Hawaii or on
the mainland. . . . I'm for catching every Japanese in America,
Alaska, and Hawaii now and putting them in concentration
camps. . . . Damn them! Let's get rid of them now![58]

Moreover, as Testsuden Kashima details in his book *Judgment
Without Trial: Japanese American Imprisonment During World
War II*, government bureaucrats had been preparing for some years
for the possible roundup and incarceration of Japanese Americans,
largely because "Yellow Peril" beliefs about the threat posed by
"disloyal" Japanese were pervasive at the highest levels of government, including the president. The bureaucratic machinery, particularly among military planners at the West Coast Command in
San Francisco, began grinding into action. By early April, they had
declared it a "military necessity" to evacuate every Japanese person,
citizen or not, from the Pacific coast.

At first, the plan was to make this a "voluntary evacuation,"
mostly to the states of the interior West. Shortly after the government announced this, however, the governors of those Western
states held a meeting with War Relocation Authority (WRA) officials in Salt Lake City. Here, they declared adamantly that they
could accept the evacuees only under armed guard and behind
barbed wire. Within a week, the WRA shut down its "voluntary"
program and proceeded to make plans for incarcerating the entire
population of Japanese Americans living on the coast—some
110,000 persons—in concentration camps in the interior.

Evacuation notices started appearing in May in communities
all along the coast, and by the end of June, nearly the entire population of evacuees had been herded into temporary "assembly centers" while the camps in the interior were being built. By summer's

end, the 10 camps, located largely in hostile desert environments, were almost finished and began to be filled. By the war's end, some 120,000 people occupied them.

The entire episode was predicated on the failure to distinguish between Japanese nationals and Japanese American citizens, not to mention the even finer distinction involving the Issei (or first-generation) immigrants, the vast majority of whom had been in the United States for over 20 years and were legally forbidden to become naturalized citizens. Throughout the war, headlines regularly referred to the enemy "Japs," as did headlines about the evacuation and subsequent events at the WRA's relocation centers. Consistent with popular sentiments prior to the war and during the evacuation debate, letters to the editor and political pronouncements often made no distinction between the citizens who once had been their neighbors and the foreign enemies their sons were fighting.

Then, as the war wound down and it became apparent that the camps were eventually going to be closed, the old agitators on the West Coast returned to the fray, demanding the government find a way to keep the "Japs" from returning. One of the leaders in this fight was Washington representative Henry "Scoop" Jackson of Everett. He had protested the formation of an all-Japanese fighting unit in the army during the war and penned a speech worrying about what would happen to his district when the war was over and the internees and veterans alike were free to return:

> What is to be the eventual disposition of the Japanese alien and native . . . is the second aspect of this problem of the Pacific. Are we to return them to their former homes and businesses on the Pacific Coast to face the active antagonism of their neighbors? Shall they again, as happened in World War I, compete economically for jobs and businesses with returning war veterans?[59]

The American Legion joined in on the rising anti-Japanese sentiments, denouncing the WRA's policy of "coddling the Japs." Longtime anti-Asian groups, like the Native Sons of the Golden West, became active in agitating alongside newer groups like the Pearl Harbor League. Some of these groups distributed signs proclaiming, "We don't want any Japs back here—EVER!" The mayor of the South King County town of Kent displayed the warning prominently in his shop and earned a *Time* magazine appearance for it, pointing at the sign.[60]

When it became evident, in late 1944, that the camps were going to be closed (thanks largely to the Supreme Court ruling in *Endo ex parte* 323 U.S. 283, which ruled that loyal citizens could not be held against their will), the agitation against allowing them to return rose to a feverish pitch. A Bainbridge Island man named Lambert Schuyler published independently a little pamphlet that had wide distribution, titled *The Japs Must Not Come Back!* His final solution: designate a passel of Pacific islands permanent territories of the United States, then remove all persons of Japanese descent to this new permanent homeland. Of course, no one of Japanese blood would be permitted to become a permanent resident of the mainland afterward.

Schuyler was hardly alone. Up and down the coast, jingoes began organizing community meetings aimed at repelling their return to a number of semirural communities that had formerly hosted Japanese families but mostly were in the process of becoming suburbs as part of the postwar boom. However, something noteworthy happened at these meetings in Washington, Oregon, and California: they all failed. In Bellevue, Washington, the community meeting broke up after some heckling erupted from the audience. An anti-Japanese meeting scheduled for the same evening in Seattle came apart as well. In California and Oregon, other "Keep Out the Japs" meetings met similar fates, and in Bellevue, a counter-meeting held two weeks later denounced any attempt to keep Japanese farmers from returning to their homes.

In the end, the forces that opposed the return of Japanese families to the newly developing suburbs won out, not so much by virtue of having scared the Japanese away or intimidated them, but largely because of economic forces interacting with the conditions created a generation earlier. At the time of the evacuation, as a lingering effect of the alien land laws, very few of the Japanese farming families owned their own farms; most still lived the itinerant tract-to-tract lifestyle of the truck farmers whose efforts had turned so many of these formerly marginal lands into valuable properties ripe for development. After the camps closed, many of the evacuees found that their former farms were slated to become suburban neighborhoods, or that in any event the white landowners were intent on joining in the transformation.

As a result, after the war the Japanese evacuees largely resettled in urban areas and took up occupations other than farming. At the time of the relocation, over 60 percent of the evacuees were employed in agriculture; after the war, less than 20 percent were.

The blindly eliminationist bigotry that had erupted during wartime—and had characterized nearly the entire history of Asian American immigration—had played its course. The exclusion of Chinese and Filipinos, both allies in the war, was dropped in 1944, as was the prohibition against their naturalization.

And the American public—instructed, no doubt, by the remarkable example of the segregated all-Japanese 442nd Regimental Combat Team, the most decorated unit of World War II—gradually shifted its attitudes about the ability of Japanese immigrants to fully become American. With the passage of the McCarran-Walter Act in 1952, even Japanese immigrants were finally permitted to become U.S. citizens.

More importantly, widespread attitudes about the inability of

Asians to assimilate in American society were, over time, demolished utterly. Nowadays, hardly an eyebrow is raised at the kind of interracial marriage between Asians and Caucasians that seemed such a horrific prospect in the 1920s.

However, influence of the eliminationist bigotry that had informed the transformation of American immigration law during these years was never fully erased. By early in the 21st century, it would come creeping back out of the woodwork.

The history of eliminationism in America, and elsewhere, shows that rhetoric plays a significant role in the travesties that follow. It *creates permission* for people to act out in ways they might not otherwise. It allows them to abrogate their own humanity by denying the humanity of people deemed undesirable or a cultural contaminant.

At every turn in American history—from Juan Ginés de Sepúlveda's characterization of the New World "barbarians" as "these pitiful men . . . in whom you will scarcely find any vestiges of humanness," to Colonel Chivington's admonition that "Nits make lice!," to the declarations that "white womanhood" stood imperiled by oversexed black rapists, to James Phelan's declaration that Japanese immigrants were like "rats in the granary"—rhetoric has conditioned Americans to think of those different from themselves as less than human. Indeed, their elimination is not just acceptable, but devoutly to be wished and actively sought.

Which is why, when we hear eliminationist rhetoric today, we need to be on our guard. The ghosts of our history tell us as much.

9

The Ongoing Legacy of Eliminationism

Probably the starkest reminders of the legacy of eliminationist racism in America are its Indian reservations. Still home to the tiny remnant of native peoples, even those places are being encroached upon by whites seeking to take over the land. The rise of the casino economy has improved conditions for many tribes, but the hard reality of life on most reservations remains one of entrenched poverty and wasted potential.

In a day and age when we like to congratulate ourselves for having outgrown racism, we acknowledge the poor conditions on Indian reservations yet write it all off to past racism. More difficult to acknowledge, perhaps, is the reality that reporters in "Indian Country" (notably Steve Hendricks, author of *The Unquiet Grave: The FBI and the Struggle for the Soul of Indian Country*) have amply documented: namely, that the squalor and cultural oppression of Indian reservations has been systematically sustained by the U.S. government well into this century.[1] The problem of white hate crimes perpetrated against Indians also persists, and the absence of an active response from law enforcement remains notable.

The great tragedy of the genocide of the Native Americans, beyond its cruel injustice, is its utter wasting of human potential: the America that could have been. Though the Indians' ecological ethic has at times been overstated, it is incontestable that for centuries before the arrival of Europeans, they lived relatively healthy lives and sustained a healthy population on the continent. At a time when we are constantly reminded of the difficulties of sustaining human civilization in a viable biosphere, a dose of the Native American conservation ethic could serve us well.

In part because white Americans have little exposure to real Native Americans, they have little reason to reflect on the costs of history; that particular episode of our eliminationist history can be easily pushed into the far corners of our consciousness. It is not so easy, perhaps, to brush aside our long effort to oppress and eliminate African Americans, as well as Asian Americans and other nonwhite immigrants, if only because their sheer numbers are so much greater and their dispersal among the population much broader. Yet we have done our best—and continue to sweep it all under our collective carpet.

Moreover, we continue to pay a price, both culturally and economically. In addition to the fissures that racial lines drawn long ago continue to generate, the cost in creativity and enterprise puts us at a disadvantage in a global economy when elsewhere those lines are disappearing.

A few years ago, Charles Mudede of the *Stranger* newspaper in Seattle wrote about the stark differences between Seattle and Tacoma, two cities twinned in much of the national perception of the Puget Sound, but starkly divided in terms of their relative vitality. Whereas Seattle's racial diversity, particularly its vibrant Asian culture, has produced an economic powerhouse and a robust public image, Tacoma's long history of exclusion and backward thinking has produced a metropolis mired in its past:

> The second self-imposed blow was Tacoma's infamous expulsion of Chinese immigrants on November 5, 1883. Granted,

every city in the Northwest experienced sometimes-deadly anti-Chinese riots, but the government in other cities stepped in at some point to restore order. (Seattle declared martial law and issued warrants for leaders of the Chinese-expulsion movement.) Tacoma's officials, on the other hand, helped force most of the city's Chinese community onto a train headed for Portland. Tacoma faced national embarrassment because of the incident, and its backward way of settling racial disputes became known as "The Tacoma Method." It has yet to recover from this humiliating recognition: Recently, the *Tacoma News Tribune* published an article titled "Tacoma faces up to its darkest hour," which posits that Tacoma might have turned out differently had it not booted out its Chinese population. "First, it is the only [city on the West Coast] that doesn't have a large Chinese American population," says the article. "[The last] census figures suggest there are fewer people of Chinese descent in the city now than there were in 1885."[2]

The *News Tribune* editorial he refers to actually lamented the absence of the energy and enterprise that Chinese Americans brought with them, and went on to say that the restrictive mindset established by the expulsion itself and the subsequent actions that allowed it to stand, produced a civic culture that was hostile to new ideas and new peoples.

Such reflection, however, is rare. Most often, we like to overemphasize the progress that has been made in racial relations since the civil-rights era; certainly, Barack Obama's election as president produced a spate of conservative proclamations about the event signifying the death of racial victimology.[3] In reality, the majority of our accomplishments have been more in the legal arena than in the larger societal one, and the bulk of that has been a small handful of laws passed during a brief period in the 1960s: the Civil

Rights Act of 1964, the Voting Rights Act of 1965, and the Fair Housing Act of 1968. Subsequent efforts to create a color-blind society, such as affirmative action and busing, have been muted over the years by ensuing efforts to do away with them.

At the same time, very little has been done to tackle the larger problem of structuralized, institutional racism. Decades of eliminationist prejudice have created a segregated society divided into largely white suburbs and rural areas, and inner cities where nonwhites remain clustered, and the resulting segregation by class and economic and political power.

Indeed, we seem to remain obdurately ignorant of the nature of these issues and reflexively fall back on old attitudes. The "problem," we may continue to think, must be with those nonwhites themselves. After all, the thinking goes, slavery ended in 1865, and we did away with Jim Crow and the officially sanctioned prejudice in the 1960s. If blacks still fail to advance, it must be something wrong with *them*. If they fail to move up and into the suburbs, it must be *their* fault.

James Loewen, in *Sundown Towns*, observes that local communities have their own ways of getting around and indeed undermining federal anti-discrimination laws when it comes to "preserving their way of life." Racial covenants remain quietly observed among home buyers and sellers, even when they have been removed from the documents and titles. Real estate agents remain careful not to cross color lines, if for no other reason than getting a reputation for crossing those lines will quickly ruin their business in those communities. Law enforcement officers will quietly harass nonwhites making any kind of unexpected appearances in formerly all-white communities.

When it comes to race in America, we've always thought of the persistent poverty and concomitant crime of the inner city as "the problem," or at least its chief embodiment. But as Loewen observes, the *problem,* or at least its *source,* is embodied in the all-white communities that have a history of making nonwhites unwelcome:

> Most people, looking around their metropolitan area, perceive inner-city African American neighborhoods as "the problem." It then follows all too easily that African Americans themselves get perceived as the source of the problem.... So whites generalize: blacks can't do anything right, can't even keep up their own neighborhoods. All African Americans get tarred by the obvious social problems of the inner city. For that matter, some ghetto residents themselves buy into the notion that they are the problem and act accordingly.
>
> ... Lovely white enclaves such as Kenilworth withdraw resources disproportionately from the city. They encourage the people who run our corporations, many of whom live in them, not to see race as their problem. The prestige of these suburbs invites governmental officials to respond more rapidly to concerns of their residents, who are likely to be viewed as more important people than black inner-city inhabitants. And they make interracial suburbs such as Oak Park difficult to keep as interracial oases.[4]

A certain dishonesty on the part of many whites on the issue of race is the chief dynamic in this situation. Most people understand that racism is deeply stigmatized in our society—"racist" is a negative, ugly word, and no one likes being accused of being one. But privately, many whites, especially those in enclaves where the stereotypes on race persist, cling to views that are most charitably framed as the lingering consequences of generations of ignorance.

Most whites claim that they eschew racism, and even justify their opposition to programs such as affirmative action on the dubious assertion that they constitute a kind of "racial preference" that is the basis of racism itself. Yet, their actions speak louder than their words. The facts show that whenever blacks attempt to make whites their neighbors, the response is white flight to more "pristine" elite suburbs.

The impulse to defend "white culture" through residential segregation has come surging to the forefront of the national consciousness with the immigration debate, which has proven, more than anything, to be a conduit through which xenophobic ideas and agendas enter the mainstream of national discourse. Probably the most prominent, and high-level, example of a conduit for such ideas is Patrick Buchanan and his race-baiting screed, *State of Emergency: The Third World Invasion and Conquest of America.* At its core, the book is an attempt to revive old eugenicist myths about race and whiteness, all couched in such terms as "defending white culture." The mindset that produced it is, in fact, infecting all levels of conservative discourse.

This is why you can now hear Bill O'Reilly declaim on national television:

> That's because the newspaper and many far-left thinkers believe the white power structure that controls America is bad, so a drastic change is needed.
>
> According to the lefty zealots, the white Christians who hold power must be swept out by a new multicultural tide, a rainbow coalition, if you will. This can only happen if demographics change in America.[5]

And then there's O'Reilly's Fox News colleague John Gibson:

> First, a story yesterday that half of the kids in this country under five years old are minorities. By far, the greatest number are Hispanic. You know what that means? Twenty-five years and

the majority of the population is Hispanic. Why is that? Well,
Hispanics are having more kids than others. Notably, the ones
Hispanics call "gabachos"—white people—are having fewer. . . .
   To put it bluntly, we need more babies. Forget about that
zero population growth stuff that my poor generation was mis-
led on. Why is this important? Because civilizations need population to survive. So far, we are doing our part here in America
but Hispanics can't carry the whole load. The rest of you, get
busy. Make babies, or put another way—a slogan for our times:
"procreation not recreation."[6]

This fetish about the birth rates of brown people compared to
white people has remained a constant of the white-supremacist set
for all of the past century; as we have seen, it was a centerpiece of
nativist agitation against Japanese immigration early in the 20th
century. It has been a central component of Klan activity since as
early as the 1920s. It was the centerpiece of David Duke's political
career beginning in the mid-1980s. As recently as 2000, he would
write:

> We are fighting for the preservation of our heritage, freedom
> and way of life in the United States and much of the Western
> World. Ultimately, we are working to secure the most impor-
> tant civil right of all, the right to preserve our kind of life.
> Massive immigration and low European American birthrates
> coupled with integration and racial intermarriage threatens the
> continued existence of our very genotype. We assert that we,
> as do all expressions of life on this planet, have the right to live
> and to have our children and our children's children reflect both
> genetically and culturally our heritage.[7]

Likewise, the "English only" movement, inextricably inter-
twined with racist immigrant-bashing, has been circulating on

the extremist Right for years. In recent years, the movement to create such a law attempted to pose itself as a legitimate organization called English USA, but it didn't take long for its racist roots to show. A 2003 Southern Poverty Law Center report detailed how its founder, John Tanton, began the organization with funding from wealthy white supremacists, and how the organization was staffed by people with longtime connections to various hate groups.

The reason conservatives are increasingly embracing these longtime appeals from the extremist Right is simple: their power base is rapidly crumbling under the weight of the Bush administration's ineptitude, both at home and abroad. Most importantly, they are losing more chunks of their base of support over the immigration issue, particularly as far-right appeals (such as the invasion and Reconquista claims) gain broader circulation and popularity. Rather than stand up to this extremism, the White House approach was to mollify it with empty gestures, such as placing overextended National Guardsmen on the border. The administration oversaw a series of "crackdown" raids by Immigration and Customs Enforcement agents, who arrested and incarcerated large numbers of suspected illegal immigrants.

The current wave of Latino migration is reaching into many precincts that, historically, were *all-white by design,* as Loewen's work demonstrates in excruciating detail. Most of the sundown towns that Loewen documents were in the Midwest and West—the same places now complaining about a "Mexican invasion." These same sundown towns have, unsurprisingly, a history of supporting racist election appeals, including broad support for George Wallace in 1968, and Republican presidential candidates in the ensuing years, all of whom made use of the Southern Strategy's core appeal to white racial interests.

The lion's share of this appeal is the notion that "white culture" is under assault from an "invasion" of brown people. And the chief culprit, predictably, is federal immigration law, the same immigration laws whose cornerstones are the anti-Asian agitation of the early 20th century.

From the nativist contingent, we mainly hear about the illegal status of these new immigrants from Latin America. "What part of 'illegal' don't you understand?" is one of the Minutemen's favorite T-shirt slogans. To which one appropriate response could be: "What part of 'bad law' don't you understand?"

The bottom line in the immigration debate is that current immigration law—as well as the proposals floated by the Tom Tancredo wing of the Republican Party (which also includes Rep. James Sensenbrenner)—is inadequate for dealing with the realities created by economic forces that no amount of border fence and no mass expulsions will overcome. This reality consists of two forces that drive the current wave of emigration: 1) a massive wage and standard-of-living gap between the United States and its immediate and most populous neighbor, and 2) the increasing demand for cheap labor in the United States.

Stressing that these immigrants are illegal begs the whole question of whether the laws on the books are adequate or just. It also creates criminals out of people who come here to work, when "coming here to work" has always been the driving force in immigration throughout our history.

But the nativists don't care. They seem to cling to simple solutions. It's easier to blame the poverty-stricken pawns in this economic game, and take their anger out on them, than to deal with the core problems. They find a scapegoat, identify "the problem," then set out to eliminate it.

Thus eliminationist rhetoric rises to the surface. You can hear it, for instance, in the right-wing blogger who wrote a post decrying those "illegal aliens" and comparing them to rats:

> We can learn from Buffalo, New York. Now in Buffalo the rat problem in the city was a huge one. Exterminators could not handle the problem. But then in 2001 the city mandated that everyone would have to begin using special anti-rat garbage totes that the rats could not open. With no way to get to the garbage, the rats left Buffalo. Now, they went to the suburbs and now the suburbs are fighting them. But it is no longer a problem for the people of Buffalo, New York. Here is how to do the same with our problem . . . [The program he then goes on to describe revolves around denying human services to illegal immigrants.][8]

Likewise, right-wing nativists have been talking almost incessantly about rounding up and deporting all illegal aliens. You don't hear any of them telling us how they intend to achieve this logistically, despite the fact that we're talking about *12 million people* and one of the pillars of an economy increasingly built on cheap labor. You can hear talk like this not just from organizations like VDare—designated a "hate group" by the SPLC but endorsed by Michelle Malkin and many others—but also from people with real influence and power.

Never mind, of course, that a substantial portion of these illegals are the spouses and parents of *legal* immigrants and citizens; never mind that deporting them means breaking up families; and never mind that these same "conservatives" talk out of the other side of their mouths, rather loudly, about "family values" and "preserving the family." One of the more pernicious anti-immigrant groups, in fact, calls itself (in classic right-wing Newspeak) "Families First on Immigration." Nor should we mind any concerns that in the process, we'll be forced to re-create the nightmare of American concentration camps.

What matters, it seems, is "defending white culture." Thus, as surely as flies follow the rendering wagon, we've been seeing an increase in hate crimes against Latino immigrants in places like Georgia and the Midwest. Latinos in these formerly all-white locales have been subjected to an onslaught of hate crimes, many of which go unreported because the victims fear deportation if they go to the police.

Again we see the nature of the eliminationist beast: it begins with rhetoric, then becomes endorsed by officialdom, a combination that gives permission for action. When right-wing pundits bandy this kind of talk, they're giving their tacit approval to violence, and voice to the darkest side of the American psyche.

The great Jewish philosopher Martin Buber, in his landmark work *I and Thou,* argued that human beings encounter and engage the world in two distinct but complementary ways: the relational and the objective, or, as Buber puts it, "I and thou" and "I and it." The former occurs when we authentically encounter another being as a whole; this encounter gives our lives meaning and ultimately reflects our relationship with the Divine. The latter describes how we deal with the world purely as objects and abstractions, dealings that allow us to navigate the material world. Both are necessary for making our way successfully in the world; according to Buber, dealing with the world exclusively in one mode or the other creates a fatal imbalance.[9]

Objectification of others is the root of eliminationism. When we engage the world and other human beings objectively, as "I and it" exclusively, we set the other's value at nothing. The desire to obtain power over others, which also expresses itself in slavery and war, requires such objectification, and thus becomes a negation of the Divine itself. Pure objectification unleashes evil upon both those others and ourselves, for in denying the Divine in those others we negate it within ourselves. This, in turn, renders us capable of the demonic.

As David Stannard puts it:

> It is tempting, when discussing . . . genocides from other times and places, to describe the behavior of the crimes' perpetrators as insane. But as Terence Des Pres once pointed out with regard to the Nazis' attempted mass extermination of Europe's Jews, "demonic" seems a better word than "insane" to characterize genocidal behavior. Des Pres's semantical preference here, he said, was based on his sense that "insanity is without firm structure, not predictable, something you cannot depend upon." And while "what went on in the [Nazi] killing centers was highly organized and very dependable indeed," thereby not qualifying as insanity, at least according to Des Pres's informal definition, "the dedication of life's energies to the production of death is a demonic principle of the first degree."[10]

The dynamic of eliminationism begins with the conceptualization of other people as less than human and finds its voice in rhetoric that portrays them as objects fit for elimination: vermin, disease, slime, traitors, killers. This rhetoric sets the stage for action by creating a rationale, which itself is seen by the likeminded as permission to act. Then, as the action occurs, the rhetoric is used to justify the violence and, indeed, to inflame it still further as both ratchet upward. In some cases, as with the internment of Japanese Americans, the action takes the form of government policy—

though in this case, it must be added, violence was largely absent; but in others, as in the case of the Nazi Holocaust or the extermination of the Native Americans, the entire enterprise is violent from start to finish.

On the other hand, the history of eliminationism is colored by the continuing presence of people of good will who opposed the base inhumanity that it revealed. But their ineffectiveness over the centuries, embodied by the crude reality of the end results, is also part of the dynamic. History has demonstrated that all the good will in the world is helpless against the determined efforts of men given over to the demonic, men whose willingness to eliminate their fellow men quickly obliterated whatever good may have been intended by others. Only in the past half-century has this ceased to be the case, when the demonic component of the American psyche has been wrestled under some semblance of control.

Many groups have been targeted for elimination in America over the centuries other than natives, blacks, and Asians, the main targets discussed in the preceding chapters. Some of them are:

- *Jews*: The Otherness of Jews in America was always present in the culture, as well as their scapegoating. Both were made starkly manifest with the lynching of Leo Frank by white thugs in Georgia in 1915, an event that helped the Ku Klux Klan return to the national scene the following year. Even starker was the anti-Semitic campaign of Henry Ford in the 1920s, particularly his publication of *The International Jew*, which gave national prominence to the "Elders of Zion" conspiracy theory that helped fuel the Nazi Holocaust in Germany. The ideas he expressed remain in the American national bloodstream to this day, embodied in "New World Order" conspiracy theories promoted by the likes of Pat Robertson and various militia-movement leaders.

- *Communists*: Red-baiting and a fear of "communist influence" actually began gaining strength under the Dies Committee as early as the 1930s, but it became a national cause célèbre when Sen. Joe McCarthy engaged in his notorious witch hunts in the late 1940s and '50s. The apotheosis of the hysteria over the "communist threat" came with the execution in 1953 of Julius and Ethel Rosenberg (whose Jewishness added an edge to their physical elimination). Likewise, the specter of the vast "communist conspiracy" and associated domestic communist traitors remained atop the Right's great enemies for the ensuing two generations in America, embodied by the enduring presence of the John Birch Society, and only faded with the fall of the Soviet Union in the late 1980s. At this point, however, the extremist Right's need for an enemy produced an inward turn that sought out new enemies at home—specifically leading officials of the U.S. government. Thus its legacy, too, remains with us in the form of the New World Order and related conspiracy theories.

- *Gays and lesbians*: Homosexuality has for many centuries been buried under a blanket of cultural stigma, some of it religious and some of it purely visceral. Those same prejudices endure today, but the increasing willingness of homosexuals to come out of the closet and live openly, beginning in the 1970s, created a significant cultural rift among those conservatives who adhered to the old taboos. It was particularly sharpened by the emergence on the scene of the AIDS epidemic, which produced such eliminationist schemes as Paul Cameron's 1992 proposal to quarantine gays, an idea that still has some currency on the Right. More significantly, gays and lesbians have in those same years increasingly become the target of hate crimes, probably the chief manifestation of the eliminationist impulse in America today.

- *Immigrants*: All colors and kinds of immigrants have historically been the subject of violent and bigoted campaigns, targeted by so-called nativists who demand that immigration cease. These campaigns range from the Know Nothings, whose main efforts focused on keeping out Irish and other Catholic immigrants, to the anti-German agitation that peaked in the 1870–1920 period, followed by the anti-Asian campaigns that flourished between 1880 and 1924. The latter were notable for the appearance, for the first time, of an effort not merely to prevent their arrival but to actively deport those already here, accompanied by the requisite eliminationist action, including violent massacres and concentration camps. The same impulse lives on today in the agitation against Latino immigration, which has proved to be a major bridge for far-right xenophobes to expand their reach into the mainstream of American discourse.

The eliminationist impulse gained new life in the wake of the terrorist attacks of September 11, 2001, especially as the flames of fearfulness were actually fanned rather than calmed by the American Right, including the Bush administration itself. Professional fearmongers leapt onto the national stage to denounce each fresh threat to national security. They particularly seized on the immigration debate, claiming that the insecure borders presented a prime opportunity for terrorists (though the reality regarding those borders was largely obscured in the racial agitation that accompanied it).

The fearmongering occurred at all levels, from Pat Buchanan proclaiming that white American culture was about to be overrun by Latinos and other nonwhites, to Lou Dobbs parroting white-supremacist nonsense on CNN, to the entire bandwidth of nativists, including the usual suspects: VDare, the Federation for American Immigration Reform, Michelle Malkin, Juan Mann, and Glenn Beck. Some of them demanded the immediate arrest and deportation of all 12 million illegal immigrants in America.

Simultaneously, these figures have provided avid media support for on-the-ground organizations, such as the Minutemen, where the eliminationist impulse runs rampant. The desire to eliminate Latinos can be found everywhere in the Minuteman ranks, such as the Minuteman who opined: "It should be legal to kill illegals. . . . Just shoot 'em on sight. That's my immigration policy recommendation. You break into my country, you die."[11] A San Diego Minuteman leader told his local paper, "If I occasionally let my language slip to a small group of people, that's my frustration with these people. I consider them less than human in the way that they conduct themselves as human beings, absolutely."

The result, as mentioned, has been a significant upsurge in hate crimes against Latinos and other immigrants. The FBI's annual hate-crime statistics release for 2006 showed a steady and noteworthy increase in bias crimes against Hispanics; 819 people were targets of anti-Latino crime in 2006, compared with 595 in 2003. In California in 2006, anti-Latino hate crimes increased even as such crimes decreased overall; and in Tennessee, state officials reported that anti-Hispanic bias crimes more than doubled in 2007.[12]

Hate crimes exist at the nexus between eliminationism's structural legacy and its human legacy. The failure of the federal government to ever pass anti-lynching legislation is mirrored in its continuing failure to pass a genuine federal hate-crime statute, particularly one that would include the requisite training and support for local law enforcement to be effective. The most recent such attempt—the Matthew Shepard Hate Crimes Prevention Act of 2007—failed in a House conference committee because Democratic leaders were unable to round up the necessary votes to push the bill out to the Bush White House, where it would have faced a certain veto in any event.

As a result, hate crimes continue to fester across the American landscape. As the nation's demographics undergo increasing shifts, the environment for creating hate crimes grows that much greater. The demographic shift occurring broadly across rural America as more Latinos move in and make their homes is already being accompanied by predictable consequences. As a report from the Department of Agriculture's Economic Research Service pointed out in 2003:

> Hispanics are the fastest-growing segment of the American population, and this growth is especially striking in rural America. The 2000 census shows that Hispanics accounted for only 5.5 percent of the Nation's nonmetro population, but 25 percent of nonmetro population growth during the 1990s. Many counties throughout the Midwest and Great Plains would have lost population without recent Hispanic population growth. Among nonmetro counties with high Hispanic population growth in the 1990s, the Hispanic growth rate exceeded 150 percent, compared with an average growth rate of 14 percent for non-Hispanics. Moreover, Hispanics are no longer concentrated in Texas, California, and other Southwestern States—today nearly half of all nonmetro Hispanics live outside the Southwest.[13]

These kinds of demographic shifts, as it happens, often become the primary breeding grounds for hate crimes—even in decidedly nonrural settings. A study published by Yale University political scientist Donald Green in 1998 focused on New York City. It found that demographic change in 140 community districts of the city between 1980 and 1990 predicted the incidence of hate crimes. The balance of whites and whatever the target group happened to be in a given district was an important factor, but the rate at which that balance changed was perhaps even more significant. The most common statistical recipe was an area that has been almost purely white, then experiences the sudden and noticeable arrival of some other group.

> In the case of New York, what occurred was a rapid inmigration of three groups: Asians, Latinos and blacks, though in the latter case the migration was often a response to the other groups' arrival; blacks were in some ways moved around, or their neighborhood boundaries changed. A number of previously white areas—Bensonhurst being the classic case, or Howard Beach—experienced a rapid inmigration of various nonwhite groups. What was particularly revealing about the hate-crime pattern was that the crimes reflected the targets who were actually moving in—that is, they revealed that this was not a kind of generalized hatred. Where Asians moved in, the researchers found a surge in anti-Asian hate crimes, and likewise with Latinos or blacks. Bias crime has more of a kind of reality-based component, at least in the aggregate, than is implicated by those psychological theories that suggest that there only exists a generalized sense of intolerance on the part of those who practice extreme forms of bigotry.[14]

Green goes on to say:

> Thinking about the kind of spatial and temporal dimensions of hate crime is a start in the right direction. . . . What it helps to think about is the difference between the static and the dynamic dimensions of this problem. People talk about the problem of hate crime being hate—of course, it is a problem, but hate isn't necessarily rising or falling in the society as a whole. What's changing is your proximity to people that you find onerous. And also your ability to organize or to take action against them.
> There are two hypotheses about why it is that hate crimes

subside when demographic change runs its course. One hypothesis is that the haters either accept the fact changes occur to them or they move away. Another hypothesis is that nobody really changes their attitude, it's just that the capacity to organize against some outsider—meeting at the back fence and conspiring against somebody—no longer becomes possible when one of your back-fence neighbors is now no longer part of the old nostalgic group.

Green says that both suburbs and rural areas are the next frontiers for hate crimes, partly because the demographic change is beginning to hit there now, "and they will lack the political will to deal with it."

What's especially notable is that, for the most part, hate crimes remain relatively effective, in terms of furthering their goals, in much of the country. Ken Toole, a native Montanan (and state senator) who runs that state's Human Rights Network, knows all about the fear minorities have of rural places like his home state. "I've experienced that firsthand, in talking with African American people on airplanes, etcetera, and their perception that Montana's not a safe place. And I think that stems from hate-crime incidents, but is more heartily reinforced by the presence of Militia of Montana, Aryan Nations, and things like that. It all feeds together.

"Here in Montana, in lily-white Montana, we spend all this time engaged in a debate whether or not these groups are white supremacist. Your average person of color doesn't even have that debate. They just know it."[15]

Toole says that when the image of a place as a haven for haters is combined with news stories of real-life hate crimes, the result is a widespread desire by minorities to avoid that place at all costs. "What you end up with is, we've heard about African American people being transferred to Montana and rejecting the transfers," Toole says, noting that it is something of a commonplace that rural people avoid the cities out of an irrational fear of crime committed by minorities. "There's very little question in my mind that, yeah, we rural folk maybe get a little nervous about the deep colors of the inner city, but that is very much a two-way street."

Perhaps of equal significance are the real-world ramifications of this fear for both minorities and the places they fear to visit: an impoverishment of the nation's democratic underpinnings. As Green points out, hate crimes succeed in making the nation a smaller place for minorities who fear driving to places like Idaho or Montana because of their reputations as havens for white supremacists.

"I think if you had to kind of step back and ask, 'Does hate crime pay?,' you'd say yes," Green says.

> If the point of hate crimes is to terrorize the population into maintaining boundaries between these perpetrators and the victimized populations, at least in some areas—certain parts of town, certain parts of the country, etcetera—you know, certain kinds of romantic relationships, whatever—then it does succeed in that. Because people really do feel that they have to constrain their behavior lest they open themselves up for attack. You know, gay men don't often hold hands in public. Black and white couples don't form spontaneously to the extent that you might expect based on their daily interactions.
>
> There are a lot of instances like that . . . we all probably have interactions with people who, when they're invited to a certain part of town, say, 'Oh, I better not go there.' From my standpoint, you tend not to attract much notice from policymakers, but I think of that as a massive dead-weight loss of freedom.[16]

There is no small irony in the conservative movement's steadfast opposition to hate-crimes legislation. Their flimsy pretense is that they are doing so in the name of protecting people's free-speech rights, that the legislation might make conservative preachers who oppose homosexuality liable for crimes committed by others. It's also worth observing that the claim that such legislation impinges on free-speech rights is flagrantly false. The Matthew Shepard bill, for instance, made clear provisions not to infringe on such rights.

The real hallmark of the right-wing rule America has endured for the better part of the new century has been its reliance on persuading the public to believe things that are factually false. The phony justification for the Iraq War (namely, the supposed presence of weapons of mass destruction that turned out not to exist) is only the most infamous example. The list—running from pseudo-science presented to deny global warming or to justify banning stem-cell research, to groundless fearmongering about Social Security—is not merely long, it touches nearly every facet of American governance and public discourse.

The immigration debate is rapidly becoming the most prominent current example of the American Right's attempt to persuade the public to launch into another monumental mistake on the basis of provably false information. And just as in those many other instances, the nation's media have played an outsize role in helping it happen.

In the spring of 2008, a coalition of progressive immigration reform groups commissioned a poll to help political candidates who were looking to change their strategy and the nature of the immigration debate. One aspect of the polling stood out as a prime example of how deeply right-wing misinformation infects the public discourse. One of the first sections of the poll, headlined "Biggest Concerns About Illegal Immigration," featured the public responses to a set of concerns identified by the pollsters as the most common issues raised in focus groups. Poll respondents named their "one or two biggest concerns about illegal immigration today." These were the results:

- Immigrants receiving free public services such as health care (48 percent)
- Immigrants not paying taxes (35 percent)
- Takes jobs from Americans and lowers wages (20 percent)
- Too many immigrants aren't learning English (20 percent)
- Weakens our security against terrorism (18 percent)
- Causing crime problems in many communities (17 percent)

If you look down that list, something stands out: each item reflects a fear based either on outright false information or on gross distortions from a highly selective set of facts. For instance:

- Only a fraction of America's health-care spending is used to provide publicly supported care to the nation's undocumented immigrants, according to a RAND Corporation study. Moreover, health-care expenditures are substantially lower for immigrants than for people born in the United States, and immigrants receive fewer services than native-born Americans.[17]
- Somewhere between one-half and three-quarters of undocumented immigrants pay federal and state income taxes, Social Security taxes, and Medicare taxes; moreover, all undocumented immigrants pay sales taxes (when they purchase something at a store, for instance) and property taxes (even if they rent housing).[18] Indeed, immigrants are boosting the Social Security system to the tune of $7 billion a year.[19]
- According to a number of studies on the subject, the only segment of the American labor population negatively affected significantly by the influx of undocumented workers

is unskilled laborers, who face direct competition from immigrants. Otherwise, most other segments of the economy where undocumented immigrants are employed—such as construction and farm work—have seen a general rise in employment that has absorbed most of the influx. The immigrant tide is helping lift all economic boats, not putting people out of work.[20]

- Nearly all Hispanic adults born in the United States of immigrant parents are fluent in English, though only a small number of their parents enjoy similar fluency. This dramatic increase in English-language ability from one generation to the next is common throughout the history of American immigration. Moreover, polling shows that Latinos, by a substantial margin, believe that immigrants must speak English to be part of American society; more pointedly, they believe that English should be taught to the children of immigrants.[21] Currently, demand for English classes at the adult level far exceeds supply.

- Experts on terrorism, using databases created from the biographical data of 373 terrorists, have found a sizeable terrorist presence in Canada (and indeed have observed Canadian-based terrorists entering the United States); however, they have found no terrorist presence in Mexico and no terrorists who entered the United States from Mexico. (Meanwhile, over 40 percent of the database is constituted of Western nationals, indicating that homegrown terrorists are one of the most significant components.)[22]

- Numerous crime studies have demonstrated that crime rates among immigrants are lower than those of the general population, by a substantial margin. Moreover, during the same period the undocumented immigrant population doubled to about 12 million from 1994 to 2005, the violent crime rate in the United States declined by 34.2 percent and the property crime rate fell by 26.4 percent. This decline occurred not only in the country generally but more specifically in cities with large immigrant populations. Immigrants also have a lower incarceration rate than native-born Americans.[23]

Undoubtedly the worst offender in this regard has been CNN's Lou Dobbs. At various times in recent years on his nightly news broadcast, Dobbs has: reported as factual the existence of a nonexistent conspiracy by Latino ideologues to return the Southwest to Mexican control as part of a plan to create an "Aztlan" homeland (complete, on one broadcast, with a map taken from one of the white-supremacist hate groups that peddles this theory); reported that immigrants are responsible for an influx of various dread diseases, including leprosy, on American shores (a claim promptly demonstrated to be an utter hoax); expounded at length on the supposed rise in criminality brought to America by immigrants, as well as dubious statistics presented as evidence that they are taking away American jobs; and at various times invited figures from white-supremacist hate groups as "experts" on immigration (while neglecting to inform the audience of the guests' backgrounds). He has also taken to claiming that most Americans are up in arms about illegal immigration—when, in fact, most polls have found that only between 4 and 7 percent of various respondents considered it among their most pressing political issues.

Their constant peddling of mistruths and smears has become so commonplace that it hardly causes a ripple when exposed anymore. Likewise, the descent of the likes of Lou Dobbs, Rush Limbaugh, and Bill O'Reilly into eliminationism, incremental as it has been, mostly elicits "what-can't-you-take-a-joke" shrugs. Hardly anyone raises an eyebrow when a popular right-wing blogger prints the home address of a Bush critic and invites his readers to pay him a violent visit (and indeed wishing aloud for his demise). Likewise, when Michelle Malkin plays a similar Radio Rwanda–like stunt on college antiwar protesters or a 12-year-old who speaks up in defense of a federal family aid program, she simply pouts and pretends that no harm was intended—and is then invited to appear on Fox News the next week.

Eliminationism, both in rhetoric and in action, is predicated on a sandcastle foundation of lies and distortions, and it always has been. The Mesoamerican and North American natives were not, in fact, soulless and inhuman savages incapable of civilization or bereft of culture. African Americans are not, in truth, subhuman brutes good only for hard labor, nor are they sexually voracious beasts lusting to rape every white woman in sight. Asians, in fact, are also whole human beings perfectly capable of assimilating and becoming full-fledged American citizens. Latinos, in fact, are not stealing our jobs and costing taxpayers billions. And in reality, none of these nonwhites are "the problem" when it comes to the failure of the inner-city poor to break out of their cycle. The problem, as we have seen, is persistent residential segregation and employment discrimination predicated on preserving white privilege at the expense of nonwhites.

Eliminationism itself is predicated on the greatest of all lies: the denial of our common humanity, what Buber called "the divine" in our relation to the world and to each other. One need not necessarily believe in God to recognize that this human element— the spark that gives us art and poetry, embodied in love itself— transcends cold material data and is the foundation for whatever meaning we obtain from life. Denying this in others kills the spark within ourselves and opens the door to the demonic. As Buber writes, in *Good and Evil*:

In a lie the spirit commits treason against itself.... Instead of completing their fellow man's experience and insight with the help of their own, as is required by men's common thinking and knowing, they introduce falsified material into his knowledge of the world and of life, and thus falsify the relations of his soul to being.

Confronting the legacy of eliminationism is necessary for our well-being as a nation. Its pernicious strand runs directly through the critical fault lines—racial, ethnic, religious, sexual, and cultural—that continue to divide the nation today. Healing those fault lines takes work.

To do so, ultimately, entails not simply standing up to the outrageous falsehoods and the cold inhumanity its purveyors spew but also creating a culture in which engaging our common humanity informs our choices, our behavior, our beliefs, our politics. It also entails looking honestly at our history and understanding how we came to be where we are today—seeing that although today the virus of eliminationism is far more hidden, it remains buried in our cultural soil, and invariably surfaces when we look the other way.

10

It Can Happen Here

Sinclair Lewis's *It Can't Happen Here*, published in 1935, is his most peculiar novel. For one thing, it's the closest thing to speculative fiction he ever wrote. It describes the rise to power of an American fascist named Buzz Windrip, who arrives on the political scene to rescue America from a plague of labor unions, welfare cheats, godless atheists, and gun-grabbing Jews.

It's an intriguing enough premise but, to be honest, Lewis fails to make it very compelling. Certainly it lacks the power of later works that envision a totalitarian society, such as *Brave New World*, by Aldous Huxley, or *1984*, by George Orwell. In most respects, it's one of his weakest works; it lacks most of the human detail and probing realism of his greatest novels. Among other problems, the plot is predictable, and the characterization, usually a Lewis strength, is very thin. It also was written after he had been awarded the Nobel, and actually marked the beginning of his decline as a writer—even though it was also a major bestseller.

Nonetheless, it's an intriguing work, in part because Lewis wrote it when fascism was already very familiar and before it had mutated into the Holocaust horror we think of when we think of fascism today. The book is a denunciation of fascism and its potential to take hold in America. Lewis may have lost his writer's touch, but he still understood Main Street better than most, and some of his detail is very telling indeed, at least in a political sense.

The title comes from an exchange in chapter 2, in which two characters discuss the political ascension of the book's central character, a right-wing politician named Buzz Windrip:

> "Wait till Buzz takes charge of us. A real Fascist dictatorship!"
>
> "Nonsense! Nonsense!" snorted Tasbrough. "That couldn't happen here in America, not possibly! We're a country of freemen."
>
> "The answer to that," suggested Doremus Jessup, "if Mr. Falck will forgive me, is 'the hell it can't!' Why, there's no country in the world that can get more hysterical—yes, or more obsequious!—than America. Look how Huey Long became absolute monarch over Louisiana, and how the Right Honorable Mr. Senator Berzelius Windrip owns HIS State. Listen to Bishop Prang and Father Coughlin on the radio—divine oracles, to millions. . . . Remember the Ku Klux Klan? Remember our war hysteria, when we called sauerkraut 'Liberty cabbage' and somebody actually proposed calling German measles 'Liberty measles'? And wartime censorship of honest papers? . . . Remember the Kentucky night-riders? Remember how trainloads of people have gone to enjoy lynchings? Not happen here?"[1]

It isn't hard to hear precursors and even parallels to today's political milieu. Especially noteworthy: the reference to "Liberty measles" ("Freedom fries," anyone?), as well as the "wartime censorship of the papers." But Lewis was speaking of the kinds of character traits that a nation has to have to lead it into fascism, and how despite (and largely because of) our blithe self-denials, we remain vulnerable to this peculiar brand of totalitarianism. What the familiarity of the scene suggests is this: the names have changed, but the traits are still with us.

As it happens, most serious scholars of fascism agree with Lewis. In his *The Anatomy of Fascism,* Robert O. Paxton writes:

The United States itself has never been exempt from fascism. Indeed, antidemocratic and xenophobic movements have flourished in America since the Native American party of 1845 and the Know-Nothing Party of the 1850s. In the crisis-ridden 1930s, as in other democracies, derivative fascist movements were conspicuous in the United States: the Protestant evangelist Gerald B. Winrod's openly pro-Hitler Defenders of the Christian Faith with their Black Legion; William Dudley Pelley's Silver Shirts (the initials "SS" were intentional); the veteran-based Khaki Shirts (whose leader, one Art J. Smith, vanished after a heckler was killed at one of his rallies); and a host of others. Movements with an exotic foreign look won few followers, however. George Lincoln Rockwell, flamboyant head of the American Nazi Party from 1959 until his assassination by a disgruntled follower in 1967, seemed even more "un-American" after the great anti-Nazi war.

Much more dangerous are movements that employ authentically American themes in ways that resemble fascism functionally. The Klan revived in the 1920s, took on virulent anti-Semitism, and spread to cities and the Middle West. In the 1930s, Father Charles E. Coughlin gathered a radio audience estimated at forty million around an anticommunist, anti-Wall Street, prosoft money, and—after 1938—anti-Semitic message broadcast from his church on the outskirts of Detroit.... *Today a "politics of resentment" rooted in authentic American piety and nativism sometimes leads to violence against some of the very same "internal enemies" once targeted by the Nazis, such as homosexuals and defenders of abortion rights.*[2]

Paxton, like his fellow scholar Roger Griffin, identifies today's far-right militia/Patriot and white-supremacist organizations—

which remain largely relegated to the fringe in the national conception of things—as the remnants of genuine proto-fascism in America. (Proto-fascism, of course, is genuinely fascist at its core—in contrast to para-fascism, which has the outward structural appearance of fascism but is different in its underlying nature.) Paxton's assumption is that any American fascism will arise in the same way fascisms of the past did: as a discrete movement that moves in to take advantage of political space created by the failures of the traditional political powers. That is, under this conception, it would have to emerge as a third party that displaces the Republican and Democratic parties.

There is, however, another possibility, namely, the transformation of an existing party into a fascist entity from within—not necessarily by design, but by a coalescence of political forces already latent in the landscape. This possibility exists because, as Paxton describes in detail, fascism is not so much an ideological "ism" as a constellation of traits that takes on a pathological life of its own. And these traits, as he details, are very much present, historically speaking, in American political life.

In fact, this very possibility was raised by one of the significant American fascist "intellectuals" of the 1930s. His name was Lawrence Dennis, and in 1936—the year after Lewis's novel appeared—he wrote an ideological blueprint titled *The Coming American Fascism*. Dennis predicted that, eventually, the combination of a dictatorial and bureaucratic government and big business would continue exploiting the working middle class until, in frustration, it would turn to fascism. The conditions he foresaw for this to happen are especially noteworthy:

> Nothing could be more logical or in the best political tradition than for a type of fascism to be ushered into this country by

leaders who are now vigorously denouncing fascism and repudiating all that it is understood to stand for. . . .

And, needless to add, these principles would mean the replacement of the existing organizational pattern of public administration by that of a highly centralized government which would exercise the powers of a truly national State, and which would be manned by a personnel responsible to a political party holding a mandate from the people. This party would be the fascist party of the United States—undoubtedly called, however, by another name. . . .

Yet how infinitely better for the in-elite of the moment to have fascism come through one of the major parties of the moment than to have it fight its way to power as the program of the most embittered leaders of the out-elite.[3]

This description has an ominous ring in an era in which the dominant party in power in America frenziedly declared war on "Islamofascism" while itself taking on many of the traits of fascism itself. It's unlikely that Dennis's thinking guided any of the intellectuals in today's mainstream conservative movement, though it is worth noting that his work is enjoying a renaissance in the paleo-conservative movement, particularly in such places as *The Occidental Review*, the far-right publication owned and operated by William Regnery.

Rather than being guided consciously (and there certainly is no evidence whatsoever for an ideologically fascist conspiracy), this transformation is occurring almost spontaneously. The primary impetus has been the transformation of conservatism into a discrete movement intent on seizing the reins of power. In the process, the means—that is, the obtaining of power—became the end, by any means necessary. This virtually guaranteed that conservatism would become a travesty of its original purpose. The nature of today's "conservative movement" is no more apparent than in how distinctly unconservative its actual conduct has been: busting budgets, falling asleep at the wheel of national security, starting wars recklessly and without adequate planning.

Specifically, two things occurred to the conservative movement in this drive for power:

- It increasingly viewed liberals not merely as competitors but as unacceptable partners in the liberal/conservative power-sharing agreement that has been in place since at least the New Deal and the rise of modern consumer society. Ultimately, this view metastasizes into seeing liberals as objects to be eliminated.

- It became increasingly willing to countenance ideological and practical bridges to certain factions of the extremist Right. This ranged from antiabortion and religious-right extremists, to the neo-Confederates who dominate Republican politics in the South, to factions of the Patriot/militia movement.

The combination of these two forces exerted a powerful rightward pull on the movement, to the point where extremist ideas and agendas have increasingly been adopted by the mainstream Right, flowing into an eliminationist hatred of liberalism. In the process, the mainstream's own rhetoric has come to sound like that on the Far Right—where eliminationism is not simply a commonplace, but a defining feature. A lot of the dabbling in far-right memes has been gratuitous, intended to "push the envelope" for talk-radio audiences in constant need of fresh outrageousness.

Fully enabled and freed of any of the traditional checks on its power by the earth-shaking effects of 9/11, the movement morphed into a genuinely radical force. And although, in its outward shape, it has come to resemble a kind of fascism, particularly in the way it has adopted nearly all of the "mobilizing passions" of fascism to some degree, at its core, it is not fascism. Remember Paxton's rather clear description of fascism in the context of the spectrum of ideologies: it is, in essence, "dictatorship against the Left amidst popular enthusiasm." There can be little doubt that what we see now is overt anti-leftism; increasingly the mainstream Right's entire raison d'être is, in Mussolini's phrase, "to break the bones of the Democrats of *Il Mundo*." Yet despite the conservative movement's efforts to create a one-party state, this is not yet a dictatorship. Neither does the movement enjoy true popular enthusiasm, particularly not since George W. Bush's handling of the reins of government proved to be so disastrous.

Regardless of the mechanism, Paxton makes clear that fascism not only can take root in America but that if it does so it will take a peculiarly American shape:

> The language and symbols of an authentic American fascism would, of course, have little to do with the original European models. They would have to be as familiar and reassuring to loyal Americans as the language and symbols of the original fascisms were familiar and reassuring to many Italians and Germans. No swastikas in American fascism, but Stars and Stripes (or Stars and Bars) and Christian crosses. No fascist salute, but mass recitations of the pledge of allegiance. These symbols contain no whiff of fascism in themselves, of course, but an American fascism would transform them into obligatory litmus tests for detecting the internal enemy.
>
> Around such reassuring language and symbols in the event of some redoubtable setback to national prestige, Americans might support an enterprise of forcible national regeneration, unification, and purification. Its targets would be the First Amendment, separation of Church and State (creches on the lawns, prayers in the schools), efforts to place controls on gun

ownership, desecrations of the flag, unassimilated minorities, artistic license, dissident and unusual behavior of all sorts that could be labeled antinational or decadent.[4]

Nearly all of these themes have played significant roles in the various political campaigns and legislative battles waged by the conservative movement this decade. Consider, for example, the brouhaha over who's wearing flag-lapel pins; the regular attempts to ban flag burning; the right-wing animus toward illegal immigrants; and the monumental attacks on gays and lesbians under the pretense of stopping gay marriage, coinciding with a de facto antagonism toward church-state separation.

What's still lacking from the basic recipe for genuine fascism, however, is the emergence of a genuine crisis of democracy. Conservatives have certainly tried to convince us that we face just such a crisis—either from the "threat" of illegal immigration, or more often and loudly, of terrorist attack. These threats, they tell us, are so overwhelming that we must suspend enforcement of our wiretap laws, or our prohibitions against torture, or overturn the 14th Amendment and thereby deny the children of immigrants their natural birthright as citizens.

Americans, particularly fundamentalist Christians, have always had a certain predilection for apocalyptic beliefs. How many times, after all, have you heard that the world was coming to an end? If you're like most of us, a lot.

Many of these beliefs have bubbled to the surface in recent years, particularly as we approached the new millennium. Remember all the fears about Y2K? Remember all the conspiracy theories by right-wing extremists that President Clinton intended to use the "Y2K meltdown" to declare martial law? Remember the "Y2K survival kits" being sold by Patriot movement believers, and the stores of generators and large bags of beans, rice, and canned goods that turned out not to be needed?

Most of these fears receded to just below the surface after Y2K turned out not to be the apocalypse after all. But then came the advent of the "war on terror" on September 11, 2001. The scenes that played out on our television screens that day, and in the ensuing weeks, were like something out of an end-of-the-world movie. They were so intense that at times they seemed surreal. It is almost natural, really, that they inspired a fresh wave of apocalypticism.

In truth, the scenes constituted a real psychological trauma for nearly all Americans. Trauma produces real vulnerability, especially to manipulation. And the conservative movement, reveling in a tidal wave of apocalyptic fears, proved adept at manipulating the public by stoking their fears and making them positively eager to participate in an ultimately totalitarian agenda. Indeed, the exploitation bears all the earmarks of psychological warfare—waged this time against the American public.

The renowned psychiatrist Robert Jay Lifton, in his book *Superpower Syndrome: America's Apocalyptic Confrontation with the World*, provides an incisive analysis of the state of the post-9/11 American psyche and the Bush administration's unmistakable manipulation of it for its own political purposes:

> As a result of 9/11, all Americans shared a particular psychological experience. They became survivors. A survivor is one who has encountered, been exposed to, or witnessed death and has remained alive. The category extends to those who were far removed geographically from the World Trade Center and the Pentagon, because of their immersion in death-linked television images and their sense of being part of a painful national ordeal that threatened their country's future as well as their own. How people deal with that death encounter—the meaning they give

it—has enormous significance for their subsequent actions and for their lives in general.[5]

Lifton identifies certain common themes in the psychology of survivors:

- Death anxiety, especially pronounced for people who witnessed the attacks or associated deaths personally, and which includes a fear of recurrence
- Death guilt, or "survivor guilt" which "has to do with others dying and not oneself"
- Psychic numbing, "the inability, or disinclination, to feel, a freezing of the psyche"
- Suspiciousness: in which survivors are "alert to issues of authenticity"
- An attempt to find "meaning and mission" from the ordeal

Much of the American response to 9/11, Lifton says, has "been a form of false witness":

> America has mounted a diffuse, Vietnam-style, worldwide "search and destroy mission" on behalf of the 9/11 dead. Here, too, we join the dance with our al-Qaeda "partner," which brings fierce survivor emotions and considerable false witness of its own.
>
> The survivor's quest for meaning can be illuminating and of considerable human value. But it can also be drawn narrowly, manipulatively, and violently, in connection with retribution and pervasive killing.[6]

Rather than helping Americans overcome the trauma of 9/11, the Bush administration—by wallowing in the worst attributes of the survivor's syndrome—in fact ensured that the nation has not healed, nor even begun to do so. Lifton's diagnosis: Bush and the conservative movement have propelled the nation into a potentially disastrous, perhaps even fatal, mindset, which he calls the "superpower syndrome": "a bizarre American collective mindset that extends our very real military power into a fantasy of cosmic control, a mindset all too readily tempted by an apocalyptic mission."

The crisis of democracy necessary to create a genuinely fascist dynamic is not as imminent as the Right would like us to think. Nonetheless, later events—particularly any further terrorist attacks, or perhaps a surge of terrorism by domestic extremists— could drastically alter that situation. Particularly in the age of the "war on terror," such a crisis remains a real potential. The key, then, is to find the path that does not take us there.

If fascism is indeed latent in our political landscape and has lately been rising to the surface, then the critical question becomes: how do we prevent it from doing so?

First, it's important to understand the conditions under which fascism's attempts to take root and gain power have failed, such as in France in during the 1920s and '30s. In France there was no "political space" for fascism to form alliances with mainstream conservatives. The same, as we have seen, was true of the previous failure of American fascism: it, too, arrived at a time of limited receptivity to its appeals. As noted, when it re-emerged in the 1930s, the ascendance of power-sharing liberalism in rural as well as urban areas again left fascism little breathing room. Where it began to take root again in the 1990s was in an economically disenfranchised rural America.

The current para-fascist phenomenon represents a different kind of mechanism, one in which the political space is created within one of the major parties, not apart from them. This tendency has finally metastasized into a genuinely dangerous situation, one in which the GOP has become host to a totalitarian movement that exhibits so many of the traits of fascism that the resemblance is now unmistakable.

As a result, calculations of any "political space" that might be created by a serious crisis of American democracy must be completely reconfigured. Instead of an alliance with conservatives offering an opportunity for a fascist movement to gain legitimacy, such a crisis instead could create a situation in which the latent fascist elements come to the surface and, in turn, come to dominate the nature of a party already in power. This makes any potential for a crisis of democracy potentially more dangerous because an opening for fascism can appear much more rapidly and without any requisite shift in the political space.

The forces the conservative movement has set in motion are going to have harmful consequences in the long term; democratic institutions like voting and privacy rights are particularly vulnerable to attack. Even more egregious is the larger harm to the health of the body politic; the divisiveness sown by conservative ideologues is not going away any time soon, regardless of how thoroughly it may have been repudiated in the 2008 election.

On the large-scale level, preventing fascism means averting a crisis of democracy and dismantling the fascist architecture of the conservative movement by repudiating its tenets. If there is going to be any healing, it will have to begin after the attack style of politics—in which smearing an opponent substitutes for the lack of any substance or accomplishment—has been relegated to the ash heap of history. This can happen when the nation's mass media are effectively reformed and the trivialization of the national discourse ceases.

But we have to deal with this on the personal level as well. The influence of this movement has also pervaded our personal lives and relationships. Families, longtime friends, and communities are being torn apart by the divisive politics of resentment and accusation that have become the core of the conservative movement's appeal.

One of the realities about coming to terms with fascism is that it is not an immediately demonizing force but rather one with long-term effects. Conservative-movement adherents are still human beings, and seeing them as participants in a form of fascism should not prevent us from understanding that many of them are simply responding naturally to the psychological manipulation inherent in the movement's appeal.

Recognizing what we are up against—namely, a form of fascism—is critical to dealing effectively with it, because even if wielding the term in discourse can be unhelpful (it remains loaded and easily misinterpreted), the concept gives us a key to understanding the thought—or rather, emotive—processes at the core of the para-fascist appeal. Getting our opponents to see, for example that dissent is not treason but patriotism, requires getting them to let go of their preconceptions. It means, in the end, getting them to see us as human beings, too. And when we do that, the fascist facade will crumble.

This raises the ultimate conundrum regarding recognizing and dealing with para-fascism. On the one hand, attaching the term to just anyone—even in a qualified way, but particularly to people we think of as our neighbors and friends—can itself be a kind of demonization. At the same time, we cannot escape confronting it when we see it.

Consider, if you will, one of the great bylaws of the blogosphere—Godwin's Law:

As a Usenet discussion grows longer, the probability of a comparison involving Nazis or Hitler approaches one.[7]

A corollary observes: "There is a tradition in many groups that, once this occurs, that thread is over, and whoever mentioned the Nazis has automatically lost whatever argument was in progress. Godwin's Law thus practically guarantees the existence of an upper bound on thread length in those groups."[8] This has become a standard for debate in the blogosphere as well, and that is particularly the case with Godwin's Law. At the very outset, as I began compiling at *Orcinus* the essays that would form this book, it became fairly clear that many of them were in gross violation of Godwin's Law. It's pretty hard not to mention Nazis and Hitler, at least by implication, when one's focus is a clearer understanding of fascism and how its essence remains alive in American society.

As someone whose reportage on many occasions has been on the subject of very real neo-Nazis, the idea that I'd lose an argument just by writing factually about the undercurrents they represent is nonsensical. For that matter, I've always viewed Godwin's Law as symptomatic of the larger problem I hoped to confront in this book: namely, an almost frightened refusal by most Americans, right and left, to come to grips with the meaning of fascism, and how that blind spot renders us vulnerable to it.

When I first began seriously studying fascism some years back, one of the first things that struck me was how little I—or anyone I knew—actually understood what it meant, in spite of the fact that, alongside communism, it was one of the two major political phenomena of the 20th century that the American system was forced to confront and defeat. Virtually every educated person I know (and many less-educated people as well) has a relatively clear and at least semi-informed understanding of communism, its origins, the basic tenets of its ideology. Moreover, wariness of communist influence is a virtual byword of the American worldview.

In contrast, hardly anyone I know understands just what fascism is. At best, most people vaguely comprehend it as a kind of heinous totalitarianism, identified specifically with Nazi Germany and the Holocaust; they also know a great deal of racial hatred and anti-Semitism was thrown into the mix. There is, however, confusion about its ideological orientation, embodied in the now-common conservative canard that "Hitler was a socialist." Expressions of this confusion are often flung about—now mostly by leftists and thoughtless liberals, but in the past decade by conservatives, too— as a catch-all term for totalitarianism, or worse yet, as a substitute for "police state" (which is not the same as fascism).

Hardly anyone can identify any tenets of fascism; most of the time it is understood largely as the extrinsic imposition of a totalitarian power fueled by virulent hatred and violence, and enabled by such influences as propaganda and "brainwashing." This model, however, is faulty; more accurately, totalitarianism of all stripes arises when certain ideologies and movements create large followings behind personalities configured by "totalist" or "authoritarian" predispositions. That is to say, fascism cannot be imposed from without unless there is concession within; its audience is not a blank slate, but rather people who willingly join in. Fascism, when it is successful, is always a popular movement.

Fascism's lack of an ideological core or easily recognizable signifiers (beyond, of course, such images from fully developed fascism as goose-stepping storm troopers and mass rallies) is a large part of the reason it's so little understood. This amorphousness also derives from the fact that although fascism arose only in the 20th century as a political force, its political strains have deep historic (perhaps even prehistoric) roots, which continue to be with us.

And it is this fact—that even though we think of fascism as a distant and unlikely threat, it sits at our elbows and dines at our tables even today—that makes a realistic discussion of fascism such an uncomfortable thing. The very threads that combine to make a fascist weave are part of the everyday fabric of our own lives.

It's much easier to declare an argument over whenever the issue of fascism arises than to confront the possibility that it lives on, even in a democratic society that we have come fondly to think of as immune from such a disease.

At the same time, I approve of the sentiment that accompanies Godwin's Law. In today's context, Nazism specifically and fascism generally are most often cited by partisans of both sides without reference to their actual contents. This is knee-jerk half-thought. Such a reflexive, ill-informed, or inappropriate reference—which describes the bulk of them—should suffice to invalidate any argument.

Without question the worst offenders are those on the Left. Back in the 1960s, antiwar radicals came to refer to anyone from the Establishment as "fascist," particularly if they were from the police. This bled over into the subsequent view that identified fascism with a police state. The confusion is alive and well today with peace marchers who blithely identify Bush with Hitler and compare Republicans to Nazis. The purpose of these analogies is to shame conservatives, but instead they give their perpetrators the appearance of shrill harpies willing to abuse the memory of the Holocaust for cheap political theater.

Robert Paxton discussed this when examining the term's overuse, by which it has become "the most banal of epithets":

> Everyone is someone's fascist. Consider Rush Limbaugh's "feminazis." A couple of summers ago, I heard a young German call Western-sponsored birth control programs in the Third World "fascist," forgetting that the Nazis and Italian fascists were, for

once, agreed in encouraging large families—except, of course,
among those considered either eugenically or racially inferior.
Those people were condemned to sterilization, if not worse. The
term "fascist" has been so loosely used that some have proposed
giving it up altogether in scholarly research.

Nevertheless, we cannot give up in the face of these difficulties. A real phenomenon exists. Indeed, fascism is the most
original political novelty of the twentieth century, no less. It
successfully gathered, against all expectation, in certain modern
nations that had seemed firmly planted on a path to gradually
expanding democracy, a popular following around hard, violent,
antiliberal and antisocialist nationalist dictatorships. Then
it spread its "politics in a new key" through much of Europe,
assembling all nationalists who hated the Left and found the
Right inadequate. . . . We must have a word, and for lack of a
better one, we must employ the word that Mussolini borrowed
from the vocabulary of the Italian Left in 1919, before his movement had assumed its mature form. Obliged to use the word
fascism, we ought to use it well.[9]

Inappropriate comparisons tend to obscure the reality of
what's taking place. The genuine proto-fascists—namely, the antidemocratic extremists of the Patriot movement—become identified with mainstream conservatives instead of being distinguished
from them. This is further complicated by the para-fascism practiced by movement conservatives, which makes fascist memes seem
normative. All this in turn gives their coalescence a cover instead
of exposing it.

The mainstream Left has been content to make jokes about the
stupidity of militiamen instead of recognizing the actual threat to
public discourse they represent. There has been little recognition of
the way the Far Right is able to insinuate its ideas and agendas into
the mainstream; indeed, the Left's generally superior, dismissive

attitude about right-wing extremists has only helped further their ability to penetrate the broader society.

No doubt, the degraded state of the word *fascism* is a large part of the reason the Left applies it willy-nilly to virtually anyone opposed to its agenda, in much the same way that the Right has debased the idea of communism. Fascism has become a black hole of a term instead of the red flag it should be, making it that much more difficult to recognize the genuine article when it sidles up alongside one.

Of course, as we have seen, liberals are hardly alone in abusing the term. Over the past decade, such abuse has become fashionable among conservatives as well; indeed, the Hitler/Nazi comparisons were particularly rampant in the identifiably proto-fascist elements of the Far Right during the 1990s, when they frequently compared Clinton to Hitler and government workers to Nazi storm troopers. Likewise, the fascism comparisons have crept into mainstream conservative rhetoric—particularly by the Rush Limbaugh and Freeper crowds, and immortalized in Jonah Goldberg's *Liberal Fascism*—as part of the attempt to paint liberal America as an oppressive police state.

In the end, this Newspeak—and its underlying eliminationism—is about naming the Enemy. For the Right, the Enemy is anyone who is Not Us. This naming is an enterprise doomed to descend into a downward and destructive spiral. Too often, those who have found themselves labeled Not Us have played into the dynamic rather than recognizing it for what it is. Escaping the spiral means refusing to become part of it.

A couple of weeks after Jim David Adkisson walked into that Knoxville church and began firing a shotgun, the Rev. Chris Buice addressed his traumatized congregation:

Some have suggested that his spiritual attitudes, his hatred of liberals and gays, was reinforced by the right-wing media figures. And it is beyond dispute that there is a plethora of books that have labeled liberals as evil, unpatriotic, godless, and treasonous.

One book has the title: *Deliver Us from Evil: Defeating Terrorism, Despotism, and Liberalism*. If that author were here in this room right now, I would introduce him to some good liberals who acted decisively on that Sunday, acted quickly and courageously to stop the terror that came into our church building. I would introduce him to some good liberals who know how to fight terror with more than just their mouths.[10]

Indeed, the men who stepped up to save the rest of the Tennessee Universal Unitarian congregation that sunny Sunday were heroic in the best sense: self-sacrificing, swift, and certain. In the process, they stopped Adkisson's rampage with only their bodies and their limbs, and no one was harmed beyond the immediate victims of his first shotgun blasts. Adkisson had envisioned firing until all 76 rounds were gone; because of their swift action, he managed to fire off only three.

It was a classic example of how progressives who believe in nonviolence and free speech can respond not merely to violence itself but to the voices of intolerance who inspire it: by remaining firm and strong and unmistakable, but true to their principles. The nature of the beast they must confront, however, poses a dilemma in that its very existence is a negation of those principles.

"I believe in rigorous debate," Buice later told the Knoxville *News-Sentinel*. "But what's the difference between a political opponent and a cockroach? You stomp a cockroach. You debate a political opponent. I believe, if you truly listen to your opponent, it will make you better."[11]

However, as Buice and his congregation learned, debate is a

moot point when someone has decided that you are the Enemy. Jim David Adkisson had named his congregation the Enemy; he believed that "all liberals should be killed," and set out to stomp them.

Naming the enemy, identifying him for purposes of elimination and purification, is the clear theme of all eliminationist rhetoric. It arises when a person takes the mantle of the hero upon his own shoulders; after all, a hero is nothing without an enemy. And so overcoming this cultural toxin means renouncing the attempt to claim the heroic role.

One of the best examinations of the mindset that relies on mythopoeic heroism can be found in sociologist James A. Aho's book *This Thing of Darkness: A Sociology of the Enemy*. Aho describes the symbiotic relationship between heroism and enemy-naming:

> The warrior needs an enemy. Without one there is nothing against which to fight, nothing from which to save the world, nothing to give his life meaning. What this means, of course, is that if an enemy is not ontologically present in the nature of things, one must be manufactured. The Nazi needs an international Jewish banker and conspiratorial Mason to serve his purposes of self-aggrandizement, and thus sets about creating one, at least unconsciously.[12]

Aho goes on to describe how the enemy is constructed in detail:

> Whether embodied in thing or in person, the enemy in essence represents putrefaction and death: either its instrumentality, its location (dirt, filth, garbage, excrement), its carriers (vermin, pests, bacilli), or all of these together. . . .
> The enemy typically is experienced as issuing from the

"dregs" of society, from its lower parts, the "bowels of the under-
world." It is sewage from the gutter, "trash" excreted as poison
from society's affairs—church, school, workplace, and family.[13]

This Thing of Darkness is an examination of right-wing extremism and the dynamic in the American body politic that creates it.
Aho's previous work, *The Politics of Righteousness: Idaho Christian*
·Patriotism (1991), was the first (and as far as I know, still the only)
serious sociological study of right-wing extremism that created a
substantive database of information about the beliefs and backgrounds of followers of the Aryan Nations and related Christian
Patriot groups. The later study, published in 1994, was an attempt
to come to terms with the dynamics underlying such cases as the
Weavers at Ruby Ridge and the murders of the Goldmark family.

Aho describes a dynamic latent in all sectors of American society but which finds a virulent expression in right-wing extremism.
In this dynamic, the two sides—the Far Right and their named
enemies, that is, Jews, civil-rights advocates, and the government—
essentially exchange roles in their respective perceptions; the self is
always heroic, the other always the enemy. Each sees the other as
the demonic enemy, feeding the other's fears and paranoia in an
increasingly threatening spiral that eventually breaks out in the
form of real violence.

Aho does, however, also argue for a way to escape this dynamic,
to break the cycle. And it requires, on the part of those seeking to
oppose this kind of extremism, a recognition of their own propensity to name the enemy and adopt the self-aggrandizing pose of the
hero:

> As Ernest Becker has convincingly shown, the call to heroism
> still resonates in modern hearts. However, we are in the habit of
> either equating heroism with celebrity ("TV Actress Tops List

of Students' Heroes") or caricaturing the hero as a bluff-and-swagger patriot/soldier making the world safe for, say, Christian democracy. In these ways heroism is portrayed as a rather happy if not entirely risk-free venture that earns one public plaudits. Today we are asked to learn that, in the deepest and truest sense. Heroism is really none of these things, but a largely private vocation requiring stamina, discipline, responsibility, and above all courage. Not just the ascetic courage to cleanse our personal lives of what we have been taught is filth, or even less to cleanse society of the alleged carriers of this filth, but, as Jung displayed, the fortitude to release our claim on moral purity and perfection. At a personal and cultural level, I believe this is the only way to transcend the logic of enemies.[14]

For all of its logic and love of science, a consistent flaw weighs down modern liberalism: an overweening belief in its own moral superiority. (Not, of course, that conservatives are any better in this regard; factoring in the religious Right and the "moral values" vote, they are objectively worse.) This tendency becomes especially noticeable in urban liberal societies, which for all their enlightenment and love of tolerance are maddeningly and disturbingly intolerant of the "ignorance" of their rural counterparts. This is not an omnipresent attitude, but it is pervasive enough that rural dwellers' perceptions of it are certainly not without basis. There's a similar stigma attached to religious believers as well, especially among the more secular liberals, and that, in turn, has given birth to a predictable counterreaction that is only partially informed by misunderstanding.

If we want to look at all those red counties and come to terms with the reasons the people there think and vote they way they do, it's important to come to terms with our own prejudices, our own willingness to treat our fellow Americans—the ones who are not like us—with contempt and disrespect.

I am not suggesting that we respond to such provocations with touchy-feely attempts at "reaching out" to the other side; these are always rejected with contempt, or viewed as a sign of weakness. Indeed, it's an absolute imperative to fight back, especially when threats and intimidations arise. But if progressives want to. win, they need to break this dynamic; and to do that, a little self-reflection will go a long way.

Respecting people from rural areas or the exurbs and suburbs, or those who hold deep religious beliefs, doesn't force progressives to compromise their own beliefs or standards. It simply means accepting being part of a democracy that is enriched by diversity of all kinds. Certainly, traditional rural values should have a place among all that diversity that liberals are fond of celebrating. Because until those liberals learn to accord it that respect, they are doomed to remain trapped in the vicious cycle being fueled on both sides. Conservatives will also have no incentive to escape that cycle. For liberals, escaping it may be a matter of simple survival—especially if the rabid Right's eliminationist fantasies ever start coming to life.

In the end, we cannot prevent fascism from happening here by pretending it is something it is not; it must be confronted directly and straightforwardly, or it will not be confronted at all. Yet, at the same time, those who are the targets of its eliminationist bile must resist the temptation to wield this recognition like a cudgel. We cannot dehumanize and demonize those who have fallen under its sway. And we cannot stop the forces of hate by indulging it ourselves.

Escaping the downward spiral of eliminationism means seeing those who indulge it as human beings, as our fellow Americans—affording them the very recognition they would deny us. We must rely on the force of persuasion and not the persuasion of force. If we are serious about defending democracy without betraying its beating heart, we have no other choice.

Notes

Introduction

1. Text taken from image of bumper sticker at www.leftinsf.com/blog/2005/06/one-busy-fascist.html. Accessed June 28, 2005.

2. J. J. Stambaugh, "Takedown of alleged shooter recounted," *Knoxville News Sentinel,* July 29, 2008.

3. Hayes Hickman and Don Jacobs, "Suspect's note cites 'liberal movement' for church attack," *Knoxville News Sentinel,* July 29, 2008.

4. Katie Allison Granju, "Timeline: Church service marred by gun fire," WBIR.com, July 28, 2008, www.wbir.com/news/local/story.aspx?storyid=61322&provider=top.

5. The entire manifesto can be read online at http://web.knoxnews.com/pdf/021009church-manifesto.pdf.

6. "Rage on the Radio," *Bill Moyers' Journal,* September 12, 2008, www.pbs.org/moyers/journal/09122008/watch.html.

7. Michael D. Shear, "McCain plans fiercer strategy against Obama," *Washington Post,* October 4, 2008, A01.

8. Andrew M. Seder, "Secret Service says "Kill him" allegation unfounded," Wilkes-Barre *Times-Leader,* October 17, 2008.

9. The video, shot by a news crew from Al Jazeera English, is available online at www.youtube.com/watch?v=zRqcfqiXCX0.

10. Josh, "Hate you can believe in: ACORN deluged with threatening and racist voicemails and emails," RightWingWatch.com, October 18, 2008, http://rightwingwatch.org/content/hate-you-can-believe-acorn-deluged-threatening-and-racist-voicemails-and-emails.

11. Heather Rutz, "Families speak out about Obama vandalism," LimaOhio.com, October 8, 2008, www.limaohio.com/news/obama_29162___article.html/vandalism_someone.html.

12. KPVI-TV, "Police investigate after swastika painted on Obama

yard sign," October 22, 2008, www.ktvb.com/news/localnews/stories/ktvbn-oct2208-obama_sign_swastika.13b27f31f.html.

13. Woody Baird and Andrew DeMillo, "Officials: Alleged skinhead plot not fully formed," Associated Press, October 29, 2008.

14. Patrick Jonsson, "After Obama's win, white backlash festers in US," *Christian Science Monitor,* November 17, 2008, www.csmonitor.com/2008/1117/p03s01-uspo.html.

15. Fred Henning's account of this incident, "Terroristic Threats," at the American Street, February 11, 2004, www.reachm.com/amstreet/archives/2004/02/11/terroristic-threats/.

16. Burke's account of the incident is online at his blog, http://weblogs.swarthmore.edu/burke/?p=439.

17. Douglas Belkin "Professor, recruiter face off at UMass," *Boston Globe,* April 4, 2003, www.commondreams.org/cgi-bin/print.cgi?file=/headlines03/0404-04.htm. See also Kristen Lombardi, "Climate of fear," *Boston Phoenix,* July 25, 2003, http://72.166.46.24/boston/news_features/top/features/documents/03044184.asp. See also "Follow-up: Charges dropped against UMass professor," *Boston Phoenix,* December 19, 2003, http://72.166.46.24/boston/news_features/this_just_in/documents/03435306.asp.

18. A word about Goldhagen: In the ensuing academic debate over his thesis, I found myself largely persuaded by the Christopher Browning camp, which doubted that "eliminationist antisemitism" was quite as pervasive as Goldhagen portrayed it, and, moreover, that it was as unique to Germany as he described it. Having some familiarity with the history of American eliminationism (particularly the lynching era and the Ku Klux Klan, as well as the "Yellow Peril" agitation and the subsequent internment of Japanese Americans during World War II), I agreed especially with the latter point.

19. Daniel Jonah Goldhagen, *Hitler's Willing Executioners: Ordinary Germans and the Holocaust* (New York: Alfred A. Knopf, 1996), 69.

20. For more on palingenesis and fascism, see Roger Griffin, *The Nature of Fascism* (London: Routledge, 1991). This will be discussed in much greater detail in chapters 6, 7, and 10.

21. David Neiwert, *Strawberry Days: How Internment Destroyed a Japanese American Community* (New York: Palgrave Macmillan, 2005).

22. Available online at www.amarillo.com/stories/120303/opi_letters.shtml.

23. Pawlik has since deleted the post from her site (www.amber pawlik.com/Rants.html), but a contemporaneous copy can be found at http://dneiwert.blogspot.com/2004/06/hate-these-days.html.

24. Available online at http://markbyron.typepad.com/ main/2003/11/the_usefulness__1.html.

25. Available online at www.humanevents.com/article.php?id= 5652.

26. Available online at www.gdnctr.com/july_30_04.htm.

27. This quote formerly appeared on Limbaugh's Web site but has since been removed. A similar version was reported in the *Denver Post,* December 29, 1995.

28. George Curley, "Coultergeist," *New York Observer,* August 26, 2002, www.observer.com/pages/story.asp?ID=6258.

29. Bill O'Reilly, *The Radio Factor with Bill O'Reilly,* June 20, 2005. Transcript available at http://mediamatters.org/items/ printable/200506220006.

30. Michael Reagan, *The Michael Reagan Show,* June 10, 2008. Transcript and audio file available at www.fair.org/index.php? page=3552.

31. Michael Barone, "Our Covert Enemies," Townhall.com, August 21, 2006. http://townhall.com/columnists/MichaelBarone/ 2006/08/21/our_covert_enemies.

32. Dinesh D'Souza, *The Enemy at Home: The Cultural Left and Its Responsibility for 9/11* (New York: Doubleday, 2007), 292.

33. David Horowitz, "The NY Times points cranks, radicals, al-Qaeda operatives and would be assassins to the summer homes of Cheney and Rumsfeld," *FrontPage Magazine,* June 30, 2006, www .frontpagemag.com/blog/Read.aspx?GUID=EC8A9F0D-EBE6-4FA0-8F5F-04B7057A5BD3.

34. Kathleen Parker, "Politics are out in a time of war," *Orlando Sentinel,* November 2, 2003.

35. CNN, "9/11 Commissioner: I've received threats," April 23, 2004, www.cnn.com/2004/US/04/17/gorelick.threats/.

36. Jamie Gorelick, "The truth about 'the wall,'" *Washington Post,* April 18, 2004.

37. Rush Limbaugh, *The Rush Limbaugh Show,* August 9, 2004. Transcript available at http://mediamatters.org/items/200508110001.

38. Dick Morris, *Hannity and Colmes,* Fox News, April 14, 2004.

39. Reuters, "California man arrested for mail threats to celebri-

ties," *Reuters Newswire,* November 13, 2006, www.reuters.com/article/
entertainmentNews/idUSN1240171820061114.

40. Michelle Malkin, *Unhinged: Exposing Liberals Gone Wild*
(Washington: Regnery, 2005).

Chapter 1

1. James A. Aho, *The Politics of Righteousness: Idaho Christian
Patriotism* (Seattle: University of Washington Press, 1990), 160–61.
2. Ibid., 219–20.

Chapter 2

1. The transcript of this broadcast does not appear to exist; the
above paraphrasing is taken from my notes.
2. William J. Clinton, "Remarks to the American Association of
Community Colleges in Minneapolis, Minnesota," April 24, 1995,
www.presidency.ucsb.edu/ws/print.php?pid=51270.
3. Charley Reese, "Clinton Exhibits All the Classic Symptoms of
the Sociopath He Is," *Orlando Sentinel,* August 23, 1998.
4. Chip Berlet, "Clinton, Conspiracism, and Civil Society," Political
Research Associates, February 12, 1998, www.publiceye.org/conspire/
clinton_networks/networks.html.
5. Hamblin's Web site disappeared after he abruptly left radio in a
2003 contract dispute with his syndicate. See http://freerepublic.com.
6. Chip Berlet, interview with author, June 1998.

Chapter 3

1. Thomas Edsall, "Lott decried for part of salute to Thurmond,"
Washington Post, December 7, 2002, A6; www.washingtonpost.com/ac2/
wp-dyn?pagename=article&node=&contentId=A20730-2002Dec6.
2. Southern Poverty Law Center, "Sharks in the mainstream: Racism underlies influential 'conservative' group," *Intelligence Report,* Winter 1999, www.splcenter.org/intel/intelreport/article.jsp?aid=360.
3. Thomas B. Edsall, "Lott renounces white 'racialist' group he
praised in 1992," *Washington Post,* December 16, 1998.
4. David Firestone, "A dealing with David Duke haunts Louisiana
governor," *New York Times,* June 22, 1999, http://query.nytimes.com/
gst/fullpage.html?res=9E01E6D8113BF931A15755C0A96F958260.

5. John Gizzi, "Sen. Smith ends bid for taxpayers' nod," *Human Events,* August 27, 1999.

6. Timothy Egan, "Terror in Oklahoma: In Congress; Trying to explain contacts with paramilitary groups," *New York Times,* May 2, 1995.

7. Eric Forman, "Ron Paul on Guns, Money and the New World Order," *Conspiracy Planet* interview, February 23, 2004, www .conspiracyplanet.com/channel.cfm?channelid=90&contentid=1659.

8. David Holthouse, "Arizona showdown: High-powered firearms, militia maneuvers and racism at the Minuteman Project," *Intelligence Report* (Southern Poverty Law Center), Summer 2005.

9. Max Blumenthal and David Neiwert, "Meet Sarah Palin's radical right-wing pals," *Salon.com,* October 10, 2008, www.salon.com/news/ feature/2008/10/10/palin_chryson/index.html.

10. CNN, "Should James Traficant Join the Republican Party?" *Crossfire,* January 4, 2001. Transcript online at http://transcripts.cnn .com/TRANSCRIPTS/0101/04/cf.00.html.

11. Jerry Cornfield, "Former lawmaker Ellen Craswell dies at 75," *Everett Herald,* April 8, 2008.

12. Chip Berlet, "Into the mainstream: An array of right-wing foundations and think tanks support efforts to make bigoted and discredited ideas respectable," *Intelligence Report* (Southern Poverty Law Center), Summer 2003.

13. Martin Durham, *The Christian Right, the Far Right and the Boundaries of American Conservatism* (Manchester: Manchester University Press, 2000), 117–19.

14. John Sugg, "A nation under God," *Mother Jones,* December 2005.

15. Mary Bruce, "McCain admits Hagee endorsement was a mistake," ABC News, April 20, 2008, http://blogs.abcnews.com/politicalradar/2008/04/mccain-admits-h.html.

16. CNN, "Gibson: 'I am not an anti-Semite'," August 2, 2006, www.cnn.com/2006/SHOWBIZ/Movies/08/01/gibson.dui/index. html.

17. Marcello A. Canuto, "Maya in the Thunderdome," *Salon.com,* December 15, 2006, www.salon.com/ent/feature/2006/12/15/maya/ .Kurt Loder, "Mel Gibson tells some brutal truths about the amazing 'Apocalypto,'" MTV News, www.mtv.com/movies/news/articles/ 1548104/20061214/story.jhtml.

18. Ann Coulter, "This Is War," *National Review,* September 13, 2001.

19. Melik Kaylan, "Dr. Johnson, meet Ann Coulter!," *Wall Street Journal,* August 31, 2002.

20. Max Blumenthal, "The Demons of David Horowitz," *Huffington Post,* April 26, 2006, www.huffingtonpost.com/max-blumenthal/the-demons-of-david-horow_b_19827.html.

21. Howard Kurtz and Dan Balz, "Clinton assails spread of hate through media; Americans urged to stand against 'reckless speech'; conservatives take offense," *Washington Post,* April 25, 1995.

22. Associated Press, "MSNBC fires Michael Savage after anti-gay comments," July 7, 2003.

23. Michael Savage, *Savage Nation,* December 31, 2005. Transcript at http://mediamatters.org/items/200501050006.

24. David Gilson, "Michael Savage's long, strange trip," *Salon.com,* March 5, 2003, http://dir.salon.com/story/news/feature/2003/03/05/savage/.

25. *Fox Report,* Fox News, February 21, 2001.

26. *Hannity and Colmes,* Fox News, July 1, 2001.

27. Michael L. Betsch, "Anti-tax group makes 'final warning' to federal government," CNSNews.com, November 16, 2002.

28. Elizabeth Schwinn, "Justice Dept. sues tax-protesting charity," MSNBC.com, April 16, 2007, www.msnbc.msn.com/id/18096539/.

29. "Oklahoma City blast linked to bin Laden," *WorldNetDaily,* March 21, 2001, www.worldnetdaily.com/news/article.asp?ARTICLE_ID=22122.

30. *The O'Reilly Factor,* Fox News, May 7, 2001.

31. Peter Hart, "O'Reilly's war," FAIR *Extra!,* May/June 2003.

32. Donna Ladd, "Conservatives, white supremacists, take to Florida streets," *Village Voice,* November 15, 2000. "Protesters on both sides rally," *Fox News,* Saturday, November 25, 2000.

33. See Lucy Williams, "Decades of distortion: The Right's 30-year assault on welfare," Political Research Associates report, December 1997, http://ajilan.pair.com/pra/welfare/Decades-of-Distortion.html.

34. *Wall Street Journal,* March 4, 1994. See also Carol Jouzaitis, "From the folks who brought you Willie Horton, here's Whitewater," Chicago Tribune, March 27, 1994.

35. Heidi Beirich and Bob Moser, "Defending Dixie," *Intelligence Report* (Southern Poverty Law Center), Summer 2003.

Chapter 4

1. Dick Anthony and Thomas Robbins, "Religious Totalism, Violence and Exemplary Dualism: Beyond the Extrinsic Model," in *Millennialism and Violence*, ed. Michael Barkun (London: Frank Cass, 1995), 30–31.

2. Michelle Goldberg, "Shock troops for Bush," *Salon.com*, Feb. 4, 2003, http://dir.salon.com/story/news/feature/2003/02/04/cpac/index.html.

3. Ibid.

4. David Frum, *The Right Man: The Surprise Presidency of George W. Bush* (New York: Random House, 2003), 148.

5. Sinclair Lewis, *It Can't Happen Here* (New York: Signet Classics, 1993).

6. Robert O. Paxton, "The five stages of fascism," *Journal of Modern History* 70 (March 1998): 3–5.

7. Anti-Defamation League of B'nai B'rith, "The Franklin 'Prophecy': Modern anti-Semitic myth making," *Facts*, April–May 1954.

8. "Fascism in America: A cell in Chehalis," and "Seattle hears a Silver Shirt 'isms' lecture," *Life*, March 6, 1939, 62–63.

9. Karen E. Hoppes, "An Investigation of the Nazi-Fascist Spectrum in the Pacific Northwest: 1924–1941" (Master's Thesis, Western Oregon State College, 1983), 10–12.

10. Ibid., 12.

11. Daniel Levitas, *The Terrorist Next Door: The Militia Movement and the Radical Right* (New York: Thomas Dunne Books/St. Martin's Press, 2002).

12. Jeffrey Gettleman and David M. Halbfinger, "Suspect in '96 Olympic bombing and 3 other attacks is caught," *New York Times*, June 1, 2003.

13. Alan Cooperman, "Is terrorism tied to Christian sect?" *Washington Post*, June 2, 2003.

14. Andrew Blejwas, Anthony Griggs, and Mark Potok, "Terror from the right," *Intelligence Report* (Southern Poverty Law Center), Summer 2005.

15. See the case of Clayton Lee Waagner, who was convicted in 2002 of sending more than 280 letters laced with powder and claiming the powder was anthrax to a variety of Planned Parenthood clinics and other abortion providers throughout the United States. These letters

were sent in the wake of the real anthrax letter attacks that occurred September through November 2001.

Chapter 5

1. Gene Owens, "Bush talks to friends off the cuff," *Mobile Register,* February 28, 2003

2. Black's Stormfront.org Web site is considered the most successful white-nationalist site on the Internet, with over 30,000 daily readers. For more on Black, see T. K. Kim, "Radical Storm," *Intelligence Report* (Southern Poverty Law Center), Summer 2005, www.splcenter.org/intel/intelreport/article.jsp?pid=908. Hale is currently serving a term in federal prison for soliciting the assassination of a federal judge. For more on Hale, see "Matthew Hale gets maximum 40-year sentence," *Intelligence Report* (Southern Poverty Law Center), April 7, 2005, www.splcenter.org/intel/news/item.jsp?site_area=1&aid=102.

3. Keith Bradsher, "Citing declining membership, a leader disbands his militia," *New York Times,* April 30, 2001.

4. Matt Bai, "Wiring the vast left-wing conspiracy," *New York Times,* July 25, 2004.

Chapter 6

1. See Jonah Goldberg, Liberal Fascism: *The Secret History of the American Left, from Mussolini to the Politics of Meaning* (New York: Doubleday, 2008), 23.

2. Giovanni Gentile, "La dottrina del fascism," in Benito Mussolini, *Fascism: Doctrine and Institutions* (Rome: Ardita Publishers, 1935).

3. Cited in Roger Griffin, "Paper tiger or Cheshire cat? A spotter's guide to fascism in the post-fascist era," *Searchlight,* November 2002.

4. Stanley Payne, *Fascism: Comparison and Definition* (Madison: University of Wisconsin Press, 1980), 7.

5. Roger Griffin, *Fascism* (Oxford: Oxford University Press, 1995).

6. Robert O. Paxton, *The Anatomy of Fascism* (New York: Alfred A. Knopf, 2004), 3.

7. Emilio Gentile, "Fascism, Totalitarianism and Political Religion: Definitions and Critical Reflections on Criticism of an Interpretation," *Fascism, Totalitarian and Political Religion,* ed. Roger Griffin (London: Routledge, 2006), 70.

8. Robert O. Paxton, "The five stages of fascism," *Journal of Modern History* 70 (March 1998), 5.

9. Ibid., 11.

10. Milton Mayer, *They Thought They Were Free: The Germans, 1933–45* (Chicago: University of Chicago Press, 1966), 111.

11. Paxton, *Anatomy*, 41.

12. Mike Soraghan, "Westmoreland calls Obama 'uppity,'" *The Hill*, September 4, 2008.

13. Antonin Scalia, "God's Justice and Ours," *First Things*, May 2002, www.firstthings.com/article.php3?id_article=2022.

14. Paxton, *Anatomy*, 49.

15. David M. Chalmers, *Hooded Americanism: The History of the Ku Klux Klan* (Durham: Duke University Press, 1981), 425. (italics added)

16. Ibid., 32–33.

17. Ibid., 33.

18. Philip Dray, *At the Hands of Persons Unknown: The Lynching of Black America* (New York: Random House, 2002), 276.

19. Sara Bullard, *The Ku Klux Klan: A History of Racism & Violence* (Montgomery, AL: Southern Poverty Law Center, 1996), 20.

20. Chalmers, *Hooded Americanism*, 200.

21. This claim had only a modicum of merit. It is true that there was a close similarity to the Klan salute devised in 1915 and that adopted by the fascists in the early 1920s and made famous by Hitler's storm troopers in the 1930s. However, there were also some differences. The Klan salute was off at a slight angle, was more relaxed, and featured the fingers splayed. Moreover, Mussolini reportedly claimed to have taken the fascists' salute from that used by ancient Romans, which is somewhat credible as well. In any case, the evidence suggests that Hitler borrowed the salute from his Italian counterparts, not from the Klan.

22. Chalmers, *Hooded Americanism*, 321–23.

23. Paxton, "The Five Stages of Fascism," 11.

24. Paxton, *Anatomy*, 23.

25. Paxton, "The Five Stages of Fascism," 13–14.

Chapter 7

1. Andrew Blejwas, Anthony Griggs, and Mark Potok, "Terror from the Right," *Intelligence Report* (Southern Poverty Law Center), Summer 2005.

2. Roger Griffin, "Paper tiger or Cheshire cat? A spotter's guide to fascism in the post-fascist era," *Searchlight,* November 2002.

3. David Neiwert, "The fence to nowhere," *American Prospect,* September 2008, 16–19.

4. Paxton, Anatomy, 16.

5. Ibid., 17.

6. See James Pinkerton, "The Devil is in the details: Another Obama connection you ought to know about," *Fox News Forum,* October 23, 2008, http://foxforum.blogs.foxnews.com/2008/10/23/jpinkerton_1023/.

7. FoxNews Chicago, "KKK warns of death threat against Obama," May 21, 2007, www.myfoxchicago.com/myfox/pages/Home/Detail; jsessionid=642F12A3869C62E309DE43C21046E7D4?contentId=3271179&version=4&locale=EN-US&layoutCode=VSTY&pageId=1.1.1.

8. Associated Press, "Feds: Alleged Pa. bomb-maker wanted Clinton, Obama dead," *Daily Item* (Sunbury, PA), June 11, 2008, www.dailyitem.com/panews/local_story_163061948.html.

9. Heidi Beirich and Mark Potok, "Silver lining: Not all white supremacists oppose black president," *Intelligence Report* (Southern Poverty Law Center), Fall 2008.

10. Ibid.

11. Charles S. Milliken, Jennifer L. Auchterlonie, Charles W. Hoge, "Longitudinal assessment of mental health problems among active and reserve component soldiers returning from the Iraq war," *Journal of the American Medical Association* 298, no. 18 (2007): 2141–48

12. For more on "dolchstosslegende"—the "stabbed in the back" legend—and its role in fascist movements, as well as in American right-wing movements, see Kevin Baker, "Stabbed in the back! The past and future of a right-wing myth," *Harper's,* June 2006, www.harpers.org/archive/2006/06/0081080.

13. David Holthouse, "A few bad men," *Intelligence Report* (Southern Poverty Law Center), July 7, 2006.

14. Federal Bureau of Investigation, "White Supremacist recruitment of military personnel since 9/11," *Intelligence Assessment,* July 7, 2008, 4–11

Chapter 8

1. Glenn Beck, *The Glenn Beck Program,* August 10, 2006. Transcript available at http://mediamatters.org/items/200608100016. (italics added)

2. Bernd Debusmann, "In U.S., fear and distrust of Muslims runs deep," Reuters, December 1, 2006, http://pewforum.org/news/display.php?NewsID=12045.

3. Jared Diamond, "The Arrow of Disease," *Discover,* October 1992, 64–73.

4. E. R. G. Robertson, *Rotting Face: Smallpox and the American Indian* (Caldwell, ID: Caxton Press, 2001), 119.

5. David E. Stannard, *American Holocaust: The Conquest of the New World* (New York: Oxford University Press, 1992), 210–11.

6. Charles M. Segal and David C. Stineback, *Puritans, Indians, and Manifest Destiny* (New York: Putnam, 1997), 134–35.

7. Richard Drinnon, *Facing West: The Metaphysics of Indian-Hating and Empire Building* (Norman: University of Oklahoma Press, 1997), 56, 99.

8. Robert J. Miller, *Native America, Discovered and Conquered: Thomas Jefferson, Lewis & Clark, and Manifest Destiny* (Westport, CT: Greenwood Publishing Group, 2006), 85.

9. Dee Brown, *Bury My Heart at Wounded Knee: An Indian History of the American West* (London: Vintage, 1991), 448.

10. David R. Montgomery, *King of Fish: The Thousand-Year Run of Salmon* (Boulder, CO: Westview Press, 2003), 105.

11. Thoedora Kroeber, *Ishi: In Two Worlds* (Berkeley: University of California Press, 1961), 64.

12. Ibid., 66–75.

13. Stannard, *American Holocaust,* 129–30.

14. Brown, *Bury My Heart at Wounded Knee,* 74–86.

15. Stannard, *American Holocaust,* 133–34.

16. James Welch, *Killing Custer: The Battle of the Little Bighorn and the Fate of the Plains Indians* (New York: W. W. Norton, 1994), 25–37.

17. Brown, *Bury My Heart at Wounded Knee,* 166.

18. Welch, *Killing Custer,* 149–97. See also Evan S. Connell, *Son of the Morning Star: Custer and the Little Bighorn* (New York: North Point Press, 1984).

19. Alvin M. Josephy, *The Nez Perce Indians and the Opening of the Northwest* (New York: Mariner, 1965), 573–633

20. Brown, *Bury My Heart at Wounded Knee,* 390–418.

21. Dennis McAuliffe, *The Deaths of Sybil Bolton: An American History* (New York: Crown, 1994).

22. Kroeber, *Ishi,* 64.

23. Stannard, *American Holocaust,* 81–95.

24. Philp Dray, *At the Hands of Persons Unknown: The Lynching of Black America* (New York: Random House, 2002), 32–47.

25. Francis B. Simkins, "The Klux Klan in South Carolina, 1868-1871," *Journal of Negro History,* XII (1927), 618.

26. Chalmers, *Hooded Americanism,* 16.

27. Dray, *At the Hands of Persons Unknown,* 116–137.

28. Edward A. Malone, *Lynching Statistics by State and Race, 1882–1968,* February 1979, provided by the Archives at Tuskegee Institute, www.law.umkc.edu/faculty/projects/ftrials/shipp/lynchingsstate.html.

29. Dray, *At the Hands of Persons Unknown,* 72.

30. Alfred L. Brophy and Randall Kennedy, *Reconstructing the Dreamland: The Tulsa Riot of 1921: Race, Reparations, and Reconciliation* (Oxford: Oxford University Press, 2003).

31. James Loewen, *Sundown Towns: A Hidden Dimension of American Racism* (New York: New Press, 2005).

32. Ibid., 28–30.

33. Ibid., 5.

34. Ibid., 30.

35. Ibid., 37–38.

36. Donald L. Horowitz, *The Deadly Ethnic Riot* (Berkeley: University of California Press, 2003).

37. Loewen, *Sundown Towns,* 112–13.

38. Andrew Wiese, *Places of Their Own: African American Suburbanization in the Twentieth Century* (Chicago: University of Chicago Press, 2003).

39. Craig Storti, *Incident at Bitter Creek: The Story of the Rock Springs Chinese Massacre* (Ames: Iowa State Press, 1990).

40. Elmer Clarence Sandmeyer, *The Anti-Chinese Movement in California* (Urbana: University of Illinois Press, 1991), 25–39.

41. Roger Daniels, *The Politics of Prejudice: The Anti-Japanese Movement in California and the Struggle for Japanese Exclusion* (Berkeley: University of California Press, 1962), 17.

42. Sandmeyer, *The Anti-Chinese Movement*, 97–98.

43. Daniels, *The Politics of Prejudice*, 20.

44. Stan Flewelling, *Shirakawa: Stories from a Northwest Japanese American Community* (Auburn, CA: White River Valley Historical Society, 2002), 22–25.

45. *San Francisco Chronicle*, May 8, 1900.

46. Daniels, *The Politics of Prejudice*, 27–28.

47. Ibid., 46–64.

48. "Deport Japanese: Demanded by Secretary of Veterans' Commission," *Seattle Star*, July 26, 1919, A1.

49. Miller Freeman, "The Japanese question," from *The Great Northern Daily News of Seattle*, a Japanese-American newspaper, January 25, 1921, Miller Freeman Archives, University of Washington.

50. "Deport Japanese," *Seattle Star*, July 26, 1919.

51. "Civic mass meeting protests Jap menace," *Seattle Star*, August 12, 1919, A1.

52. David Neiwert, *Strawberry Days: How Internment Destroyed a Japanese Community* (New York: Palgrave, 2005), 55–61.

53. "The Fight is on!" *Seattle Star*, August 14, 1919, A1.

54. Freeman, "The Japanese question."

55. "Whites try to buy them out at low price, say Japanese," *Seattle Times*, March 21, 1942, 12.

56. *Congressional Record*, February 26, 1942.

57. Henry McLemore, "This is war! Stop worrying about hurting Jap feelings," *Seattle Times*, January 30, 1942.

58. *Congressional Record*, December 15, 1941.

59. Speech draft in Henry M. Jackson Archives, University of Washington Archives, 3560-2156/31.

60. *Time*, December 20, 1943. See also Audrie Girdner and Annie Loftis, *The Great Betrayal: The Evacuation of Japanese-Americans During World War II* (London: The Macmillan Company, 1969), 361.

Chapter 9

1. Steve Hendricks, *The Unquiet Grave: The FBI and the Struggle for the Soul of Indian Country* (New York: Thunders Mouth Press, 2006).

2. Charles Mudede, "How Tacoma fought Seattle for the future and lost," *Stranger*, August 10, 2000, www.thestranger.com/seattle/Content?oid=4609.

3. See, for example, Bill Bennett's election-night suggestion on CNN that "You don't take any excuses anymore from anybody who says, 'The deck is stacked, I can't do anything, there's so much in-built this and that,'" CNN Newsroom, Tuesday, November 4, 2008.

4. James Loewen, *Sundown Towns: A Hidden Dimension of American Racism* (New York: New Press, 2005), 374–375.

5. Bill O'Reilly, *The O'Reilly Factor,* May 16, 2006. Transcript available at http://mediamatters.org/items/200605170006.

6. John Gibson, *The Big Story,* May 11, 2006. Transcript available at http://mediamatters.org/items/200605120006.

7. David Duke, DavidDuke.org, cited in "David Duke: In His Own Words," Anti-Defamation League Report, May 2000, www.adl.org/special_reports/duke_own_words/on_immigration.asp.

8. Radaractive, "Illegal immigrants? Take the Buffalo approach!," April 13, 2006, http://radaractive.blogspot.com/2006/04/illegal-immigrants-take-buffalo.html.

9. Martin Buber, *I and Thou* (New York: Free Press, 1971).

10. David E. Stannard, *American Holocaust: The Conquest of the New World* (New York: Oxford University Press, 1992), 150.

11. David Holthouse, "Arizona Showdown," *Intelligence Report* (Southern Poverty Law Center), Summer 2005.

12. FBI Uniform Crime Reports: Hate Crime Statistics 2006, www.fbi.gov/ucr/hc2006/index.html.

13. William Kandel, John Cromartie, "Hispanics Find a Home in Rural America," *Amber Waves* (U.S. Department of Agriculture), February 2003.

14. Donald Green, interview with author, August 21, 2003. The study in question is Donald Green, Jack Glader, and Andrew Rich, "From lynching to gay-bashing: The elusive connection between economic conditions and hate crime," *Journal of Personality and Social Psychology* 75 (July 1998): 1–11, www.yale.edu/isps/publications/green1.pdf.

15. Ken Toole, interview with author, January 23, 2004.

16. Donald Green, interview with author, September 18, 2003.

17. Dana P. Goldman, James P. Smith and Neeraj Sood, "Immigrants and the cost of medical care," Health Affairs 25, no. 6 (2006): 1700–11.

18. Immigration Policy Center, "Assessing the Economic Impact of Immigration at the State and Local Level," April 17, 2008.

19. Eduardo Porter, "Illegal immigrants are bolstering Social Security with billions," *New York Times,* April 5, 2005.

20. Rakesh Kochhar, "Growth in the Foreign-Born Workforce and Employment of the Native Born," Pew Hispanic Center Report, August 10, 2006.

21. Shirin Hakimzadeh and D'Vera Cohn, "English Usage Among Hispanics in the United States," Pew Hispanic Center report, November 29, 2007; and "Hispanic Attitudes Toward Learning English," Pew Hispanic Center Fact Sheet, June 7, 2006.

22. Robert S. Leiken and Steven Brooke, *The Quantitative Analysis of Terrorism and Immigration: An Initial Exploration* (London: Routledge, 2006). The information here is included in the abstract, www.informaworld.com/smpp/content~content=a759220249~db=all.

23. Andrea Nill, "From Anecdotes to Evidence: Setting the Record Straight on Immigrants and Crime," Immigration Policy Center, September 10, 2008.

Chapter 10

1. Sinclair Lewis, *It Can't Happen Here* (New York: Signet Classics, 1993), 21–22.

2. Robert O. Paxton, *The Anatomy of Fascism* (New York: Alfred A. Knopf, 2004), 201–2.

3. Lawrence Dennis, *The Coming American Fascism* (New York: Harper and Brothers, 1936), ix, 257.

4. Paxton, *Anatomy,* 271–72.

5. Robert Jay Lifton, *Superpower Syndrome: America's Apocalyptic Confrontation with the World* (New York: Nation Books, 2003), 137.

6. Ibid., 146–47.

7. See the discussion of "Godwin's Law" at Usenet FAQs, www.faqs.org/faqs/usenet/legends/godwin/.

8. From the Public Domain Jargon File, http://catb.org/esr/jargon/html/G/Godwins-Law.html.

9. Robert O. Paxton, "The Five Stages of Fascism," *Journal of Modern History* 70 (March 1998), 7.

10. "Rage on the Radio," *Bill Moyers Journal,* PBS, September 12, 2008, www.pbs.org/moyers/journal/09122008/watch.html.

11. Hayes Hickman, "Pastor full of curiosity, doubt," *News Sentinel* (Knoxville, TN), August 7, 2008.

12. James A. Aho, *This Thing of Darkness: A Sociology of the Enemy* (Seattle: University of Washington Press, 1994), 26.

13. Ibid., 109.

14. Ibid., 182–83.

Index

Acknowledgments

This book was many years in the writing, compiled and built upon from work originally published at my blog, *Orcinus* (http://dneiwert.blogspot.com), which debuted in 2003. As such, it owes a great debt to the many readers I've had over the years, because their constant and consistent input—through comments, e-mails, and the usual blogospheric interaction—has had a significant impact on the ideas that emerged on those pages.

I'd particularly like to thank and acknowledge my many fellow bloggers who, over those years, have both supported and nurtured my work. Some of these bloggers are deservedly well known: Duncan Black (Atrios), Heather Parton (Digby), John Amato (Crooksandliars), Jane Hamsher (Firedoglake), Matt Stoller (Open Left), Markos Moulitsas Zuniga and Joan McCarter (DailyKos), TBogg, Glenn Greenwald, Tom Tomorrow, Amanda Marcotte (Pandagon), Melissa McEwan (Shakespeare's Sister), and Jesus' General. Lesser known, perhaps, but every bit as important to the development of this text were my friends David Goldstein (Horses Ass), John McKay (archy), Spocko, Kyledeb (Citizen Orange), Eric Muller (Is That Legal?), and Blue Texan (Instaputz). A great debt is especially owed my cohort at *Orcinus,* Sara Robinson, whose broad range of knowledge and consistent thoughtfulness and insight was always a perfect complement to my work.

There have also been writers, journalists, and thinkers outside the blogosphere (though many of them have blogs of their own now, too) who have helped this text progress, in one form or another: Joe Conason, Chip Berlet, Rick Perlstein, Jeffrey Feldman, Frederick Clarkson, Mark Potok, David Holthouse, Roger Daniels, Roger Griffin, Eric Ward, and Devin Burghart. I owe the ultimate debt of gratitude to my friend and mentor, the late Reverand Bill Wassmuth.

I also owe a big thanks to the folks who helped shape a messy block of manuscript into a well-honed text: Jill Marsal, my agent at Sandra Dijkstra Literary Agency; Peter Richardson, my editor at PoliPoint Press; Beth Nauman-Montana, for her editing help; and Katherine Silver and David Peattie of BookMatters.

My greatest debt is owed to the two women who have kept me going through the years: my wife, Lisa Dowling, and my daughter, Fiona Rose Neiwert. They have made it all possible, and necessary too.

About the Author

DAVID NEIWERT is a veteran journalist based in Seattle. The author of two books on the effects of the extremist right on mainstream society, as well as *Strawberry Days: How Internment Destroyed a Japanese American Community* (a Washington State Book Award finalist), his reportage on domestic terrorism for MSNBC.com won a 2000 National Press Club Award for distinguished online journalism. He is also the editor of the award-winning weblog *Orcinus* and the managing editor of the popular "vlog" Crooksandliars. com. His work has appeared in *The American Prospect, Salon.com,* and various regional publications. Neiwert has been married to Lisa Dowling for 20 years and is the doting father of seven-year-old Fiona, who both like to visit killer whales with him.